HOUSE OF LORDS

SELECT COMMITTEE ON
THE EUROPEAN UNION

THE FURTHER LIBERALISATION OF COMMUNITY POSTAL SERVICES

WITH EVIDENCE

Ordered to be printed 12 December 2000

LONDON: THE STATIONERY OFFICE
£15.50

HL Paper 6

CONTENTS

	Paragraph	Page
PART 1: INTRODUCTION	1	**5**
THE BASE POSITION—THE 1997 DIRECTIVE.	1	**5**
House of Lords' Interest	9	**5**
The current proposals	10	**7**
PART 2: THE VIEWS OF THE WITNESSES	19	**8**
What Benefits would be likely to result from the proposed liberalisation measures?	24	**8**
The Commission's view	24	**8**
Reducing the reserved area by weight/price formula	29	**8**
Opening outgoing cross-border mail to competition	30	**9**
Removing the price limit on express mail	31	**9**
The definition of special services	32	**9**
The further step in 2007	33	**9**
The Views of other witnesses	34	**9**
What problems could result from the proposed liberalisation particularly in terms of maintaining universal service with an affordable and uniform tariff structure?	50	**11**
Are there any measures not identified in the Commission's proposals, which would help the Commission's stated aims for postal services?	68	**14**
PART 3: THE OPINION OF THE COMMITTEE.	74	**15**
Direct Mail	91	**18**
Special Services	92	**18**
Compensation Fund	97	**19**
PART 4: SUMMARY OF CONCLUSIONS AND RECOMMENDATIONS	98	**20**
Appendix 1—Membership of the Sub-Committee		**21**
Appendix 2—List of Witnesses		**22**
Appendix 3—Call for Evidence		**23**

ORAL EVIDENCE

European Commission
Written evidence 1
Oral evidence, 11 October 2000 5
Supplementary evidence ....

The Post Office
Written evidence 20
Oral evidence, 18 October 2000 23
Supplementary evidence by the Post Office 34

The Communication Workers' Union/Communication Managers' Association
Written evidence 38
Oral evidence, 25 October 2000 41

The Mail Users' Association
Written evidence 52
Oral evidence, 1 November 2000 55

The Direct Marketing Association (UK) Limited
Oral evidence, 1 November 2000 61

TNT Group N.V.
Oral evidence, 8 November 2000 65

Written evidence 73
Mr Alan Johnson, MP, Minister for Competitiveness, Department of Trade and Industry
Oral evidence 15 November 2000 75

Free and Fair Post Initiative (FFPI)
Written evidence 82
Oral evidence 15 November 2000 85

WRITTEN EVIDENCE

	Page
The Association of International Courier and Express Services (AICES)	91
Consumers in Europe Group	93
Mr W Maschke, Deutsche Post	96
Anton van der Lande, Chairman, EEA Postal Committee	97
La Poste, France	100
National Federation of Subpostmasters (NFSP)	102
Posten AB, Sweden	106
Royal National Institute for the Blind	107
Brian Simpson, MEP	108
Ross Clark, Journalist, The Spectator	109
United Parcel Service	110

SECOND REPORT

12 December 2000

By the Select Committee appointed to consider European Union documents and other matters relating to the European Union.

Ordered to Report

THE FURTHER LIBERALISATION OF COMMUNITY POSTAL SERVICES

10544/00 COM (2000) 319 final

A proposed European Parliament and Council Directive Com (2000) of 30 May 2000 amending Directive 97/67/EC with regard to the further opening to competition of Community postal services

PART 1: INTRODUCTION

THE BASE POSITION—THE 1997 DIRECTIVE.

1. The European Commission's proposals are the second stage in a process of liberalising postal services in the European Union. They seek to build on the 1997 Directive (97/67/EC). The proposals, which, if agreed, would come into effect from 1 January 2003, include a requirement to review progress in 2004 and to set a date for full and final liberalisation by 1 January 2007. EU postal services are estimated to handle 135 billion items a year, generating turnover of about 80 billion euro or about 1.4 per cent of the European Union's GDP. About two-thirds of this turnover is generated by mail services, including the reserved area. The remainder is generated by parcels and express services, which are already in the competitive area.

2. Directive 97/EC of the European Parliament and Council of 15 December 1997 established a harmonised regulatory framework for the Community postal sector, and defined the process for opening the postal market to further competition.

3. The 1997 Directive defined:

- the minimum characteristics of the *universal postal service*;
- the quality standards for cross-border services;
- tariff principles, and principles governing transparency of accounts;
- common maximum limits for those services which may be reserved by a member state to its universal service provider(s) to the extent necessary to ensure the maintenance of the universal service (effectively 350 grams and five times the standard tariff for an item in the first weight step);
- the principles to govern the authorisation/licensing of the provision of non-reserved postal services, and the separation of regulatory powers and operational functions in the postal sector.

4. The transposing of this postal directive into national law was required to be completed by February 1999. Some problems remain. They concern chiefly the adequacy of the arrangements for ensuring that the required regulatory authorities are legally separate from, and operationally independent of, the postal operators; and the extension of domestic postal monopolies to value added services.

5. The 1997 Postal Directive continued the process of gradual and controlled opening to competition of the postal markets foreseen by the Council in its Resolution of 7 February 1994 on the development of Community postal services. At that time the timetable was that:

- the Commission should present a proposal by 31 December 1998 for the further gradual and controlled opening of the postal market in particular with a view to opening cross-border and direct mail to competition; as well as on a further review of the price and weight limits;

- The Council and Parliament should decide on this proposal by 1 January 2000;
- The measures should take effect from 1 January 2003.

6. The Commission proposal was delayed mainly by the resignation of the previous Commission on 15 March 1999 and by the need for the new Commission to re-examine the issue.

7. The European Council of the Heads of State and Government, in March this year, recognised the importance of further opening the postal market and called upon the Commission, the Council and the Member States to act in accordance with their respective powers to achieve the following objectives:

- to set out by the end of 2000, a strategy for removing the barriers to postal services;
- to speed up liberalisation with the aim of achieving a fully operational internal market in these areas.

8. In the United Kingdom, the Postal Services Act 2000 is designed to achieve similar objectives.

HOUSE OF LORDS' INTEREST

9. When the Commission's original proposal and draft notice were published in 1995, the Select Committee decided to conduct an inquiry.[1] The main conclusions of the Committee were:

- The Committee welcomed the fact that the Commission had published proposals to harmonise Community postal services and to establish common standards, but believed that the over-riding aim ought to be to secure the provision of a good quality universal service rather than to promote liberalisation. Postal services had a vital social role as well as an economic one.

- The Commission proposals were unlikely to equip the postal sector to face the growing threat of substitution by electronic means of communication.

- The Commission should issue a Notice only after the Directive had been adopted and in a revised form that took account of criticisms made in evidence.

- Universal service providers should be afforded sufficient monopoly protection to ensure their long-term economic viability without reliance on subsidy or compensation from other operators.

- The Directive should impose on Member States an obligation to set uniform tariffs within their own borders and to permit postal operators to offer discounts only where costs had been avoided.

- The Commission's proposed universal service obligations and quality of service standards were satisfactory, but should be regarded as the minimum acceptable.

- The extent of liberalisation of domestic mail proposed was acceptable, though a simple price threshold would have been preferable. The liberalisation of outgoing cross-border mail was unobjectionable, but the proposed automatic liberalisation of new services should have been replaced by a presumption in favour of their continued reservation

- Direct mail and incoming cross-border mail should be maintained within the reserved area. At the very least the decision whether to proceed with a second stage of liberalisation should not be taken until the effects of the first stage of liberalisation had become apparent and should only involve liberalisation by content if the issues of verification and enforcement had been satisfactorily resolved.

- Universal service providers should not be required to offer downstream access to their networks at cost-effective tariffs.

- Universal service providers' accounts should distinguish between reserved and non-reserved services and should be independently audited.

- The United Kingdom Post Office combined efficiency with a high level of service and should be treated as a model for other Member States. The Government should be prepared to give the Post Office greater commercial freedom in future and to consider the case for an independent regulator.

- The liberalisation measures effected in Sweden and the Netherlands did not provide a suitable model for the United Kingdom or for the Community as a whole.

---

[1] The Report of the inquiry was published on 21 May 1996 as the Tenth Report in the Session 1995-96 (HL Paper 81).

THE CURRENT PROPOSALS

10. The Commission now proposes from 1 January 2003:

- to reduce the existing weight/price limits from 350 grams and 5 times the basic standard tariff for letters, to 50 grams and 2.5 times the basic standard tariff for letters, and for direct mail (i.e. addressed advertising material);

- a full opening to competition of all special (value added) services (without price limit) — including express mail, delivery on appointment, tracking and tracing, and guaranteed time delivery;

- full opening to competition of outward cross-border mail [the *de facto* position in the United Kingdom];

- a review to be carried out in 2004 with a view to possible further liberalisation in 2007;

- special tariffs to be based on transparency, non-discrimination and on avoided costs;

- cross-subsidy of universal services outside the reserved area out of revenues in the reserved area, to be prohibited except as necessary to fulfil the universal service obligation (USO) in the competitive area.

11. It is the first two of these proposals which could potentially have the greatest impact on postal services in the United Kingdom.

12. The Commission sees the current proposals as a move toward the completion of the internal market for postal services while ensuring the maintenance of the universal service obligation. Further liberalisation is expected to allow the benefits of greater competition to improve the service levels, in terms of both quality and prices, available to posting customers. The focus is intended to be on markets where opening has already occurred and on the fastest-growing segments where the impact of competition on universal service providers can be offset by market growth. The Commission argues that the steps should be significant enough to create actual competition. The central concern surrounds the pace of reform. The Commission argues that timidity of approach will reduce the likelihood of real competition emerging and thus delay the delivery of improved quality of service and efficiency.

13. In our inquiry we sought to determine what effect the Commission's proposals would have on the United Kingdom Post Office, and whether or not they should be supported. We asked three questions:

(i) **What benefits would be likely to result from the proposed liberalisation measures?**

(ii) **What problems could result from the proposed liberalisation, particularly in terms of maintaining a universal service with an affordable and uniform tariff structure?**

(iii) **Are there any measures, not identified in the Commission's proposals, which would help to secure the Commission's stated aims for postal services?**

14. This report is based on an inquiry conducted by Sub-Committee B (Energy, Industry and Transport). The membership of the Sub-Committee is given in Appendix 1.

15. We took written evidence from many of those who had supplied evidence to the inquiry in 1996. The witnesses are listed in Appendix 2. In addition we heard oral evidence from the European Commission, the United Kingdom Post Office, the Communications Workers Union and Communication Managers Association (CWU/CMA), the Mail Users' Association, the Direct Mail Association, TNT Post NV (Netherlands), the Minister for Competitiveness, Mr Alan Johnson MP, "Free and Fair Post", Senator Philippe Bodson, and in private, from Mr Graham Corbett and Mr Martin Stanley, Chairman and Chief Executive respectively of the new postal services regulator, Postcomm. We sought evidence from the Post Office Users' National Council (POUNC) but because this organisation was in the process of transmogrifying into the new Consumer Council for Postal Services (CCPS), set up under the Postal Services Act 2000, it felt unable to comply with our request. We are conscious that consumers' interests, reflected only in the evidence from the Consumers in Europe Group (CEG), are perhaps under-represented in the evidence, though not, we hope, in the report.

16. Appendix 3 sets out the terms on which written evidence was sought.

17. We should like to thank our Specialist Adviser, Chris Nicholson of KPMG, for the assistance he provided during the inquiry and towards the drafting of this report. We are also grateful for the assistance provided by the Posts Division of the Department of Trade and Industry.

PART 2: THE VIEWS OF THE WITNESSES

18. The current proposals are aimed at opening up a further 20 per cent of the European postal market to competition. The Post Office believes that in the United Kingdom this would leave it with 60 per cent of its existing revenues in order to sustain its universal service obligation (Q74). Change is controversial. In evidence, many witnesses believed that further liberalisation was both desirable and, ultimately, inevitable. The differences appear over the pace of change.

19. The commercial mail users, those companies which see opportunities in a liberalised postal market, and those Member States which have already liberalised their postal services or, like Germany, are in the process of so doing, argue for rapid liberalisation and the setting of a date by which all Member States will have opened their postal markets to competition.

20. Those who argue against haste are those organisations which feel they have most to lose by rapid change: the Post Office, the Unions and the Consumers in Europe Group (CEG).

21. All witnesses believe that it is vital for all Member States to maintain a universal service obligation at a uniform and affordable tariff. The existing definition of what the EU considers should constitute the universal service obligation is set out in Chapter 2, Article 3 to 6 of the Postal Directive (97/67/EC dated 15 December 1997).

22. Witnesses have responded, directly or indirectly, to the three questions posed in the Call for Evidence. This evidence is reviewed below. The first question was:

What Benefits would be likely to result from the proposed liberalisation measures?

THE COMMISSION'S VIEW

23. The *Commission* argues that liberalisation will produce more efficient markets and therefore better services, that it would be implementing the internal market, that in many cases it would be catching up with what is actually happening in the market already, and that opening the market is not only an opportunity, but is essential if post offices are to compete with the new technologies. The *Commission* adds that its proposals form part of a gradual opening.

24. Before the implementation of the 1997 Directive, 27 per cent of universal service providers' postal revenues, on average, was open to competition. The 1997 Postal Directive opened approximately an additional 3 per cent of the universal service providers' revenues from postal services, leaving 70 per cent of total postal services revenues, on average, in the reserved area. The total market opening proposed as the next step to be implemented from 2003 would represent an additional 20 per cent of these revenues which would mean that up to 50 per cent of the universal service providers' revenues from postal services could be maintained within the reserved area (Para 2.4 of the Explanatory Memorandum covering the Commission's draft proposals).

25. For a second level of benefit, the *Commission* argues that their proposals constitute a controlled market opening because Member States will be acting on the basis of consensus and will be reflecting the reality of the market.

26. The *Commission* claims to have examined the financial equilibrium of the universal service obligation and to have concluded that the universal service obligation would be economically viable in a situation of progressive market opening.

27. National legislators and regulatory authorities would be empowered to ensure a smooth implementation according to national political requirements.

Reducing the reserved area by weight/price formula

28. The specific benefits of the proposed measures, particularly in the reduction of the 50 grams weight limit, would be that it will be easy for regulators to enforce and will allow limited competition thus ensuring that the implementation of the proposal would be gradual and controlled. The *Commission* argues that a lower limit — 20 grams — would be too much, too quickly, as it would increase the market opening from 20 per cent to 32 per cent of Postal Revenues. On the other hand, a larger limit, say 100 grams, would reduce the increase in market opening from 20 per cent to 14 per cent, which would not lead to substantial market entry, and would not, therefore, make the required difference to postal operators to oblige them to be efficient.

Opening outgoing cross-border mail to competition

29. This is already the *de facto* position in ten Member States including the two countries with the highest volumes of outward cross-border mail (Ireland and Luxembourg).

Removing the price limit on express mail

30. There is a principle already well established in the existing postal directive that new services in the sense of services that are "quite distinct from conventional services" do not form part of the universal service and consequently there is no justification for their being reserved to universal service providers.

The definition of special services

31. These services are already out of the reserved area under the existing directive and the current proposals do not seek to change this. *The Commission* in seeking to reinforce the definition of special services characterises special services as those which must meet three conditions:

(a) they must be clearly distinct from the universal service;

(b) they must meet specific customer requirements; and

(c) they must have added value features not offered by the standard postal service.

The further step in 2007

32. When the current proposals are implemented there will be a further review in 2004, which will focus on how to guarantee universal service in an appropriate manner in a fully competitive market. The Commission proposes that the review last for two years and aim for complete liberalisation from 2007. (In the first draft of these proposals the Commission had hoped to agree 1 January 2007 as the final date for full liberalisation, but they were obliged to accept the current compromise position.)

THE VIEWS OF OTHER WITNESSES

33. *The Association of International Courier and Express Services (AICES)* recognises the need for the European Commission to find common ground in favour of further liberalisation but is disappointed that the final (i.e. current) proposals have been diluted in comparison to earlier drafts. It argues that the Commission was widely expected to propose full liberalisation as of 2003, but the final proposals presented by Commissioner Bolkestein reserve the majority of direct mail items (items up to 50 grams) for Europe's monopoly holders. *AICES* claims that the level of liberalisation proposed is the bare minimum necessary. It is also concerned about the lack of a final date for full liberalisation, partly because it implies not only delays in much needed reforms of the public postal operators, but also because it implies a delay in the completion of the single market. *AICES* states that liberalisation encourages competition and that increased competition will stimulate the reform of public postal operators into efficient, cost-aware and above all, customer-orientated companies. The abolition of monopolies will end distortions of competition between different parts of the communications market.

34. The *Direct Marketing Association (United Kingdom) Limited* argues that full liberalisation will lead to growth in the postal sector and stimulate new services, new job opportunities, and an overall increase in employment. It will not undermine the ability of the universal service providers to sustain the universal service obligation at an affordable and uniform price. The *Association* adds that the entry of new private operators through full liberalisation will help to develop a better and more efficient postal service. The *Association's* main concern is, of course, direct mail where the *Association* argues that full liberalisation of direct mail should occur by 1 January 2003. The *Association* adds that direct mail is already liberalised in six European Union countries (see paragraph 90).

35. The *European Express Association (EEA)* regrets that the Commission's proposals do not adequately address the need for increased competition in Europe's postal market. The *EEA* argues that customers increasingly want a wider range of new services with a good price/quality ratio and also freedom of choice between service providers world-wide. Therefore, the single market for postal services should be completed as in all other sectors. The price/quality ratio of the postal product must be improved and only increased competition can guarantee this. The development of new products will be stimulated; increased competition will stimulate the reform of public postal operators into efficient, cost-aware and above all customer-orientated companies. The abolition of monopolies will end distortions of competition between different parts of the communications market. The *EEA* goes onto argue that the Directive should include 1 January 2007 as the final date for full liberalisation

claiming that without a final date the public postal operators (PPO) will have no real incentive to improve their services, or to take advantage of the dynamics of the internal market.

36. The *Mail Users' Association* stresses the benefits of fair competition in the postal market place. Not only does competition offer choice to the customer and therefore downward pressure on prices but it also acts as a catalyst for increased quality of service levels. It regards the reserved sector of the market — the Royal Mail's £1 monopoly — to be disproportionate to the sums needed to support the universal service. The *MUA* argues that business mailers expect the benefits likely to result from the current proposals to be limited and could only be regarded as firm steps in the right direction if they are inextricably linked to a published timetable for further liberalisation.

37. *United Parcel Service (UPS)* lists the benefits likely to flow from liberalisation, thus:

- The single market for postal services should be completed as for other sectors;
- The price/quality ratio of postal products should be improved — increased competition alone can bring this about;
- Liberalisation will stimulate the development of new products and encourage innovation in the postal sector;
- Increased competition will stimulate the reform of public postal operators into more efficient cost-aware and above all customer-orientated companies;
- The abolition of monopolies will end distortions of competition between alternative segments of the communications market.

38. *UPS* further insist that the Directive should include a final date for full liberalisation and that this should be 1 January 2007.

39. *Deutsche Post* together with *TNT Post Group NV, Posten AB* and *Finland Post Limited* declares itself to be "*in favour of a full and swift, and yet gradual and controlled liberalisation of the European postal market*", but *Deutsche Post* itself does not spell out the benefits it expects the current proposals to bring.

40. *TNT Post Group NV's* position is admirably summarised in its evidence:

- Without competition there is no innovation;
- Without innovation, postal services will be substantially substituted by other media within a decade!

Liberalised postal services are essential for the future of the sector. *TNT* goes on to argue that liberalisation should be as rapid as possible, claiming that the Postal Directive, far from being a first step towards a liberalised postal market, had re-monopolised postal services in more than half EU Member States.

41. *Posten AB*, the Swedish Post Office, is one of the few liberalised postal services in Europe. This was achieved in 1993 when the monopoly on letters was abolished in a single step. *Posten AB* argues that to safeguard the universal service, the European postal industry must compete on equal terms with other service providers in expanding European communications and logistics' markets. Not only is liberalisation itself desirable, it should come as quickly as possible. A prolonged process will jeopardise the long-term future of the postal sector including employment, affordable prices, and last, but not least, the universal service itself.

42. The *United Kingdom Post Office* supports the view that the introduction of competition in the postal market will produce benefits in efficiency and service quality, reductions in price and increases in choice for all customers. Competition provides an opportunity to encourage innovation and to increase efficiency and productivity. Nevertheless, *The Post Office* sees potential conflict between the introduction of competition as required by the European Commission's proposals and the universal service obligation (USO) as set out by the Government in the Postal Services Act 2000.

43. The *CWU/CMA* also state that they are not opposed to a measure of liberalisation in the provision of postal services but, quoting the Postal Directive, believe that such liberalisation should be gradual and controlled and not at the expense of universal service and uniform tariffs. The proposals cannot, in their opinion, be considered either gradual or controlled.

44. The *National Federation of Sub-Post Masters* is less attracted to the idea of liberalisation. It prefers to regard modernisation of the postal sector as the catalyst for exploiting new technology and delivering an efficient high quality service to members of the public and businesses. *"NFSP is*

concerned as to whether liberalisation will in fact produce benefits in efficiency, reductions in price and increases in choice for all customers."

45. The *Royal National Institute of the Blind (RNIB)* does not take a view on whether the postal sector should be liberalised/privatised or not. *"The central concern of blind and partially sighted people and their organisations is that any moves towards further liberalisation of postal services should not threaten the continuation of vital freepost Articles for the Blind services..."*The *RNIB* draws heavily on the experience of New Zealand where it claims liberalisation did not improve the position of visually-impaired people.

46. The *Consumers in Europe Group (CEG)* offers no judgments on benefits likely to accrue from the current proposals for further liberalisation. Their concern focuses exclusively on the maintenance of the universal service obligation at a uniform tariff and affordable price. The CEG also emphasises the social importance of the continued existence of post offices, especially in rural areas.

47. The *Government* does not express an overt opinion in its evidence about the benefits of liberalisation though its position can be inferred from the fact that the *Government* is already putting in place a new legislative framework for the regulation of the United Kingdom domestic postal market to give the Post Office the commercial freedom to operate effectively in a dynamic and changing global market. The *Government* supports further liberalisation of the European postal market consistent with maintaining the universal service obligation.

48. The second question was:

What problems could result from the proposed liberalisation particularly in terms of maintaining universal service with an affordable and uniform tariff structure?

49. The proponents of liberalisation claim to see no real problems in the Commission's current proposals and, by and large, expect them to allow national licensees to operate a viable universal service with affordable and uniform tariff structures though they do not attempt to define any of these terms. For example, *AICES* regards the price and weight limit, as proposed by the Commission, as a modest step in the right direction and argues that it is the absolute minimum necessary at this time. *AICES* favours full liberalisation of the market. It welcomes the Commission's proposals on outbound cross-border mail recognising that this is effectively liberalised already in all Member States. *AICES* appeals to the Commission to re-examine the issue of inbound cross-border mail and strongly opposes the view that it is necessary to maintain the monopoly in this area of the market.

50. The *Direct Marketing Association* argues that the proposed measures would have no effect on the universal service obligation nor The Post Office's ability to provide a universal service at an affordable price and standard tariff. It welcomes full opening to competition of outward cross-border mail but argues it should be accompanied by full opening to competition of inward cross-border mail. Its own specific theme is that direct mail should be fully liberalised by 2003 and if this is not possible under the present proposals, then a fixed deadline for liberalisation should be set.

51. The *European Express Association* takes a similar line. The *EEA* argues that the Commission's current proposals do not change the obligation to provide a universal service and that the position of a universal service and a fully liberalised market are not mutually exclusive. The *EEA* adds however that the universal service obligation should meet the most important criteria: the provision of a good and affordable basic postal service. If postal services lag behind the communications market as a whole, they risk losing the very basis on which the social role (i.e. universal service) is built. The current Commission proposal liberalises a mere 20 per cent of the currently reserved area, which *EEA* regards as sufficient to guarantee the universal service obligation. *United Parcel Service*'s evidence makes the same claims in almost identical language.

52. The *Mail Users' Association* argues that it is extremely unlikely that any potential competitor would regard it feasible to develop a national network based on the present proposals, that the existing universal service to all postal addressees in the country will continue to be provided by the national carrier. The *MUA* considers the universal service obligation will be maintained satisfactorily but is concerned about The Post Office's future investment in infrastructure, given the heavy burdens they are being allowed to take on in terms of their international acquisitions, allowances and joint ventures. *MUA* concludes that while maintaining the universal service is likely to continue in much the same fashion as today, sending items that fall outside the postal monopoly is likely to cost the customer more.

53. *Posten AB* is required by the Swedish Postal Services Act to maintain a universal service. *Posten AB* argues that the liberalisation of the European postal industry has to be put into effect as swiftly as possible in order to safeguard the universal service and that it is important to concentrate

more on the content of the postal service than on the structure of how to offer a service. A flexible organisation enabling postal operators to adapt to market changes, quickly shifting customer demands, and different local solutions for service is the best way to safeguard the maintenance of universal service to all citizens. *Posten AB* ends its evidence by quoting the Swedish Regulator, the National Post and Telecom Agency's statement in their latest report on Swedish liberalisation.

> *"There is nothing in the Swedish experience that may indicate that competition in the entire postal market should be regarded as a problem. Instead it should be considered a solution to the challenges facing the Postal World in a new environment dominated by Information Technology and globalisation."*[2]

54. *TNT Post NV* also argues that a universal service can be maintained in a liberalised market, that the purpose of the universal service obligation is to safeguard the ability of the general public to communicate regularly at a reasonable cost. TNT Post N.V. goes on to suggest that the concept of universal service needs to be flexible and dynamic to take account of the rapidly changing ways in which we communicate. *TNT Post NV* also points to fully liberalised postal markets in Sweden, New Zealand and Argentina which, they claim, demonstrate that a universal postal service can be preserved even in a fully liberalised market. If they have a problem with the Commission's proposals, it is that they do not go far enough, fast enough.

55. *Deutsche Post* ignores the issue and argues only that a final date for full liberalisation must be set.

56. The *United Kingdom Post Office* finds considerable difficulty in accepting that the reduction of the reserved areas to 50 grams would enable it to maintain a universal service. It argues that the directive proposes a reduction in the scope of the reserved area of such an extent that, if implemented in 2003, would lead to a financial impact on the Post Office that would almost certainly push it into loss. This would undermine the ability of The Post Office to continue to meet the social obligation laid down in the Postal Services Act 2000 to provide a universal service at an affordable and uniform tariff. *The Post Office* therefore strongly prefers a reduction in the reserved area limited to 150 grams arguing that if this proved too generous, further reductions could be made. If the reduction was made immediately to 50 grams, the process would be irreversible. If it was subsequently found that the universal service obligation could not be sustained by a reserved area measured by the 50 grams weight/price figure, it would be too late to do anything about it.

57. *The Post Office* also has problems with the Commission's definition of special services which it believes could be used to undermine the integrity of the reserved area in that it would remove legal certainty from the definition of the reserved area, and would risk opening up all bulk mail to competition through what would, in effect, be deregulation by means of court actions.[3]

58. The *CWU/CMA* is also concerned that the proposed reduction of the reserved area by weight/price to 50 grams would lead to a substantial loss in postal operators' revenues which would have the effect of undermining The Post Office's profitability. In addition, the proposal constitutes a direct threat to the uniform tariff currently operated by universal service providers. It adduces evidence from a study by Toulouse University which estimated that a fully competitive market would generate highly differential prices with rural customers paying tariffs more than four times those paid by commercial customers.

59. *CWU/CMA*'s final point is that these proposals would also lead to a dramatic loss in jobs. It points to the experience of countries which have already liberalised such as Germany, Sweden or New Zealand where cuts in jobs in the main postal operator have been as high as 40 per cent. *CWU/CMA* also believe that a review in 2004 — only one year after the next step in the liberalisation process, is too sudden and does not accord with the "gradual and controlled" liberalisation process which Member States had agreed in the original directive.

60. The *National Federation of Sub-Postmasters (NFSP)* also believes that a sudden reduction to 50 grams might eliminate Post Office profits and that The Post Office would be left unable to maintain a viable business or to sustain a universal service for customers. The *NFSP* also makes the point that liberalisation tends to be irreversible and therefore needs to be carefully thought out before implementation. It is concerned that too radical a liberalisation would result in a serious reduction in the funding available through The Post Office to support sub-post offices.

---

[2] National Post and Telecom Agency, "The Liberalised Swedish Postal Market". Available at www.pts.se.

[3] What The Post Office means by this is that the proposed definition of special services is so imprecise that competitors might establish services, which could be challenged in court for transgressing The Post Office's monopoly. If the court nevertheless found such services to be "special", as defined in the current proposal, they would then be held to be outside the reserved area.

61. The *RNIB* is concerned with safeguarding political support for the freepost Articles for the Blind service at European Union level. Such a commitment has been less forthcoming at a European Union level than in the United Kingdom. The European Parliament did demonstrate support for such schemes by amending the 1995 Directive Proposal to ensure that liberalisation would not threaten free post schemes in different Member States, but the European Commission was not enthusiastic about such amendments. The compromise, eventually agreed to, was to permit Member States to continue such schemes. The *RNIB's* main worry is that the current proposals might lead to a reduction in the commitment to continue to support this scheme.

62. The *Consumers in Europe Group (CEG)* believes that the letter monopoly held by most European Post Offices should be reduced as far as possible in order to encourage lower prices, better service, and more choice for consumers. Consumers want the universal service at a uniform and affordable tariff to be maintained. *CEG* therefore favours a step-by-step approach to liberalisation reducing the monopoly of the universal service providers for direct mail to 150 grams as a first step, with further reductions depending on the outcome of the Commission's review of the situation at the end of 2004. *CEG* adds that 2004 might in practice be too early for a full assessment. *CEG* goes on to argue that the reserved area should be strictly proportional to the cost of providing the universal service and would wish the Commission to provide strict guidelines for the operation, transparency and control of any compensation fund that each Member State might be allowed to set up to ensure the maintenance of the universal service in the event that the reserved area could not cover the universal service providers' costs. *CEG* also urges the Commission to provide a definition of "affordable" as specified in the 1997 Postal Services Directive.

63. *Mr Brian Simpson MEP*, stresses the threats that the current proposals make to levels of employment and argues that a cut in the reserved area from 350 grams to 50 grams in one move is not, in his opinion, either controlled or gradual. He adds that Postcomm must ensure that its decisions are consistent with European Union decisions. The proposal to reduce the reserved area to 50 grams puts at risk the financing of the universal service throughout the United Kingdom, and a reserved area of 150 grams including direct mail is necessary in order to ensure a viable universal service throughout all parts of the United Kingdom. *Mr Simpson* adds that further liberalisation after the present proposals have been implemented should be taken carefully and not hurried.

64. The *Government's* position has been affected by domestic legislation. The Postal Services Act 2000 is designed to establish a new regulatory framework and a regulator, the Postal Services Commission, PostComm, with responsibility for preserving the universal service obligation. Under this new framework The Post Office will no longer have a monopoly but will be licensed to operate in a reserved area. This reserved area which is broadly similar in scope to The Post Office's current monopoly area, will be regulated by PostComm who will be able to license other players in the market consistent with its obligation to ensure a universal service obligation. The Government identifies two particular problems from the European Commission's proposals:

(i) a new definition of "special services";

(ii) the reduction of the reserved area by price/weight.

On the special services issue, the *Government* argues that further work needs to be undertaken to define such services to ensure that they do not put at risk the legal certainty provided by the weight/price definition of the reserved area nor be used as a device to render the reserved area void. On the question of the definition of the reserved area by weight/price, the *Government* recognises that this is currently consistent with United Kingdom practice except that the levels proposed do not match the current tariff structure of the Post Office. The *Government's* position, however, is that this is a matter for the new regulator and that in the words of the minister, Mr Alan Johnson MP, the regulator's report would be a major input in the government's considerations (Q 344).

65. The *French Post Office, "La Poste"*, finds little virtue in liberalisation, approves the European Commission's willingness to maintain a reserved sector and to fix its contours on the basis of weight and price, but does have strong reservations. It thinks the proposed weight/price limits are too low and the introduction of new concepts of special services and traditional services misleading. The announcement of new proposals for 2004 and beyond without assessing the measures expected to come into effect in 2003, is too sudden a step. The *French Post Office* also suggests that liberalisation of special services poses problems of legal certainty. As regards the weight/price limits, the *French Post Office "like most other European operators"* will accept a reduction to 150 grams and three times the base tariff. The *French Post Office* adds that the Commission's proposals go against the principle of a gradual and controlled opening to competition.

66. The third question was:

Are there any measures not identified in the Commission's proposals, which would help the Commission's stated aims for postal services?

67. Fewer witnesses responded to this question. The *Mail Users' Association* argues that the key issue for business mailers is that liberalisation in the market place needs to be sustainable. For the *MUA* the current proposals do not go far enough to support long term competition. MUA argues from the experience of the telecommunications market, that it would be feasible to offer potential postal operators access to the national carriers distribution network "downstream", and thus enable them to provide competitive services for all mail streams aimed at a specific region. By licensing competitors in this way it would be possible to analyse the effects of competition on the universal service (both financially and socially) while at the same time offering the competitor a viable platform from which to grow. Provided that the end results of this competition did not compromise the universal service obligation, and that the licensed carrier was proficient and in a position further to develop its systems, the postal regulator could then expand the controlled test-bed further afield.

68. The *CWU/CMA* argues that the process of liberalisation should be "gradual and controlled" and that after a couple of years' experience of the current proposals, there should be a thorough review which looked at the impact on service levels, prices, profitability and employment. Only in the light of such a review should further proposals be drawn up in respect of any further liberalisation in 2007 or at any later date. This is a view echoed by the *National Federation of Sub-Postmasters*.

69. The *Government* suggests that Postcomm will want to see whether the European Commission's proposed directive leads to equivalence across Member States. The United Kingdom postal services operate in a completely open market outside the reserved area. EC legislation permits licensing regimes outside the reserved areas but the Government believes there should be consistency between the two areas.

70. The *French Post Office* is critical of the failure of the Commission to address the consequences of its proposed amendment to Article 7 of the Postal Directive. The Commission's proposal envisages a two-stage approach to the market-opening process. The first step is the reduction, with effect from 1 January 2003, of the maximum weight and price limits of the postal services which Member States can reserve to their universal service providers. The second is a decision on a further step towards opening the postal market with effect from 1 January 2007. That decision would be taken by the European Parliament and the Council by 31 December 2005. The French Post Office's concern centred on the Commission's statement: "Failing such a decision, the amended Postal Directive would cease to apply on 31 December 2006". The *French Post Office* said that the introduction of "the notion of nullity" would create "a strong element of legal uncertainty prejudicial to the whole postal sector". Further, there was "a major contradiction.... The Commission cannot plead for the universal service at the same time as proposing the removal of the regulatory framework, which guarantees it, in the event of disagreement on review of the directive".

71. According to the Commission, this French reference is to the lapsing mechanism which is in the 1997 Directive, and which has not so far been challenged there. The Commission now seeks to transfer it to the amended Directive. The Directive is a balance between obligations and the reserved area required to meet those obligations. The balance includes moving towards further liberalisation. If that balance were to be broken through decisions on future liberalisation not being taken as required by the Directive, then the whole Directive would lapse and the competition rules would apply. A Directive would then be brought forward under Article 86 of the EC Treaty. That is of course possible now but the political choice has so far been made to try to open the market through harmonisation. In short, either the postal services accept controlled liberalisation through consensus and political compromise, or the Commission could put forward a Directive based on internal market competition rules which would, it is implied, look less kindly on reserved areas.

72. The *French Post Office* also observes that "the European market today is the market most open to competition in the postal sector world-wide. In comparable countries such as the United States, Japan or Switzerland, the monopoly is guaranteed within the following limits:

- Japan: 2 kg

- Switzerland: 2 kg, including parcels

- USA: US$3 (this monopoly changes in line with the weight of items dispatched and can, for example, reach US$6 for a package weighing 1 kg)."

The *French Post Office* concludes that the continued opening of the European market would be to the detriment of European interests, which would, in addition, be weakened in negotiations at the World Trade Organisation (WTO).

PART 3: THE OPINION OF THE COMMITTEE.

73. In 1996 when the Committee last looked at the issue of Community Postal Services, it was powerfully impressed by the performance of The Post Office and recommended that The Post Office serve as model for other Member States. Furthermore, the Committee was unimpressed by the then recent decision of the Swedish Government to liberalise the Swedish Post Office completely.

74. Five years on, the Committee would be hard put to sustain the admiration it once held for The Post Office. Services have deteriorated (QQ 66, 125, 150, 230, 259, 260, 339 and 361), though contrary to common assumptions, possibly more in urban areas than in rural areas. The Post Office admits that it has not considered the interests of its customers as it should have (Q 69). Criticism in the national press focuses on the preservation of practices under the monopoly which would not be possible in the market place."[4] *"The Post Office is said to be the best known brand in the United Kingdom after Coca-Cola. It is also the country's biggest retail chain. But it is also an organisation that loses a million items of its customer's business per week; delivers a service at midday — when most recipients have gone to work; does not take credit cards; offers bureaux de change without computer access to exchange rates; and one that many people only visit because they have to."*[5]

75. The Swedish experiment with liberalisation may still be viewed askance by national post offices which have yet to liberalise, and indeed there are features about it which might not accord with the sort of freedoms which we would associate with liberalisation. Nevertheless, according to the Swedish Regulator, it has proved to be successful in that it provides a top quality service and has maintained the universal service obligation. But it does so at a cost. Its tariff is higher than the European average, though the Swedes argue that much of this was the result of the imposition of VAT on services which had hitherto been excluded by virtue of the monopoly, and a one-off increase provided by a loophole in the legislation (now closed!). The Bureau Européen des Unions de Consommateurs (BEUC) quotes reports from the Swedish consumer organisation which contradict this. Sveriges Konsumentrad records increased uncertainty about the time for mail to arrive.[6]

76. What is more the Swedish example has been followed by Finland, though with different national features, and the Netherlands has privatised its postal services and part liberalised them. The most recent member of the liberalising tendency has been Deutsche Post which has bought a number of companies to create a postal services group which covers all aspects of mail, express, logistics and finance. The German government has unilaterally reduced the weight/price limit for Deutsche Post from 350 grams to 200 grams for letter mail and from 350 grams to 50 grams for direct mail pending the acceptance of the current EC proposals. Deutsche Post has gone to the money markets and offered 25 per cent of its shareholding to the public, raising 6.6 billion euros (£4.6million) in new capital, as part of the process of turning itself into a large global logistics company. This activity is likely to put Deutsche Post in a strong position as the postal market liberalises.[7] Deutsche Post's "competitive instincts" can be seen in the formal anti-trust proceedings which the Commission launched against it on 8 August 2000![8]

77. Against this background, the Committee was disappointed that the attitude of The Post Office appeared to be one of the dogged defence of existing markets under as high a reserved area as possible. We concur with those witnesses who have observed (Q 13 and 240) that the universal service *obligation* could as easily be called a universal service *opportunity* in that the incumbents have in place an infrastructure which would be prohibitively expensive for competitors to replicate. *The Post Office* argues that this is one of the grounds for their concern — that opening the market will simply permit "cherry picking" i.e. companies set up to exploit the most profitable areas of the postal service while ignoring the obligation to provide a universal service at a uniform and affordable tariff. This view is supported by the CWU/CMA, the Government and the National Federation of Sub-Postmasters, all of whom fear that any attack on the Post Office's income from competition would inevitably affect the ability of the Post Office to continue to offer the universal service at a uniform and affordable tariff.

78. It was difficult for the Committee to establish from the figures available to it whether or not the Post Office's fears were justified. Currently within the tariff structure of most national postal operators there are two elements of cross-subsidy:

---

[4] *Spectator* 11 November 2000, "Not Sorted". *The Times* Fourth Leader, 11 December 2000

[5] *The Times* 14 November 2000, Christine Buckley.

[6] BEUC's comments on the Commission's proposal for a Directive amending Directive 97/67/EC with regard to the further opening to competition of Community Postal Services and its BEUC/284/2000 quoted in CEG's evidence, page (93).

[7] See "Postal groups grow ambitious" by Frances Williams, Financial Times 19 November 2000.

[8] European report No. 2533, 7 October 2000.

- geographical cross-subsidy such that a geographically uniform tariff may be levied;
- cross-subsidy between users, typically from large users (businesses) to less frequent users (individuals).

Competition may put pressure on the universal service provider to:

(a) abandon a uniform tariff structure; or

(b) reduce service standards in high cost areas.

If the universal service provider maintains the universal service obligation at a uniform and affordable tariff and is unable to make improvements in efficiency, then competition could lead to a reduction in profits, which, in turn, could affect the viability of the operator. It is also likely that competition will lead to downward pressure on tariffs for business users and corresponding upward pressure on tariffs for individual users of postal services as The Post Office believe will happen (based on a study from the University of Toulouse) — although the no price discrimination clause of the draft directive, as well as the powers of the United Kingdom regulator, are presumably designed to seek to avoid this.

79. The Commission's proposals specify a system known as *avoided cost* to quantify the cost of sustaining the universal service obligation. *"In a postal context [this system] focuses on answering the big political question: 'If the universal service provider could choose NOT to provide the universal service, by how much would its profits increase?'"* In other words, on some routes costs which could be avoided from not offering a service are greater than the uniform price received for offering such service. *"Adding up the difference between revenue and avoidable cost on each of these loss-making routes is the financial (net avoided) cost to the operator of having to run these services."*[9]

80. The Post Office has, with the consultants, PricewaterhouseCoopers, developed a different method of calculating - the *entry pricing* method. This seeks to identify *"under specific liberalisation assumptions by how much the profit of the business [would] be reduced if there remain[ed] the requirement to provide the universal service at uniform prices"*. In short, this approach was designed to model a dynamic market based on a pessimistic assumption that competition would reduce significantly The Post Office's revenues.

81. On the basis of the *avoided cost* method, the Commission argues that the implementation of the current proposals would put the cost of supporting the universal service obligation at no more than 5 per cent of revenue (Q 21). The Post Office disagrees saying that by its method of calculation. *"The total amount of traffic that we think we would actually lose if there were a reduction in the monopoly down to 50g is only about 7 or 8 per cent of the total traffic we have at the present time. It is the loss of that traffic which will then equate, in terms of loss of profits, to the ability to finance the Universal Service Obligation, to a figure between £250 million and £300 million"*. (Q 76)

82. The Committee asked the Commission to say why it had chosen the net avoided cost method and how it responded to The Post Office's advocacy of the entry-pricing method. The Committee is persuaded by the Commission's argumentation, in its supplementary evidence[10], though it recognises that the Commission's method measures the current market environment and does not address the consequences of liberalisation in the way that the entry-pricing method does. The Committee feels that while there is merit in the entry-pricing method, too much depends on sensitive and subjective assumptions. The Committee regrets that The Post Office did not provide figures based on the net-avoided cost method while at the same time advancing the entry-pricing method as its preferred system for measuring the cost of the universal service obligation.

83. The difference produced by the two methods is so wide as to make it difficult to establish what the true picture might be. The Committee is, however, more inclined towards the Commission's view that the impact on the Post Office will not be as great as alleged by The Post Office, partly because the proposed liberalisation to 50 grams would still leave the incumbent with 60 per cent of its revenues from the reserved area, which many "businesses and companies would be delighted if that were the position which they faced" (Q 79), and partly because of the elusive nature of The Post Office's evidence. At one point the Committee was startled to be told by The Post Office that it had no means of determining revenues and costs on a regional basis. Nevertheless, the real problem here is not so much which of the two estimates of the true cost of the universal service obligation is accurate but whether disinterested evidence could be adduced to define the cost of maintaining the universal service obligation.

---

[9] The Post Office's Supplementary Evidence Page (36)
[10] Supplementary evidence from the European Commission. Page (15)

84. The Government argues that it is precisely because it is so difficult to define this particular cost, it would be unwise to support the existing proposals for a reduction on the weight/price basis from 350 grams to 50 grams, and that if a reduction has to be made as part of a negotiation, then the sticking point should rest at 150 grams. This figure was advanced with virtually the same supporting argument by the Post Office, the CWU/CMA, the National Federation of Sub-Postmasters, Mr Brian Simpson MEP, the Scottish Parliament (in a separate letter to Commissioner Bolkestein), and the French Post Office. It might appear that the figure has more to do with the bargaining process than with any reflection of the real cost of maintaining the universal service obligation — the Minister admitted he had no idea whether this figure would preserve The Post Office's ability to fund the universal service obligation (Q 343). The Government added that having enacted legislation — the Postal Services Act 2000 — it could not intervene further to determine this particular cost and that this was a matter for the newly established regulator, PostComm . Whatever PostComm came up with would be regarded as a major input into the Government's considerations (Q 344).

85. Under the Postal Services Act 2000, The Post Office is to be vested with public limited company status on 26 March 2001 and the regulator's first concern will be to license The Post Office within the reserved area. The Committee understands, however, that PostComm is heavily engaged in examining financial and other issues around maintaining the universal service obligation in the United Kingdom. The problem for the Committee in terms of the current proposals is that it is unlikely that PostComm will report until mid-2001 at the earliest.

86. In the United Kingdom, there is full competition outside the reserved monopoly area. Within the reserved area, the regulator can opt to lower the ceiling, as the European Commission proposes, or he can select services for which he issues licences to competitors. He can also exempt types of mail or permit downstream access and third party access to the postal route. It is not possible at this stage to predict which route PostComm will adopt, indeed the regulator might choose more than one.

87. If the European Commission's current proposal is adopted, then one of the tools which the regulator might wish to use will be blunted. PostComm, therefore, has an interest in preserving a higher ceiling in the reserved area than the actual cost, however calculated, which the universal service obligation might demand, in order to retain flexibility in pursuing its objectives. But if the ceiling is left at a high level, whether this be 350 grams or 150 grams, and the regulator proceeds to introduce competition by other methods, then The Post Office could be disadvantaged compared to its European competitors who would be able to continue to shelter the national incumbent beneath the higher ceiling without opening the reserved area by the introduction of selective competition.

88. A second problem is one of timing. The United Kingdom's Government's approach to liberalising the United Kingdom's postal system is out of step with the Commission's timetable. The French Presidency has called for the Commission's proposals to be considered at the Council on the 22 December 2000. The Minister told the Committee that little would probably be decided on this occasion, it would be an orientation debate only, and the Commission's proposals would not impact on PostComm's programme. But there is always the possibility that the French Presidency might see advantage in achieving an agreed position on 22 December on the basis of the Commission's proposals but with a compromise figure of a weight/price reduction to 150 grams. If the proposal was unresolved at this meeting then it would fall to the Swedish Presidency to pick it up. The Swedish attitude might be far more favourable to the proposal as the Commission has put it forward because Member States which have liberalised are at a competitive disadvantage in cross-border markets where such markets are still protected. Even if the French Presidency does advance compromise proposals on 22 December, there can be no certainty that the Council will give them a fair wind.

89. The Committee accepts the argument made by the Post Office, The CWU/CMA, the National Federation of Sub-Postmasters and the Government that it is important to get the right weight/price reduction because the process of liberalisation is irreversible. In the absence of a neutral and accurate means of assessing the cost of the universal service obligation, and given the apparent intention of PostComm to use competition within the reserved area to stimulate better services and innovation in the incumbent, the Committee concludes that at this stage it would be wiser to proceed more cautiously than the draft directive envisages. Having said this, the Committee still believes that only the rapid introduction of competition will effectively reform an organisation which is failing to offer the services, that the public has a right to expect. The Committee's preference would be to support the Commission's proposals for a reduction to 50 grams. The Committee was not convinced by the arguments put forward by those who sought to resist the Commission's proposal. However, the difficulty of reconciling the UK's national agenda — the implementation of the Postal Services Act 2000 — with the progress of the Commission's proposal in the EU institutions prompts us to withhold judgment until we are able to see how PostComm proposes to deal with its management of the reserved area.

DIRECT MAIL

90. The Commission's proposal couples letter mail and direct mail. Direct mail is already outside the reserved area in five Member States (Finland, Italy, Netherlands, Spain and Sweden) and partly liberalised in a sixth (Germany, where the Government has reduced the monopoly ceiling on direct mail to 50 grams). Many witnesses (AICES, EEA, MUA, DMA, UPS) argue that direct mail should be fully liberalised immediately. Direct mail constitutes a substantial proportion of items below 50 grams. The Committee does not think that it makes sense to break the link with the ordinary letter post until the regulator has been able to rule on the cost of maintaining the universal service obligation at a uniform and affordable tariff.

SPECIAL SERVICES

91. The Commission witnesses rehearsed clearly the definition of special services. *"There are three criteria that are established in the Directive in order to qualify for a special service. One is that they have to be clearly distinct from the universal service; secondly, that they have to meet specific customers' needs and they have two or more value-added features"* (Q 44).

92. The Post Office argues that not only is it unnecessary for the Commission to pronounce on this issue but confusing because the European Court of Justice has, in the Corbeau case[11], already established principles about the extent to which it is possible to reserve "new services". In considering whether Article 90 (2) (now Article 86) (2)[12] could be used to justify extending the postal monopoly to "new services" the court held that such an extension was not justifiable provided that;

(1) the new services in question were distinct ("dissociable") from the postal services offered by the incumbent postal administration, and

(2) that placing such service in the competitive area would not undermine the economic equilibrium of the incumbent postal administration in providing the postal service of general economic interest.

93. The Post Office therefore rests its case on the second limb of the test in the Corbeau case, namely that "special services" (however defined) must not undermine the economic equilibrium under which the incumbent postal administration provides the service of general economic interest (the universal service obligation as defined in Article 3 of the Postal Services Directive). The Post Office goes on to say that it follows from the Commission's proposal that once a service is found to be *"a special service then it is incapable of reservation, irrespective of the effect on the universal service provider's ability to provide a universal service"*.

94. In the new proposal, the Commission seeks to re-define more tightly the characteristics of special services to reinforce the distinction between special services and universal services because special services are excluded from the reserved area. The Commission argues that the Corbeau judgment applied only in the absence of harmonised Community rules; the 1997 Directive had since provided a harmonised maximum reservable area to sustain the universal service obligation. Hence, there was no conflict between the Corbeau judgment and the exclusion of special services from the reserved area as laid down in the 1997 Directive. On the contrary, "The Directive 97/67/EC and the proposed modification integrates the principles established in the Corbeau judgment…"[13] In any case, the issue of what constitutes special services will have to be considered by PostComm when the regulator licenses the universal service provider in March 2001 because the terms of such licence will presumably define the characteristics of the universal service obligation and, by implication, services which do not fall into the reserved area.

---

[11] Case C-320/91, *Corbeau*, [1993] ECR I-2533. Mr Corbeau, a Liège trader, was prosecuted for providing postal services within the city and outskirts of Liège. He undertook to collect correspondence from the sender's address and deliver it the next morning provided the addressee was located within the area which he served. He also arranged to forward by the postal service correspondence for addresses outside that area. Belgian law reserved to the Belgian postal administration (the *Régie des Postes*) the activities of collecting, carrying and distributing correspondence. The Tribunal Correctionel de Liège (Criminal Court, Liège) sought guidance from the European Court of Justice on the compatibility of the Belgian rules with Community law. The court of Justice held that it was contrary to Article 86 (formerly 90) of the EC Treaty for a Member State which confers on a body the exclusive right to collect, carry and distribute mail, to prohibit an economic operator established in that State for offering certain specific services dissociable from the service operated of general interest which meet the special needs o economic operators and call for certain additional services not offered by the traditional postal service, in so far as those services do not compromise the economic stability of the service of general economic interest performed by the holder of the exclusive right.

[12] The competition rules of the EC Treaty (in particular Articles 81 and 82) apply to both public and private undertakings. Article 86 (2) provides a limited exception: undertakings entrusted with the operation of services of general economic interest are subject to the competition rules of the Treaty in so far as the application of such rules does not obstruct the performance, in law or in fact, of the particular tasks assigned to them.

[13] Commission's supplementary evidence page 19.

95. The Committee considers that the Post Office has failed to make a persuasive case on special services. We accept the Commission's attempt to define special services in a way that will lead to legal clarity and thus help preserve the reserved area. In our opinion, the Corbeau judgment has been overtaken by the provisions of the 1997 Postal Directive.

COMPENSATION FUND

96. *"The Postal Directive enables a Member State to set up a compensation fund where it determines that the universal services obligation in Article 3 represents an unfair financial burden to the universal service provider. Since such a fund or any other state resource for this purpose might contain state aid elements, this Directive includes a recital which recall the notification requirements for such aid under Articles 87 (1) and 88 (3) of the Treaty".*[14] The Committee notes that provision for a compensation fund remains an option under the 1997 Postal Directive. None of the evidence we have seen supports the setting up of a compensation fund. Nevertheless, the Committee believes it should remain an option which national regulators might use.

---

[14] (Paragraph 2.9.3 of the Explanatory Memorandum covering the proposed draft Directive)

PART 4: SUMMARY OF CONCLUSIONS AND RECOMMENDATIONS

97. Further liberalisation is both desirable and unavoidable because it introduces competition. Competition is needed in order to improve services and efficiency. Therefore, the Commission's proposals are, in principle, acceptable.

98. Everyone — incumbents, competitors, and consumers — recognises the importance of maintaining the universal service obligation, though there is considerable variation in different Member States about the extent to which they go beyond the definition in Articles 3–6 of the 1997 Directive. It will be important for the regulator to define the universal service obligation for the licensed United Kingdom universal service provider.

99. In the United Kingdom, it is equally important that the universal service obligation be delivered to a uniform tariff at an affordable price. Given the tendency of liberalisation to push up costs for individual users while reducing them for business users, it is important that the regulator rule on the tariff structure. People need to know exactly how much the change to a more liberal regime will cost them in terms of the price of stamps and levels of service.

100. The core issue is: what does it cost the universal service provider to continue to sustain the universal service obligation at a uniform and affordable tariff? The Commission argues that to reduce the reserved area (monopoly) by weight and price from the current 350 grams to 50 grams will not imperil the universal service obligation at a uniform and affordable tariff because the vast majority of letter post, including direct mail, falls beneath a 20 gram ceiling. The incumbent will retain 50 per cent, on average (60 per cent in the UK case) of all existing postal services revenue and the impact of competition on the incumbent's revenues can be both stimulating as well as damaging. The Post Office appears to ignore the element of opportunity deriving from greater competition and sees only potential losses. The Post Office, the Unions, the NFSP, the consumers (CEG), and the Government urge caution and a reduction to 150 grams until the effects of further liberalisation can be assessed. The Committee is not persuaded that the reduction of the ceiling on the reserved area by weight and price to 50 grams will have the consequence The Post Office predicts — too many of the latter's assumptions are questionable.

101. Therefore the Committee accepts the Commission's case. However, there is a problem for the United Kingdom. The United Kingdom regulator, PostComm, established under the Postal Services Act 2000, whose task is to maintain the universal service obligation, will not be in a position to report on the cost of sustaining the universal service obligation until mid-2001. The Committee believes that it would be illogical to shackle the regulator before he has had a chance to examine the universal service obligation and to indicate how he intends to use his powers under the Act to introduce competition into the reserved area.

102. Therefore, pending a clearer view of the cost of the universal service obligation, and assuming that the Commission's proposals will continue to be negotiated in the EU, the Committee **recommends that the Government support a reduction to 150 grams at this stage.**

103. The Committee does not believe that the Post Office has made a sufficiently persuasive case on special services and **recommends that the Government support the European Commission's proposal in this respect.**

104. It is unlikely that the Government will wish to use state aid to support the establishment of a compensation fund, but the Committee **recommends no change to the provision contained in the text of the proposed directive**[15].

105. The Committee believes that the Commission's proposal for a Directive amending Directive 97/67/EC with regard to further opening to competition of Community postal services raises important issues to which the attention of the House should be drawn, and we make this report for information.

---

[15] Recital 26

APPENDIX 1

Sub-Committee B (Energy, Industry and Transport)

The members of the Sub-Committee which conducted this inquiry were:

- L. Bradshaw
- L. Brooke of Alverthorpe (Chairman)
- V. Brookeborough
- L. Cavendish of Furenss
- L. Chadlington
- L. Faulkner of Worcester
- B. O'Cathain
- L. Paul
- L. Sandberg
- L. Skelmersdale
- L. Woolmer of Leeds

APPENDIX 2

List of Witnesses

The following witnesses gave evidence. Those marked * gave oral evidence.

    Association of International Courier and Express Services (AICES)
* Communication Workers' Union/Communication Managers' Association

    Consumers in Europe Group
* Department of Trade and Industry
* Direct Marketing Association (UK) Limited
* European Commission
* Free and Fair Post Initiative (FFPI)

    La Poste, France
* Mail Users' Association

    Mr W Maschke, Deutsche Post

    Posten AB, Sweden
* Mr Axel Rindborg of Free and Fair Post

    Royal National Institute for the Blind

    Brian Simpson, MEP

    The Post Office

    Ross Clark, Journalist, The Spectator
* TNT Group N.V.

    United Parcel Service

    Mr Anton van der Lande, Chairman, EEA Postal Committee

APPENDIX 3

CALL FOR EVIDENCE

FURTHER LIBERALISATION OF THE POSTAL SERVICES

I am writing to invite you to submit written evidence to the inquiry on postal services to be conducted by Sub-Committee B of the House of Lords European Union Committee. The inquiry is based upon the Commission's proposal to open up further parts of the postal services market to competition by January 2003 (Proposal for a European Parliament and Council Directive amending Directive 97/67/EC with regard to the further opening to competition of Community postal services). The Commission proposes to:

reduce the existing weight/price limits from 350 grams / 5 times the basic standard tariff for letters to 50 grams/ 2.5 times the basic standard tariff for letters;

reduce the existing weight/price limits from 350 grams / 5 times the basic standard tariff for letters to 50 grams / 2.5 times the basic standard tariff for direct mail (i.e. addressed advertising material);

full opening to competition of outward cross-border mail;

full opening to competition of all express mail services (without price limit).

The inquiry will build on the Sub-Committee's previous consideration of postal services liberalisation in Session 1995-96 (House of Lords European Communities Committee, 10th Report, Session 1995-96, "Community Postal Services" HL 81].

The Sub-Committee is particularly interested in the views of witnesses on the following points:
What benefits are likely to result from the proposed liberalisation measures?
What problems could result from the proposed liberalisation, particularly in terms of maintenance of a universal service with an affordable and uniform tariff structure?
Are there any measures not identified in the Commission's proposals which would help to secure the Community's stated aims for postal services?

Evidence should be submitted to Patrick Wogan, Committee Office, House of Lords, London SW1A 0PW. Fax 020 7219 6715. E-mail woganp@parliament.uk OR sampsonm@parliament.uk. **Evidence must arrive by 15 September 2000.**

Evidence should be written in short numbered paragraphs and accompanied by a brief summary of the main points. It should not exceed six sides of A4 except by prior arrangement with the Clerk. If drawings or charts are included, these must be black-and-white and of camera-ready quality.

Evidence should be signed and dated, with a note of the author's name and status, and of whether the evidence is submitted on an individual or corporate basis. Only one copy is required. All submissions will be acknowledged. Evidence submitted in response to this invitation becomes the property of the House and may be printed.

You may follow the progress of the inquiry from the Weekly Agenda of House of Lords Select Committees. This is free, and may be ordered from Geoffrey Newsome, Committee Office, House of Lords, London SW1A 0PW, telephone 020 7219 6678. Alternatively, consult the UK Parliament web site, at http://www.parliament.uk.

[END]

MINUTES OF EVIDENCE

TAKEN BEFORE THE EUROPEAN UNION COMMITTEE (SUB-COMMITTEE B)

WEDNESDAY 11 OCTOBER 2000

Present:

Brooke of Alverthorpe, L.
    (Chairman)
Cavendish of Furness, L.
Faulkner of Worcester, L.

O'Cathain, B.
Paul, L.
Skelmersdale, L.
Woolmer of Leeds, L.

Memorandum by the European Commission

Why a Commission proposal?

Requirement in current Directive and request from the European Council at Lisbon in March 2000;

Need to assist Postal sector's evolution:

— Market players are gearing up for competitive market (through international alliances and acquisitions), resulting in distortions to Internal Market and growing competition concerns;

— Technological competition is starting to put at risk segments of traditional mail, requiring further competitiveness.

Benefits of the Commission's proposal

Adapting the regulatory framework to market reality will decrease current market distortions and improve efficiency;

Increased competition will lead to benefits for both businesses and consumers from more competitive prices, improved quality of service and increased market innovation;

A gradual and controlled approach is proposed, creating real competition while taking full account of both the need to preserve universal service and the reality of uniform tariffs:

— Reduction in the weight limit to 50 grams is reasonable as it is practical, while allowing competition and safeguarding universal service;

— Opening all outward cross-border mail to competition reflects market reality and will result in improved quality of service;

— Safeguards for universal service and the uniform tariff remain, eg the national legislator's and regulator's powers to set tariffs, licensing conditions and to set up a compensation fund if needed;

— Other provisions strengthen regulatory framework by promoting innovative services and increasing consumer protection;

— Further step in 2007 dependent on review of universal service provision in 2004 and no preconditions are set now.

Budgetary impact of Commission's proposals will be positive since they aim at sustained greater profitability for incumbents.

CONTEXT OF THE COMMISSION'S PROPOSAL

1. On 30 May 2000, the European Commission agreed on a proposal for a European Parliament and Council Directive amending Directive 97/67 EC with regard to the further opening to competition of Community postal services. The proposal, including the explanatory memorandum, is attached for reference. This proposal responded first to the requirement in Article 7 of the existing Directive for the Commission to make a proposal for the further gradual and controlled opening of the postal market. Second, the proposal responded to the European Council of Heads of State and Government in Lisbon in March of this year which called upon the Commission, the Council and Member States to act in accordance with their respective powers to achieve the following objectives:

— to set out by the end of 2000 a strategy for the removal of barriers to services (including postal services);

— to speed up the liberalisation in areas such as . . . postal services, with the aim of achieving a fully operational market in these areas.

11 October 2000] [*Continued*

A. BENEFITS OF THE COMMISSION'S PROPOSAL

2. There are three levels of benefits involved with the Commission's proposal:
   1. General benefits inherent to improving access to the postal market;
   2. Benefits of the approach proposed by the Commission;
   3. Specific benefits of the main elements of the proposed measures.

GENERAL BENEFITS INHERENT TO IMPROVING ACCESS TO THE POSTAL MARKET

More efficient markets and services

3. Experience over a wide variety of different sectors, for example telecommunications, largely proved that liberalisation brings important market benefits, particularly for business but also for consumers: more competitive prices, improved quality of service and increased market innovation to tailor solutions according to customer needs. There is no reason to expect different results in the postal sector provided that prices are geared to costs and licensing conditions are adequate. This is also backed up by experience in Member States where postal services have been further liberalised than required by the current postal Directive.

Implementing the Internal Market

4. The benefits inherent to the implementation of the internal market (free movement of goods and services and freedom of establishment) will become available within this important sector which is already partly open to competitor access. Apart from removing trade barriers and creating new business opportunities for operators, the market opening will also allow current distortions to be reduced through increasing the level of harmonisation of market access.

Catching up with market reality

5. The postal sector has already anticipated market opening. Posts which used to be government administrations have been turned into commercial organisations; mergers, acquisitions and alliances bloomed during the past few years in order to fulfil increasing demand for pan-European and global services. Furthermore, half of the Member States have already opened their postal markets further than required by the existing postal Directive.

Opening the postal market is not only an opportunity: it is a must

6. The status quo is not a viable option if the requirements of increasing service quality and developing employment opportunities are to be met. The letter mail market is a maturing market under severe threat from indirect technological competition and needs increased innovation in order to continue growing. Some mail segments, such as banking mail, are already starting to migrate to electronic means of communication eroding letter volume growth. Moreover, competition concerns are important and increasing and there is a real risk that lasting damage is done to the market if current distortions are not corrected and innovation is not promoted.

Budgetary consequences of market opening

7. Greater competition will further the efficiency and profitability of the incumbent operators, making these companies more valuable.

BENEFITS OF THE APPROACH PROPOSED BY THE COMMISSION

A gradual market opening

8. The Commission's proposal is a gradual opening of the market for postal services within a step-by-step approach spread over at least a decade since the adoption of the existing 97/67 EC Directive in December 1997. At that time, 27 per cent of the USPs' postal revenues on average were open to competition. The initial postal Directive opened approximately a further 3 per cent of the USPs' revenues from postal services leaving 70 per cent of these revenues on average in the reservable area.

9. The total market opening proposed as the next step to be implemented from 2003 represents an additional 20 per cent of these revenues, which means that up to 50 per cent of the USPs' revenues from postal services can be maintained within the reserved area. The proposed additional opening is set at a reasonable

level to ensure that actual competition can take place without jeopardising the provision of the universal service.

10. An additional step will take place in 2007, based on a proposal from the Commission following a review of the sector which will focus on assuring universal service in a competitive environment.

A controlled market opening

11. The means proposed to achieve the gradual market opening have been chosen on the basis of consensus and market reality following consultations with operators and regulators, which will ensure a fully controllable implementation:
   — Consensus means: reducing weight and price limits for the maximum reservable area is considered generally as the best approach by all postal industry stakeholders;
   — Market reality: liberalising *de jure* growing market segments already opened *de facto* to competition (eg outgoing cross-border mail).

The economic viability of the universal service

12. The Commission has examined the financial equilibrium of the universal service and has concluded that universal service is economically viable in a situation of progressive market opening. USPs are generally in an improving financial situation and some make substantial profits drawn from the letters monopoly which may help to finance acquisitions of private operators.

13. Although it is not the objective of the current or the proposed Directive to guarantee additional social obligations (for example, relating to a uniform tariff) the proposal gives sufficient scope for Member States to implement such tariffs. Member States must take account of how to finance them when they impose such obligations (also ensuring that such obligations do not distort competition).

National Legislators and Regulatory Authorities are empowered to ensure smooth implementation according to national political requirements

14. National legislators and regulatory authorities are empowered to implement the proposed Directive and have powers to adapt the Community regulatory framework to the domestic environment. First, they can maintain the uniform tariff, including setting it at a level appropriate to ensure universal service. Second, they can impose licensing conditions on all operators in the universal service area. Third, they can establish a compensation fund if the universal service represents an unfair financial burden for the USP.

A feasible approach

15. The proposed gradual approach makes the proposal economically feasible, providing the time necessary for the holders of postal monopolies to prepare for the possibility of increased competition, which in any case they have already been doing for several years. The current growth of the letter mail market (+3 per cent per year in volumes on average) makes it even more feasible since the market growth can allow the potential impact of competition on the incumbents to be compensated.

SPECIFIC BENEFITS OF THE MAIN ELEMENTS OF THE PROPOSED MEASURES

(a) *50 gram weight limit*

16. The reduction in the weight and price limits to 50 grams and 2.5 times the tariff for ordinary, direct and inward cross-border mail (which amounts to 16 per cent of USPs' postal revenues) is easy for regulators to enforce and will allow a limited amount of competition, ensuring that the proposal should be gradual and controlled.

17. In particular, the nearest alternatives appear flawed: 20 grams might be too much too quickly, as it would increase the market opening from 20 per cent to 32 per cent of universal service providers' postal revenues. Moreover, a 20 gram limit would encourage small changes in weight to bring letter mail items outside the reservable area, leading to regulatory uncertainty. On the other hand 100 grams would reduce the market opening from 20 per cent to 14 per cent which would not result in market entry and would not therefore make the required difference to postal operators to be effective. A 50 gram limit can allow sufficient revenues to be open for some actual competition to be attractive for new entrants, particularly for heavier direct mail and packages which are growing with the development of advertising and electronic commerce. 50 grams is therefore a reasonable level that is also practical.

18. Only a significant percentage opening of the market (secured by a reduction to 50 grams) will enable the incumbent operators to maintain in so far as possible employment and allow for increased employment

11 October 2000] [*Continued*

with the private operators. Liberalisation is not the main driver for reductions in employment in the sector (currently reducing by 0.8 per cent per annum as a result of technological and management changes). However, if no modernisation were to take place under pressure from a realistic market opening, projections show a substantial and sudden decline in customer demand for mail services. This demand would migrate to other means of communication and would mainly concern the growing advertising market, business mail and bank correspondence. The consequences of doing too little would thus be an accelerated decline in employment in traditional mail services.

19. The effect on mail volumes and profitability is also expected to be positive. Significant market growth is still predicted for the letter market over the medium term (for example, in the UK, direct mail volumes are currently growing by around 10 per cent per annum). Given that most of the costs of incumbent universal service providers are fixed labour costs, the boosts to overall volumes will benefit the universal service providers by providing additional profits at very little extra cost. It is estimated that most universal service providers will generally see an increase in profitability as a result which will compensate for the loss of volumes to new market entrants. Experience shows that typically incumbents with good quality of service can expect to retain 80–90 per cent of the market opened to competition over the medium term.

20. The reduction proposed will benefit household consumers as senders of mail, and not only businesses with large volumes, since the increased efficiency and quality of service accorded to business mail will automatically flow through to the treatment of individual consumer mail which goes through the same process. In addition, household consumers will also benefit as receivers of mail. Around two thirds of all mail items are sent to households who will benefit indirectly from quality improvements granted to business mail.

(b) *Opening outgoing cross-border mail to competition*

21. Outgoing cross-border mail is already "de facto" open to competition in 10 Member States, including the two countries with the highest volumes of outward cross-border mail (Ireland and Luxembourg). It accounts on average for 3 per cent of universal service providers' postal revenues. Opening this segment will bring the regulatory framework into line with market reality. It will also allow existing and new postal operators to form partnerships with other operators. It will lead to an improvement in the quality of service for cross-border mail delivery by improving the outward transit times and reducing the disruptive effects of borders on the mail flows.

(c) *Removing the price limit on express mail*

22. There is a principle already well established in the Directive that new services, in the sense of services which are "quite distinct from conventional services", do not form part of the universal service and consequently there is no justification for their being reserved to universal providers. Express services are a prime example of such services and therefore it is not appropriate for a price limit to apply to express mail services. Experience shows that it may be possible to provide a small number of localised express services at a price below the price limit. This is estimated at 1 per cent of universal service providers' postal revenues. Removing this limit would allow such services to proceed and bring the Directive into line with the general principle on new (ie distinct) services which it has already established.

(d) *The definition of special services*

23. These services are already out of the reservable area according to the existing Directive. There is no change to this basic principle. The reason to define special services in the Directive proposal is to promote these services for users and to clarify their status following recent complaints received by the Commission concerning the provision of such services in individual Member States. Innovation in the postal market is thereby encouraged within a clear regulatory framework.

24. A definition in the articles of the Directive is considered necessary (to supplement the existing reference in the recitals) so as to give sufficient guidance to national regulatory authorities over criteria which determine when a service is a special service outside of the reservable area.. Accordingly, special services are better defined in the proposal in that they must meet three conditions. They must:

— be clearly distinct from the universal service;

— meet specific customer requirements; and

— have certain added-value features not offered by the standard (ie conventional) postal service.

(e) *Special tariffs*

25. The proposal includes a revision to ensure that special reduced tariffs offered by the universal service provider to users, particularly to businesses or consolidators of mail, are provided in a transparent and non-discriminatory manner and are available to all users posting under equivalent conditions. A practical benefit

will be to ensure that consolidators can access bulk mail discounts related to avoided costs for the universal service provider on all the consolidated mail they handle. That will enable small and medium-sized businesses, which post lower volumes, to have indirect access to the discounts given to larger mailers. The result will be a lowering of their postage costs.

(f) *Rights of consumers*

26. The proposal includes a revision which ensures that procedures for dealing fairly with customer complaints will apply equally to postal services which are outside the universal service. The proposal also states the principle of non-discrimination between business and consumers in accessing postal services. Both provisions will increase consumer protection.

(g) *The further step in 2007*

27. With regard to the time schedule of the proposal for a next phase proposed to take place from 2007, a review of the sector will be undertaken prior to a new proposal in 2004 focusing on how to guarantee universal service in an appropriate manner in a competitive environment. The postal market requires clarity as the market is dynamic and changing and cannot therefore wait longer. Moreover, for the next stage of market opening, a two-year review is proposed; the last directive had only a period of one year and this was from the date of adoption, not the date of transposition. There are also no preconditions set in advance on the nature or extent of market opening which may be proposed, enabling the effects for universal service to be assessed first.

B. THE PROPOSED MARKET OPENING ALLOWS FOR THE MAINTENANCE OF THE UNIVERSAL SERVICE AND A UNIFORM TARIFF

28. The Directive proposal is aimed at establishing a framework for further implementation of the internal market in postal services. A substantial part of the progress towards this goal is left to the national regulator or legislator. The objective of the Directive proposal is not to regulate every detail but it seeks instead to establish a co-operation with the national authorities.

29. With regard to universal service, Member States remain free to maintain a reservable area of up to 50 per cent of incumbent postal revenues to finance the universal service. In addition, national authorities remain competent to determine the price level for all mail, including the application of a uniform tariff or maximum tariff. The level of tariffs set is a major factor affecting the profitability of universal service operators. National authorities also have the facility to establish both licensing conditions for private operators and a compensation fund if such a fund is needed. This will allow Member States to ensure that the universal service is provided in an adequate manner according to national requirements.

30. Finally, with regard to the provision of rural services, the 1997 Directive allows full liberty to the Member States to organise their postal networks and maintain rural post offices as they see fit, allowing operators to maximise the benefits that can be gained from having such a network. The Commission continues fully to support that objective and has ensured that the tools to do this will be maintained.

C. ARE THERE ANY OTHER MEASURES NOT IDENTIFIED IN THE COMMISSION'S PROPOSALS WHICH WOULD HELP SECURE THE COMMUNITY'S AIMS IN THIS AREA?

31. No. At this stage, the Commission considers that the proposals made constitute a balanced package which takes account of the mandate which was given by the European Council at Lisbon and the requirements of the existing Directive.

19 September 2000

Examination of Witnesses

MR PAUL WATERSCHOOT, Director, Postal Services Unit, MR PHILIP GROVES, Postal Services Unit, Directorate General Internal Market, European Commission, called in and examined.

Chairman

1. Good morning, gentlemen. We are very pleased to see you and hope you have had a pleasant journey across to us.
(*Mr Waterschoot*) Certainly.

2. We hope you will enjoy a pleasant time with us this morning. We are grateful to you for finding time in your busy diaries. We would like to conclude the evidence-taking probably around five to twelve or noon, if that is acceptable to yourself. Is there any opening statement at all you wish to make, or shall we dive straight into questioning?
(*Mr Waterschoot*) I can make a short statement, if you agree. I am Paul Waterschoot, I am a Director of DG Internal Market with the European Commission

11 October 2000] Mr Paul Waterschoot and Mr Philip Groves *[Continued*

Chairman *contd.*]

and I am responsible, among other things, for postal services. Just a brief word about the existing Directive. The existing Directive, which was adopted in 1997, harmonises a minimum level of postal services, and in order to make the provision of this universal service possible there is a reserved area. It also provides for a separation of the regulatory authority from the operator, and it provides for accounting standards and licensing conditions. It also establishes criteria for the quality of services. It also has asked the Commission to come forward with a proposal for a new Directive, which should be a controlled and gradual market opening. That was the mandate it gave to the Commission. The Commission came forward with a proposal in May this year and the main content of that is to reduce the reserved area from 350 to 50g, to liberalise out-going cross-border mail, and to reduce the price limit for express mail. It also foresees a further step to be taken in 2007. The three main issues which are discussed presently, both in the European Parliament and in Council, are the definition of special services, the reduction of the price weight limit to 50g and the timetable for further market opening. That is what I can say as an opening statement.

3. That is very helpful indeed. Thank you very much. You have set the scene for us. I am wondering if you could please explain what you see as the principal benefits to arise from the Commission's proposals for the economy and for consumers more generally?
(*Mr Waterschoot*) Our opinion is that introducing competition will improve the quality of service. The pressure of competition leads to innovative services and more flexible services for users. Also, the proposal perceives more flexible access to the postal network by small and medium sized enterprises. It also, we think, will improve the speed and reliability of cross-border mail. One of the weak points is the interface between different postal operators, and we think there can be substantial improvement. Substantial improvements have already taken place under the first Directive. It also, we think, will improve the sustained and lasting employment in the postal sector. With technological competition, by e-mail and other means, if there is not modernising action undertaken the employment in the postal sector will be reduced. It will promote investment because it gives a clear legal framework about further developments.

4. Just following up, really, on your introduction on the three principal issues which are presently being discussed, could we also have a look at it from an extreme position? Some of the newer Member States, such as Finland and Sweden, have totally demonopolised the postal services. Why have you not gone for that more radical approach?
(*Mr Waterschoot*) I think the main reason was that we had a political mandate, which was in the first Directive, to take a controlled and gradual approach. We also have to take account of the fact that this is a harmonisation Directive, so it should harmonise situations in different Member States and these situations are quite different, which means that for some Member States we could have gone faster, but we have to take account of the slowest ship in the convoy.

Lord Skelmersdale

5. Who is the slowest ship in the convoy?
(*Mr Waterschoot*) I think that a number of Southern Member States—Italy, Spain and Greece—are rather slow and France is also one of the slower ones.

Chairman

6. Where does the United Kingdom fit in the pattern?
(*Mr Waterschoot*) Fairly average. Quite well as regards the quality of service but average as regards market liberalisation. We also have to take account of the fact that incumbents need quite some time to make the structure of adaptations which are necessary. There is very large employment in this sector and it takes time to adapt to the new environment. So these are the main reasons why we have this progressive approach.

Baroness O'Cathain

7. Thank you very much for your comments in answer to my Lord Chairman's first question. I took down the points that you made about competition in general and how you felt that competition would improve the quality of services, lead to greater innovation and flexibility, access to the network by SMEs etc. It all had a horrible ring of déjà-vu for me (if you can actually say "ringing", which is aural, in relation to déjà-vu, which is seeing). We had a situation in this country, in another industry, where it was said that all these things were going to happen. It was actually the dairy industry in this country, and what actually happened when competition came in was that it just decimated the producer base. I know there is not a producer base for postal services but are we actually convinced that by bringing in this sort of liberalisation the people who live on tops of mountains in Scotland or Wales or down the middle of valleys where there are very few chimney pots—as they say—are going to have as good a service as they have at the moment? The way we put up, those of us who live in cities, with the cost and the lack of flexibility of the postal services is actually to support those areas where it costs an awful lot more to both collect and deliver mail because there are not the chimney pots. How convinced are you that by bringing in this great idea of competition, which is a sort of mantra, if you like, that we are going to end up with a universal postal service where people are not going to be desperately disadvantaged if they live in rural areas?
(*Mr Waterschoot*) I think one can make several arguments. One is that as a reference model I would rather look at the telecom than the dairy industry. That has more similar factors. In the telecom industry the deregulation has been quite a success. Prices have gone down, new services have been provided and there has been, I think, even an increase

Baroness O'Cathain *contd.*]

in employment, if you compare all the operators in the market. As regards universal service, I think, to be honest, we have to assess what the universal service is which people need. Perhaps until now we have looked at this universal service as something which has been defined by regulators instead of asking the consumers what they want. My impression is that often the consumer would be quite happy to pay something extra to have the mail sooner or on time on a more regular basis. This said, I know that the quality of service here in the United Kingdom is excellent. The experience we have is that there are a number of Member States where there has been total market liberalisation. One of the countries I would mention is Sweden. Sweden is not a country which is demographically very favourable for the provision of a universal service; it is a very large country with a population which is in all areas. Sweden has one of the best quality services in Europe. Finland is another case, but Finland has no real competition in the market. It has been liberalised but there is no real competition in the market outside parcel services, of course. For mail there is very little competition. I would mention that in Sweden the quality of service, even if you liberalise the market completely, can be excellent.

Chairman

8. Is it not also very expensive in Sweden?

(*Mr Waterschoot*) Prices have gone up because when you open up the market you have to treat all operators in the same way. That means that you have to apply VAT also to the incumbent, which means that prices have gone up because of this fiscal measure.

Lord Woolmer of Leeds

9. I understand that there are a number of studies which have been carried out for the Commission prior to the issue of the new Directive. What were the key issues studied and how does the outcome of your studies affect the proposals that you have made?

(*Mr Waterschoot*) You are quite right, there were a number of studies carried out in 1997, 1998 and 1999. One dealt with the evaluation of the cost of the universal service—the additional cost. The other study dealt with the liberalisation of direct mail. There were a number of others regarding cross-border mail; the different scenarios regarding price and weight limits—50, 100 and 150g, and so on. Then we also had a study about what we call "downstream access". That is what I mentioned when I referred to small and medium sized enterprises having access to the mail stream at different points. So these were the studies which were carried out, and of course they were extremely useful for us in order to prepare the new proposal. The most important one was the cost of the universal service, but, also, the studies on direct mail had a direct impact on the proposal. So there were a number of direct effects of these studies on the proposals.

10. If I could turn to the question of universal service obligations, what alternative ways of funding the USO did you consider? Is it clear to you that the cost of a USO justifies continuing reserved areas? This is particularly a way of providing a framework in which funds can be made available. So two questions: do your studies justify continuing the reserved area approach to maintaining universal service obligations; secondly, did you consider alternative ways in which universal service could be maintained while increasing competition?

(*Mr Waterschoot*) As regards the alternative ways to deal with the universal service obligation, the existing Directive already foresees a number of alternatives. One is the Compensation Fund, which is a fund which could be financed by other private operators which would enter into the market and would contribute to finance the extra costs of universal service. There are a number of Member States who have implemented this in their legislation. The other element is that the national regulator has the possibility of defining the tariff applied for postal services. The only reference in the Directive in this respect is that tariffs should be related to cost, but there is a very large discretionary power by the national regulator to determine the price in such a way that universal service can be financed. There are also in the existing Directive—and we have not touched on this in our new proposal—licensing conditions that can be provided for those private operators that provide services within the universal service. So outside the reserved area but within the universal service. These licensing conditions can be established in such a way as to avoid cherry-picking and which have an effect to increase the cost for the incumbent when he provides the universal service. These are the alternatives to finance the universal service. Then I come to the second part of the question, which relates to the reserved area. We have to be aware that the reserved area really means that as long as this reserved area exists there is a *caveat* on the functioning of the internal market, because there is no freedom to provide services or establishment. I think what we have in these Directives is a change from the emphasis on the reserved area towards these other means which the national regulator can use in order to ensure that universal service can be provided. As for other advantages, it creates better transparency because if you have a reserved area there are all kinds of cross-subsidies within that reserved area, and when you have compensation from the licensing conditions this creates greater transparency as regards the cost allocation of the incumbent.

Chairman

11. Can that not undermine the universal service obligation as well?

(*Mr Waterschoot*) I do not think so. I think greater transparency on costs is something which is a management requirement, and I think that in a competitive environment there is no way you can avoid this. It is also a requirement within the existing Directive to have analytical accounting. So greater transparency as regards to cost and cost allocation is a requirement and you cannot avoid that.

12. I do not think we have any problem with transparency. We would like to see more of it. Which

Chairman *contd.*]

is the most important: competition or retaining the universal service obligation?

(*Mr Waterschoot*) They are both requirements which the Community has to take into account when it makes proposals.

Baroness O'Cathain

13. If they are mutually exclusive.

(*Mr Waterschoot*) I do not think they are. We have looked into, for example, the situation in Sweden and I have talked to the chief executive officer of Deutsche Post, and what they will tell you is that universal service is not an obligation, it is a market opportunity. I will tell you why. About 60 to 70 per cent of all mail dealt with by the incumbent is business mail to private customers. That is the main market share. These business customers are not going to deal with somebody who cannot deliver mail to all customers. That is the big market advantage of the incumbent, that he has access to all citizens and can deliver mail to all citizens. So it is seen by these incumbents as a market opportunity more than an obligation. Some of the private operators would be disadvantaged if they could not deliver mail widely, and this is the main handicap of entering into this market.

14. Which is why the incumbent in Sweden, even though there is no longer a monopoly, has the majority of the business.

(*Mr Waterschoot*) Exactly.

15. But at a high price.

(*Mr Waterschoot*) The high price has to do with the introduction of VAT on the incumbent. I told you this. When you open up the market you have to deal with all operators in the same way. You cannot say "You, the Post Office, do not pay VAT".

Chairman: Who is the gainer, other than the recipient of the VAT?

Lord Skelmersdale

16. First of all, I would like to declare an interest in that I am one of the contributors to the 60 per cent you have just mentioned. I am a Director of a pan-European mail order firm. The first thing that struck me when I read all these papers was that it is an enormous drop from a level of 350g to 50g. Why did you choose it?

(*Mr Waterschoot*) It is an enormous drop, if you look at the figures for the weight limits, but I think you have to look at what this means in terms of volume of mail and revenues generated from this mail. What we found out is that this drop from 350 to 50g corresponds to 16 per cent of the revenues of the incumbent. I think that this is the right way to look at it. In practice, this means that the incumbents keep, as a reserved area, 50 per cent of the mail market. Fifty per cent, we think, is a reasonable reserved area in order to finance whatever the additional costs are for the universal service. Because some of the arguments have been that we have opened up the most profitable part of the market, we have been very careful about this. We have left the most profitable part of the market in the reserved area. This most profitable part of the market is around 20g. That is where the bulk occurs of the mail delivery and transport. This is where the incumbents finance their fixed costs of the network. That is where they make their profits. We have left that in the reserved area. Secondly, we have left the direct mail below 50g in the reserved area and that is a very increasing part of the market and a very profitable part of the market. Thirdly, we have kept the incoming cross-border mail, which is important for a number of Member States, in the reserved area. So not only is the reserved area the share of the market as important as 50 per cent of the revenues in the mail sector, but secondly the most profitable part of the market remain reserved.

17. I would certainly agree with you that as the weight steps decrease the profit to the operator increases. This is why the British Post Office is concerned that they are going to be made to drop their minimum weight step from 60g to 50g, because that comprises an enormous amount of their volume and an enormous amount of their profit. Have you done any sort of study into this and what the effect would be?

(*Mr Waterschoot*) We have looked at the weight step between 150, 100 and 50g, but I must say we have not looked at the weight step of 60g because it is very particular to the United Kingdom.

18. Exactly. It is unique. It is this particularity which is going to cause a lot of consternation in the subsequent discussions in Brussels. I have no doubt.

(*Mr Waterschoot*) I am aware of that but the volume of mail between 60g and 50g is not comparable to the big bulk, which is around 20g. So I can understand the point about the regulation, that that is difficult because you have another weight step than most of the other Member States, but not the point on the impact on the revenues of the operator, because that part of the market is in no proportion to the big bulk, which occurs around 20g.

Lord Skelmersdale: Have no fear, I shall put exactly the same question to the British Post Office when the time comes.

Lord Woolmer of Leeds: Because that is particular to the United Kingdom, surely you have made an estimate of the proportion of business that is affected by the shift from 60 to 50g? Your job is to see what is practical and the problems that will arise. What advice can you give us? You must have studied this.

Chairman

19. The British Post Office maintain that you will eliminate totally their profit. Would you agree with that view? Have you done any work on it at all?

(*Mr Waterschoot*) They argue that we reduce their profits by moving down to 50g (that is from 150 to 50). It is a different argument from 60 to 50. I would not agree with that at all. The experience we have had is that if you open up the market, even if you open up the market totally (and you have said it yourself, in Sweden the incumbent retains 90 to 95 per cent of the market) there will, in practice, be very little change as regards the market share in the market. What will change is that there will be competitive pressure on the incumbent to be more profitable, to make

Chairman *contd.*]

productivity gains and to provide new services. That is the pressure on the incumbent which flows from the market opening. It does not necessarily mean that large market shares will be lost. This is the experience we have in several Member States. For example, in Germany the weight limit is lower than the Directive allows, and you will see that they maintain a large part of their market.

20. What is the weight limit in Germany?
(*Mr Waterschoot*) 200g. 50 for direct mail.

Lord Skelmersdale

21. As it happens, that is 2.5 times the minimum step in the United Kingdom, which is 60g.
(*Mr Waterschoot*) I do not agree with that assessment. First of all, the incumbent will retain 90 to 95 per cent of the market anyway. That will be the case especially in the United Kingdom because it is an efficient operator. I would not necessarily say so in all Member States where you sometimes have bad quality of service. There the incumbent would be losing more market share and more revenue. Secondly, the estimate by the Post Office does not take account of their own adaptation to the market. If you have a competitive environment the incumbent will change and will become more competitive and will make productivity gains. I think that is important. The third element is that the United Kingdom Post Office over-estimates the cost of providing a universal service. They are using a method which is not really the most appropriate one and our estimate is that the additional cost of providing the universal service is around 5 per cent of the revenues of the universal service provider. These are the additional costs, but in the meantime they are making substantial profits. That is where the profits are made—in providing the universal service. So I think that estimate is not realistic.

Lord Paul

22. It is a very short question. You have mentioned three times now that the United Kingdom Post Office is an efficient operator. Are things much worse in other Member States?
(*Mr Waterschoot*) I honestly think that the quality of the United Kingdom Post Office is excellent and this is why I think they are not going to lose very much market share. This is why I think that they will maintain their profitability.

Baroness O'Cathain

23. Did I hear you correctly that the cost of producing a universal service only amounts to 5 per cent of the value of that service?
(*Mr Waterschoot*) It is even less, because the 5 per cent is the additional (and this is the average for the Community) costs, because in the meantime for other parts of the universal service the incumbent makes profits. This is the area where the incumbents make the most profits. What we have not done is to compensate profitable areas of the universal service with non-profitable ones, but the extra costs—only the extra costs—are estimated to be 5 per cent.

Chairman

24. That is your calculation, using your method of calculation?
(*Mr Waterschoot*) That is our method of calculation.

25. However, there are other methods of calculation?
(*Mr Waterschoot*) Yes, exactly.

Lord Skelmersdale

26. In that case, can I ask why you are loading the chips against the incumbent by not having universal service provision for people coming in and competing with the incumbents?
(*Mr Waterschoot*) That is possible in the sense that the national regulator can apply licensing conditions, and in these licensing conditions you can have certain universal service obligations.

27. Where do I find that in the Directive?
(*Mr Waterschoot*) That is already in the existing Directive.

28. Is it?
(*Mr Waterschoot*) Yes. I think it is Article IX.

29. There is no change to that?
(*Mr Waterschoot*) There is no change on that part, no change at all. I must say that the country that has the most experience with licensing conditions is Germany, and it has worked very well.

Chairman

30. I think, in some respects—maybe you will agree with this—that whilst Sweden and Finland have gone ahead of most other States, Germany is more comparable with us than Sweden.
(*Mr Waterschoot*) Yes, certainly.

31. In terms of the size of the economy and the numbers involved and so on. Really, what has happened in Sweden may not necessarily be replicated here; that, in fact, the private sector might see far greater opportunities here for the kind of market open to them similar to Germany than in Sweden. So their efforts to penetrate could be much more vigorous here.
(*Mr Waterschoot*) Yes. It also has to do with the technology which is implemented. A substantial amount of these new services are services which have new technology features. In as far as there is a demand for such new technology services, I think that the United Kingdom situation is more similar to Germany than Sweden.

Lord Cavendish of Furness

32. My Lord Chairman, if I put my question it might help my colleague, Lord Paul. If you want to post a letter in Italy people go to the Vatican City. I

11 October 2000] MR PAUL WATERSCHOOT AND MR PHILIP GROVES *[Continued*

Lord Cavendish of Furness *contd.*]

think I understood rightly in your opening remarks that you felt your proposals would be, in employment terms, neutral or, maybe, even slightly positive. You may know that the Communication Workers' Union and the Communication Managers' Association, to name but two, are concerned that the proposals would lead to dramatic job losses. I assume you have done an analysis to back up your original statements made in your opening remarks. I would like to ask you how you respond to those anxieties and, perhaps, particularly, whether there may be job losses in the interim while the proposals are working through?

(*Mr Waterschoot*) The estimate we have made is that there is loss of employment of about 0.8 per cent per year, whatever the regulatory environment is. This job loss depends on productivity gains, which the incumbents do whatever the regulator requires. So there is already a tendency to have job losses in this area which are not very big but which are substantial. The argument we are putting forward is that if we do nothing there will be a substantial increase in job losses because the main change in the market is not the regulatory change but it is technological competition. As you all know, e-mail is becoming the kind of way people communicate rapidly and efficiently. This means, of course, there is less work for the post offices of this world. If we do not do anything about this there will be a certain decrease in employment. So the only way to prevent this is to make the incumbents more competitive and, also, to provide these new services. The way to do this is to allow for competition. This also allows for small firms to enter into the market with innovative type of services. On the employment side there are about 1,400,000 people working in the postal service for the incumbents, and about 400,000 for the private operators. What we expect is that there will be a shift and a progressive reduction of employment with the incumbents and an increase in the private operators, in exactly the same way as we have seen for telecoms.

33. I think you suggested that there is still growth in the postal industry, which I find interesting. Do you feel your job is to keep the postal services as competitive for as long as possible, while acknowledging the inevitable transition—ie, electronic mail?

(*Mr Waterschoot*) I would not say that. I think the growth rate of postal services is about 3 per cent a year, so it is substantial. They also benefit from electronic mail in the sense that if you order something by e-mail it has to be delivered, and it is the postal service or the private operator which delivers the parcel. Also, for example, one recent development is that a substantial increase in the mail market has followed the introduction of the GS17 telephones, because all the people need to receive the bills, and this is a huge increase in the market of mail. So I would not share the view that we expect a decline in postal services. I think there is a place for the postal service in the future and it will be quite important, but this requires that the postal service adapts to the new environment. This is what we are looking at.

Lord Faulkner of Worcester

34. The Directive does not provide for a uniform tariff structure, does it? Can I ask you why you have not done that and whether the proposals that you have made will make a uniform tariff difficult or impossible to achieve in the future?

(*Mr Waterschoot*) The Directive allows for uniform tariffs to apply. It does not require it. There are a number of tools which the national regulator can use in order to facilitate the implementation of a uniform tariff. Those are mainly how the national tariff is priced. If you have a very low tariff for first and second-class mail it is very difficult to apply a uniform tariff. If you have a higher level it is more easy to cross-subsidise within that tariff. So the other tools which are available are licensing conditions. If you apply tougher licensing conditions to private operators, which avoid cherry-picking, then it is easier to apply a uniform tariff. Also the Compensation Fund can contribute to this. What it really means, in practice, is that the way the Directive defines the universal service is a minimum level, so it is a minimum level that everybody has to comply with. However, Member States can have a higher level of universal service, and one of the requirements in that national definition of universal service can be a uniform tariff. Tools are available on the national level in order to implement the uniform tariff.

Chairman

35. We do not have a regulator, as yet, in the United Kingdom, although one will be established in the spring of next year. How many of the other States are in the same position as the United Kingdom in that they all have proposals for establishing regulatory regimes?

(*Mr Waterschoot*) I have met the United Kingdom regulator, and they are keen on starting up the business. I think that the United Kingdom has sorted this out in a reasonable way, compared to the requirements of the existing Directive. We have a number of infringement procedures on-going against other Member States where we have problems about how the regulator was set up, and, mainly, the problem of independence of the regulator compared to the part of the administration which has to deal with the management of the incumbent. What we want to avoid is conflicts of interest between the regulator as an authority that has to deal with independent service providers and the responsibility to manage the local incumbent post office.

36. Are all the other States now in the process of establishing?

(*Mr Waterschoot*) They are in the process of establishing. As I say, we have infringement procedures on-going in four or five Member States because they have not established an independent regulator.

Lord Faulkner of Worcester

37. Can I ask a practical question about the mechanics of posting a letter in a country which has deregulated and removed any sort of monopoly? I

Lord Faulkner of Worcester contd.]

was in New Zealand in September where they have gone a long way down this road, and now increasingly you find, on streets, there are two post-boxes; one for one operator and one for the original incumbent. Is that what is happening in Sweden, where you have got open competition? Do you envisage that happening elsewhere in Europe?

(*Mr Waterschoot*) That is one model but I do not expect it to happen very much in the Community. What happened in Sweden is that you have a private operator which delivers mail between the three main cities. It is mainly business users who use this facility. We have to be realistic about it; the independent consumer will not be the first target for newcomers in the market, it will be mainly business-users. The model of having several post-boxes, and so on, I do not think is realistic. The individual consumer, of course, will be able to use express mail, for example, and then they can go to whichever private operator is available.

38. In New Zealand one of the services is the express service. It is a lot more expensive, but that is aimed at the individual customer, not just business-users.

(*Mr Waterschoot*) You have that in the United Kingdom already. You have got private operators who provide express services, and the difference is that you do not have a post-box; you have to go to the office or call the people and they come and fetch the mail.

Baroness O'Cathain

39. When you told us about the 1997 Directive, the 2000 Directive proposal and then the further step you mentioned for 2007, the first item you mentioned was "special services" and "defining special services". You are obviously going to have some input on this, so can we hear from your own lips the definition of special services you would prefer to see in the 2007 Directive?

(*Mr Waterschoot*) Within the Commission there was a long debate about this and how far the 2007 step should be defined—yes or no. The political decision was not to pre-empt the discussion which should take place as regards what would happen in 2007. I think what can be said is that we are moving towards a more integrated internal market, which means that the progressive reduction of the reserved area will take place. I think, also, that in the next proposal we have to look at the definition of universal service, because there is a minimal definition in the Directive but there are all kinds of different levels in Member States, and we might have to harmonise that further to have a of more level playing field. Apart from that I do not think we can say very much about what the next step will be. The only criteria which is foreseen is to look at how the universal service can be provided in a competitive environment. That is going to be the main criteria for the next step.

40. Getting back to this point about special services, could you envisage a situation where competitive demand—people feeling that there is greater competition, which would result in greater efficiency—could lead to the abolition of the continuing reserved areas and, actually, total abolition of the reserved areas and then it all becoming special services?

(*Mr Waterschoot*) Special services is something quite particular in the sense that these are new services which provide additional features. I do not necessarily think that the main part of the market will go that way. I think that a lot of the market will remain in the traditional services, so I would not relate that argument to the special services. Special services is a very small part of the market.

41. That brings me back to my original question to you, which is how can you define special services? Are they going to be, say, 2, or 3 per cent of the total market or do you envisage them being 60 per cent of the total market? What would they be?

(*Mr Waterschoot*) My impression is that these services are probably going to remain a fairly small share of the market in the future. That does not mean that the reserved area will remain as it is. It is a different type of argument. The estimate we have done in making this proposal is that the definition of special services does not change in any respect the degree of market openings, so small is that part of the market.

42. So it is not really terribly important?
(*Mr Waterschoot*) No.

43. So we should not read anything into the fact that the first requirement you stated about the 2007 proposal was the definition of special services?

(*Mr Waterschoot*) No, I do not think so. I think the main requirement for providing the next proposal is to look at how the universal service can be provided in a competitive environment, but it does not relate to special services.

Chairman

44. I think the British Post Office has a particular worry about special services; that because of the lack of a definition this may be used as a means to circumvent the reserved area.

(*Mr Waterschoot*) It is one of the difficult subjects which are discussed presently in the Council working groups and Parliament. I think one has to emphasise that there are three criteria which are established in the Directive in order to qualify as a special service. One is that they have to be clearly distinct from the universal service; secondly, that they have to meet specific customers' needs (so it is not the needs of all customers, it is special needs for particular customers), and they have to have two or more value-added features. So it is a very tight definition, and there is no reason why this should undermine the definition of the reserved area.

Lord Skelmersdale

45. I was interested in your reference earlier to the Compensation Fund. I find that a very untidy way of dealing with problems such as the subsidy to keep the universal service provision. Can you go a little further and say what reinforced your decision to propose this mechanism of subsidy?

Lord Skelmersdale contd.]

(*Mr Waterschoot*) I have to stress that the Compensation Fund was foreseen in the initial Directive, which is applicable now, so we have changed very little as regards the Compensation Fund.

46. There is no reason why you should not. This is a new Directive. I agree, it is loosely based on the old one.

(*Mr Waterschoot*) I think the main rationale for a Compensation Fund is that it creates greater transparency than the cross-subsidies that occur within the reserved area. In other words, if you have a Compensation Fund you have to clearly evaluate what the additional costs of the universal service are and, secondly, how you want to finance that. So there is a budgetary constraint on how this universal service is provided.

47. Why does that matter? Why do you need to identify those costs, given that you are getting, through all this, a new minimum level?

(*Mr Waterschoot*) One of the main arguments about introducing competition in this market is that you have price and cost transparency; that costs are allocated to where they belong and that we have a level playing field in order for cross-subsidies not to occur within different services. That means that you have to define more clearly where your loss-making areas are within the universal service and where you are making profits. I think that the Compensation Fund, if you ask my personal preference, is not my preferred tool to deal with it but it is one way to make a more competitive environment work and, also, to make more transparency and impose better financial management on the incumbent.

Chairman

48. What would be your preferred tool?

(*Mr Waterschoot*) I think licensing conditions is the most progressive and adequate tool in order to have a controlled market.

Lord Paul

49. Mr Waterschoot, you have given me the answer to the question I was going to ask at the outset, but I need a little clarification. You mentioned that the comparison with the dairy industry is not really a fair comparison, and I have some sympathy with that. However, you also mentioned that the right comparison would be the telecommunications industry. In view of the very big developments in the technology field as far as the telecommunications industry is concerned, do you think there is a danger of misleading ourselves if we compare these two industries?

(*Mr Waterschoot*) You are quite right. I think that technological progress is much greater and technological leaps made in the telecom sector are much greater than one can expect in the postal services. However, also in the postal services there are innovative services which are made possible by the use of telecom means. So, for example, I spoke to one of the post offices the other day and they said "We are establishing electronic post and mail boxes where people can receive all official communications, and they know they will find them at that particular point". So that is a totally innovative service which is extremely useful for citizens and which uses telecommunication means. The question which can be put is "How far is that still part of the mail market?".

Lord Paul: That would be the kind of area that my colleague mentioned, that in telecommunications it will be much easier to serve that area than the post office.

Baroness O'Cathain: With satellite or whatever, but not with people running up and down mountains with vans.

Chairman: Can we come to the issue of the timetable for the proposed Directive? The view is being advanced, not just by the Post Office here but by a number of others, that it is too tight, that the next changes are coming in too quickly and that it should be taken over a longer time-scale. They are prepared to embrace change but need more time for it. What is your view on that?

(*Mr Waterschoot*) First of all, I think that regulatory developments have to take account of the speed of developments in the market place. As things stand now, we are running behind on the development in the market place. There are a lot of mergers, acquisitions and new technology introduced in this, so we are, as it were, coming behind the developments as they already occur. Secondly, I think compared to the existing Directive we are allowing for an additional year. We are really doubling the time which is provided for in between new proposals. I think that that is quite reasonable. As the next step is not really defined it allows us quite a lot of flexibility so far as what we propose in the next step. The timetable is tight. It is tight for different reasons. It is tight because of the very lengthy process of putting proposals through the Community system. You have to have the reading in Parliament, the council working group, and so on, this is why it is a tight timetable. It is not a tight timetable because of what is required in the market.

Baroness O'Cathain

50. You are going to go away thinking the only thing we think about here is the dairy industry. I am really very concerned that—this is just one of three items I am concerned about, after your magnificent answers to questions—first of all, the market is not homogeneous throughout Europe for mail service, it could not possibly be, they are just not identical. When you talk about Sweden, if you are living 400 miles from Stockholm and you want to buy a new dress or a new skirt you use mail order. You do not have mail order in the same way in highly developed markets like we have in the United Kingdom, although there is some. I take your point about the development of e-mail encouraging mail order as well. Getting back to this universal delivery of mail, the problem is, of course, that the competition from e-mail is not actually the competition that the telecom industry has. There is huge competition for the postal service from e-mail at the moment and anecdotes are something that one should not actually

Baroness O'Cathain *contd.*]

build market projections on, however I am convinced that there are a lot of people like me, where at least 50 per cent of our personal mail is now going via e-mail rather than going in vans and by a chap on a bicycle. If you are forecasting developments in the postal services from the basis of telecom and other issues I just fear that there might be a huge problem in a number of years when you find that people are not using postal services.

(*Mr Waterschoot*) You are quite right in saying that the market is not homogeneous. There are big differences. The biggest difference you can find is between, for example, the Netherlands and Greece. In Greece you have to deliver all the mail to all the different islands, which is quite costly, and in the Netherlands you have a small area which is very densely populated, so the market is not homogeneous. This is also why I started out by saying that it is a harmonisation Directive and we have to take account of the slower countries and the faster countries. We are somewhere in the middle with regard to those other areas. With regard to the dangers of the less populated areas not having a proper universal service, I do not have any fear at all because there are safeguards in place in the existing Directive, and they have even been enhanced in this new Directive, in order to ensure that a universal service is provided and can be provided at a reasonable cost.

51. As a final question, you are actually convinced that those changes in the new Directive will stick, and that people will not come and cherry pick the urban areas for delivery?

(*Mr Waterschoot*) What you have to be aware of is that the Directives give a lot of power to the national regulators. These powers are determining the national tariff, licensing conditions and compensation funds which are very powerful tools. We are always talking about subsidiarity, and this is really a case of subsidiarity. Post offices do not necessarily like this because they have a national regulator which is going to be on their back in order to ensure that there will be good service, productivity gains and profitability. The reality is that there are lots of tools which can be used by the national regulator in order to ensure that there is a competitive and very good universal service provided for.

Lord Woolmer of Leeds

52. Can I just bring this down to what it means for the average citizen, not through business to business. Politicians are always concerned about what the citizen thinks. If I understood you correctly—I want to ask you two questions—the implication of all this is that VAT is going to be imposed on all postage. From the citizens' point of view in the United Kingdom that is going to add two and a half pence on second class mail and nearly five pence on first class mail. The politicians will have to present this as a considerable step forward. Secondly, in the United Kingdom the current point is 60 grams; if it went down to 50 grams your argument is that most postage is 20 grams anyway, so let as assume that has little effect. In Germany and France, to take two equivalent countries, what in sterling is currently the cost of posting 50 grams? What is the current United Kingdom equivalent in Germany and France? I assume you will have looked at what it means in concrete terms as opposed to theoretical terms. I am just trying to understand what message the British Parliament would give to the ordinary citizen of what this means for them.

(*Mr Waterschoot*) On your last point, I do not have the exact figures here but Germany is known as having one of the highest tariffs in the Community. This is something that we have looked at from a competition point of view. There are complaints about the level of the national tariff in Germany. In France it is rather higher than in the United Kingdom also. I do not have the exact figure, I can provide them to you, if you want.

Lord Woolmer of Leeds: That would be helpful.

Chairman

53. That would be very helpful.

(*Mr Waterschoot*) I do not have it with me but we have a table about the tariffs in all Member States for different categories.

Lord Faulkner of Worcester: That could show those which have some form of VAT attached to them as well.

Lord Woolmer of Leeds: I understand the argument entirely. I sympathise with the desire to increase competition, and you are bound to face objection from all incumbent post offices, I understand that. The citizen is a very practical person who will say, first of all, "You are going to add five pence onto my fist class post with VAT", and secondly "You are telling us we ought to be in line with France and Germany, but look, we are already much cheaper than those". There is a political argument here.

Chairman

54. What is the trigger for the introduction of VAT?

(*Mr Waterschoot*) VAT?

55. Yes.

(*Mr Waterschoot*) When you open up the market and you have different categories of operators you have to treat them in the same way. It is the argument about the level playing field. You cannot say, "You guys have to compete against the incumbent who does not pay VAT". It just does not work. You have to treat them in the same way. I also think that there are fiscal policy reasons for dealing with it in that way, but I am not familiar with those.

56. This would come in the next stage of liberalisation?

(*Mr Waterschoot*) That is possible.

Lord Woolmer of Leeds

57. You do not pay VAT on e-mails.

(*Mr Waterschoot*) It is not part of the same package. It is not something that we would deal with. I would expect that once you open up—

Chairman

58. What do you mean, it is not something that you deal with? Is it a different part of the Commission?
(*Mr Waterschoot*) It is the same Commissioner but a different part of the Commission.

59. We hope there is some joined-up Commission work taking place.
(*Mr Waterschoot*) He is co-ordinating everything we do.

60. It is a very significant factor.
(*Mr Waterschoot*) I know it is.

Lord Woolmer of Leeds

61. At a stroke, that adds 17.5 per cent on to the costs. You are not offering the average consumer in Britain, the ordinary household, improvements on reducing costs. You have to get a 17.5 per cent reduction in costs, in what is already, by your own admission, an efficient post office compared to other parts of Europe. It is pretty unlikely that the average household will actually see a fall in postal prices.
(*Mr Waterschoot*) I can tell you what they have done in Sweden. When they introduced VAT on postal services they provided a certain number of stamps for each household which corresponds approximately to their annual consumption of mail requirement.

Baroness O'Cathain

62. For nothing?
(*Mr Waterschoot*) I think it was for nothing or for a reduced price. I think it was for a reduced price, I am sure that was it. That took up the price differential which would flow from that.

63. A one-off.
(*Mr Waterschoot*) I think it is a permanent feature.
Baroness O'Cathain: That is free mail!

Chairman

64. We have to come to the end now. This is a very important point, it is not one of the three major issues that is being debated.
(*Mr Waterschoot*) It is not part of this proposal.
Lord Woolmer of Leeds: It sounds as if it was almost an inevitable consequence of harmonisation.

Chairman

65. My final question to you was going to be that given the opposition have some very substantial incumbents throughout Europe, given the opposition from a good many of the trade unions, because of the threat of job losses, given some consumer resistance and consumer organisations' resistance too, did you feel you were going to keep to a timetable and keep to the Directive broadly as it is now defined, and did you believe it was practical to be able to deliver that. I suspect if the VAT issue was thrown into the pot as well, that would be a further issue that would create a lot of problems for you?
(*Mr Waterschoot*) First on the VAT, I think that would also be a concern for the national regulator insofar as he has to ensure that there is a level playing field. I suppose that there would be concerns on a national level, also, that competition should be introduced in such a way as not to make undue advantage for the incumbent. I would not know about that yet, but I would expect that it would be a concern on a national level also. Secondly, as regards the opposition, yes, we have a lot of opposition, that normally occurs with postal Directives, and there was lot of opposition in the last one. What I think is important is that postal services should be seen as part of an infrastructure which is essentially for other businesses. If you do not have an efficient postal service then there are a lot of businesses which suffer from this. I would say that the big users of postal services are really the banks, the publishers of magazines and newspapers and the distance selling people. Those are people who really require efficient postal services. They often work through direct mailing shots, this is also something which is delivered by the postal services. I think that the postal service infrastructure is something that is essential for a well-functioning economy. I think we all have to ensure that this really occurs. One way to do that is to ensure that there is competition in the market.
Chairman: I think that is a very useful point at which to conclude and to express the gratitude from the Committee. I am very impressed, indeed, with the frank and open way you answered all of our questions helpfully. Indeed, we look forward to getting additional evidence from you on relative costs throughout Europe. Thank you very much.

ASSESSING THE EXTRA BURDEN OF THE USO

Why entry pricing is not a reliable method

INTRODUCTION

When assesssing the extra burden of the USO, one has to define a relevant methodology, favouring reliable assessments. A range of methods is available opposing two different main approaches:

— Direct assessment of the extra burden through identification and quantification of the losses arising on those parts of the post office business which are covered by universal service obligations, and which would not be provided by a commercial organisation (eg Full Distributed Costs or Net Avoided Cost methods);

— Indirect assessment of the extra burden as the potential profitability impact from market opening on the USP (eg Entry Pricing method).

The assessment made by N/e/r/a for the European Commission is based on direct assessment methods while some USPs (eg The Post Office) favour indirect assessment methods (ie Entry Pricing), which may lead to higher estimations of the extra burden from the USO.

The following sections aim at:

— Explaining why Entry Pricing is a questionable method in principle;

— Illustrating the limitations of the method and express reservations with the specific implementation made by The Post Office;

— Explaining why direct assessment methods produce more reliable results;

— Describing the conservative approach taken by the European Commission in this respect.

WHY ENTRY PRICING IS A CONTESTABLE METHOD

Principle objections

The following objections are inherent to the Entry Pricing method as such, independently from the assessment made by the Post Office, even if they apply to it:

— The Entry Pricing method does not actually measure (directly) the extra burden of the USO but the potential consequences of it (ie potential profitability impact of different liberalisation scenarios);

— One resulting issue is that the profitability impact measured by the Entry Pricing method may not solely result from the extra burden of the USO (eg efficiency and competitiveness of the USP, market entry strategies from competitors, expected marginal costs of entrants, USP's management capabilities within a competitive environment, pricing strategy of the incumbent . . .);

— A good example of this issue is that the Entry Pricing method suggests that the extra burden of the USO is related to the targeted profit level by the USP, which can be questioned. Indeed, the extra burden assessed using the Entry Pricing method establishes a connection between the cost of the USO and the target profit level. Obviously, the higher the target profit is, the stronger the competitive impact will be and it can be strongly contestable that the extra burden of the USO would vary simply because a USP wants to achieve higher profits.

— The Entry Pricing method requires more numerous and difficult assumptions, which makes it a less reliable method. More concretely, the method requires assumptions such as average prices and volumes for various mail streams, incremental costs for hundreds of routes (eg 2,520 routes in the case of UK), volume growth assumptions for different mail streams, assumptions related to the efficiency of the USP, marginal costs of entrants on hundreds of routes, extent of entry on to liberalised routes, relative importance of price vs quality and other non-price factors (eg customer loyalty), incorporation of second round impacts, sensitivity of the results . . . In total, hundreds of inter-linked assumptions are needed, which greatly impact the results. The Post Office itself acknowledges this limitation when stating: "the results are most sensitive to assumptions on the relative impact of price and non price factors, the extent of linkage of traffic from other routes and assumptions on the growth of volumes prior to liberalisation". The high sensitiveness of the results to numerous assumptions most likely requires defining maximum values for some impacts in order to avoid unrealistic scenarios (which reinforces the need for care with interpreting the results);

NOTES:

The connection of some of the assumptions needed for using the entry pricing method with the individual situation and strategy of each USP also make the entry pricing not uniformly applicable throughout the Union.

Some of the required assumptions (eg efficiency of the USP) are highly controversial, including at USPs' level (the Entry Pricing method requires assumption on an efficiency notion which many USPs are paradoxically totally opposed to at a regulatory level).

Implementation reservations

Further from principle objections inherent to the Entry Pricing method as such, there are additional reservations to the specific implementation of the method by The Post Office.

Indeed, the assumptions made by The Post Office can be questioned in the light of some results contradicting both other studies and reality in Member States where postal services are already liberalised.

WHY DIRECT ASSESSMENT IS A BETTER APPROACH

Direct assessment is a better approach than Entry Pricing for the following reasons:

More reliable results:

— Direct assessment actually measures the extra burden, contrary to entry pricing that attempts to assess the extra-burden only through its potential consequences on the USPs' profitablity;
— Direct assessment avoids the risk of the results being muddied by factors not related to the USO burden as such (ie factors impacting profitability independently from the USO such as market entry strategies of the entrants);
— Direct assessment does not require assumptions from USPs but is based instead on tangible data provided by the same UPSs out of their accounting systems;
— Direct assessment does not require using controversial notions (such as efficiency of the USP).

More uniformly applicable throughout the European Union:

— Direct assessment is much more easily applicable throughout the Union because it is based on tangible and actual accounting data rather than on a set of numerous parameters largely influenced by each USP's specific situation and strategy.

11 October 2000] [*Continued*

Comparison of postal charges in the EU

		-20	-25	-50	-60	-100	-150	-200	-250	-350	-500	-1000	-1500	-2000
B	Euro 40.339	17	32	32	36	36	50	50	50	58	80	100	120	120
		0.42	0.79	0.79	0.89	0.89	1.24	1.24	1.24	1.44	1.98	2.48	2.97	2.97
DK	Euro 7.4537	4.00	5.25	5.25	5.75	5.75	9.75	9.75	9.75	17.00	17.00	21.00	28.00	30.00
		0.54	0.70	0.70	0.77	0.77	1.31	1.31	1.31	2.28	2.28	2.82	3.76	4.02
D	Euro 1.95583	1.10	2.20	2.20	3.00	3.00	3.00	3.00	3.00	3.00	3.00	4.40	-	-
		0.56	1.12	1.12	1.53	1.53	1.53	1.53	1.53	1.53	1.53	2.25	-	-
E	carta basica	35	45	45	75	75	125	125	225	225	325	325	500	500
		0.21	0.27	0.27	0.45	0.45	0.75	0.75	1.35	1.35	1.95	1.95	3.01	3.01
EL	Euro 336.386	120	170	170	200	200	220	220	250	350	350	-	-	-
	Euro 336.35	0.36	0.51	0.51	0.59	0.59	0.65	0.65	0.74	1.04	1.04	-	-	-
F	Euro 6.55957	3.00	4.50	4.50	6.70	6.70	11.50	11.50	11.50	16.00	16.00	21.00	28.00	28.00
		0.46	0.69	0.69	1.02	1.02	1.75	1.75	1.75	2.44	2.44	3.20	4.27	4.27
I	posta prioritari	1200	2400	2400	2400	2400	3600	3600	3600	3600	9600	9600	15600	15600
	Euro 1936.27	0.62	1.24	1.24	1.24	1.24	1.86	1.86	1.86	1.86	4.96	4.96	8.06	8.06
IRE	Euro 0.787564	0.30	0.30	0.35	0.45	0.45	0.70	0.70	0.70	1.15	1.15	1.80	4.20	5.20
LUX	Euro 40.3399	18	24	24	36	36	52	52	52	64	64	80	100	100
		0.38	0.38	0.44	0.57	0.57	0.89	0.89	0.89	1.46	1.46	2.29	5.33	6.60
		0.45	0.59	0.59	0.89	0.89	1.29	1.29	1.29	1.59	1.59	1.98	2.48	2.48
NL	Euro 2.20371	0.80	1.60	1.60	2.40	2.40	3.20	3.20	3.20	5.00	5.00	6.00	7.50	7.50
		0.36	0.73	0.73	1.09	1.09	1.45	1.45	1.45	2.27	2.27	2.72	3.40	3.40
P	Correjo Azul	85	120	120	120	120	290	290	290	290	520	800	800	800
	Euro 200.482	0.42	0.60	0.60	0.60	0.60	1.45	1.45	1.45	1.45	2.59	3.99	3.99	3.99
A	Euro 13.7603	7	8	8	9	9	14	14	14	20	20	34	45	45
		0.51	0.58	0.58	0.65	0.65	1.02	1.02	1.02	1.45	1.45	2.47	3.27	3.27
FIN	Euro 5.94573	3.50	3.50	3.50	4.80	4.80	7.20	7.20	7.20	12.00	12.00	20.00	32.00	32.00
		0.59	0.59	0.59	0.81	0.81	1.21	1.21	1.21	2.02	2.02	3.36	5.38	5.38
S	Euro 8.243	5	10	10	10	10	20	20	20	30	30	40	50	60
		0.61	1.21	1.21	1.21	1.21	2.43	2.43	2.43	3.64	3.64	4.85	6.07	7.28
UK	Euro 0.5896	0.27	0.27	0.27	0.27	0.41	0.57	0.72	0.84	1.09	1.58	3.32	-	-
		0.46	0.46	0.46	0.46	0.70	0.97	1.22	1.42	1.85	2.68	5.63	-	-

Basis: first class, single domestic letter, franked by stamps, within the foreseen format
Source: Web sites and other information from the USPs

11 October 2000] *[Continued*

The special services exception and the Corbeau Judgement

GENERAL PRINCIPLE

New services can be provided on condition that they do not endanger the financial equilibrium of the service of general interest.

QUESTION AT ISSUE

It has been argued by some that the Commission's proposal will undermine financially the ability of universal service providers to safeguard the service of general interest entrusted to them. This principle was established in the Corbeau Judgement in 1993 in which the ECJ ruled that a new service (such as Corbeau's rapid letter delivery service in the city of Liège) could be provided in competition provided that its provision in this way did not engdanger the economic equilibrium of the service of general interest. The interpretation of this principle was left to the national courts.

Certain postal operators argue that the Commission's proposed market opening measures, if agreed, would conflict with Corbeau by preventing them from ensuring universal service in conditions of financial viability.

RESPONSE

A. *Funding the existing cost of universal service:*

1. New mechanisms to safeguard universal service

First, the Corbeau Judgement applied only in the absence of harmonised Community rules and therefore before maximum reservable area had been harmonised in the 1997 postal directive. The judgement is consistent with that harmonisation.

A consequence of this harmonisation was that other services, even though they might fall within the definition of the universal service, remain outside the reservable area. In the case of "new" services, quite distinct from conventional services, they are outside the universal service and therefore there is no justification under the current Directive for their being reserved.

The Directive established that if the maximum reservable area is insufficient in certain Members States, then recourse can be had for example to a compensation fund. These developments went further than Corbeau in establishing or reinforcing alternative or supplementary mechanisms to ensure universal service in a more competitive environment.

The safeguards in the Directive are: the compensation fund, licensing conditions within the universal service area and the ability of the regulator to set prices. Justified cross-subsidisation within the universal service area is in the proposed modification as a further safeguard. Taken together, these safeguards provide a guarantee for universal service to be provided in conditions of financial equilibrium. This includes the maintenance of an extensive network of rural post offices, particularly if a Member State feels that it is particularly vulnerable to the market opening proposed due to the current situation of its operator or the spread of its population.

2. Case of special services

The UK Post Office argues that the Commission's proposal on special services does not comply with the Corbeau judgement yet on account of the fact that this judgement applies in the absence of harmonised Community rules, which are no longer absent, the argument is not valid.

The Post Office argument highlights difficulties in establishing what is or is not a valid special service at the moment. So this is not a problem that is unique to the proposal. Furthermore, it is precisely what the Commission seeks to clarify through a clear definition.

It is also not in the Commission's view acceptable, as argued by the Post Office, for innovation to be limited to the incumbent through a wider scope of the monopoly. It is for national regulators to ensure that falsely labelled services (which promise much but deliver little extra) do not undermine the legitimate reserved area.

Special services will vary between Member States since what is quite distinct from the universal service as established and enforced in one Member State will vary from another. But the principles applying remain the same. That is why the examples of features are just that, examples, and why special features in themselves do not make a service special and non-reservable. Two other conditions have to apply, as made clear in the Commission's submission to the House of Lords.

The standard postal service is drawn from the existing reference in the Directive (recital 21) to the conventional service and refers to the normal service offered to everyone as part of the standard letter price, without extra payment for additional features.

Finally, the Commission seeks to remove the price limit which, while not applying to new services, is applied to express services through recital 18 read in combination with Article 7. Such a price limit is illogical given that express services are innovative in nature and are outside the universal service.

3. Profitability of universal service providers

Third, developments in recent years show that almost every universal service provider now makes profits. Currently, only Italy is loss making but the Poste Italiane is predicted to break even by 2002. In the last reporting year, exceptional losses were declared by Sweden Post and the UK Post Office but these were related to one-off charges (pensions and writing off benefits payment automation) and in both cases their respective letters services remain profitable.

Moreover, most universal service providers would remain profitable following a reduction in the weight limit to 50 grams on account of the expected growth in volumes. The universal service providers would be likely to hold on to the vast bulk of the mail opened to competition in such a step if they had a good level of quality. The Post Office would arguably only expose 15 per cent of their profits to competition, as this is the proportion of postal volumes between 50 grams and 350 grams.

4. Primary importance of level at which uniform tariff is set

Fourth, the financial equilibrium of the USP will primarily depend on the levels of prices which the regulator sets. There are a wide variety of domestic tariffs applied across Member States. Small changes in the uniform tariff can cause large increases or decreases in profitability given that demand is relatively inelastic. This will remain the case as long as substitution of mail by other media does not occur on a large scale.

5. Proposal does not seek to open specific more profitable segments

The opening of a further 20 per cent of universal service providers' postal revenues proposed would be achieved through weight and price reductions which do not focus specifically on more profitable flows of traffic or on the bulk of mail volumes which fund the fixed costs of the postal network. This approach is designed with the guaranteeing the financial equilibrium of USPs in mind. It allows the incumbent to benefit from the high postal volumes in the weight limit between 0 and 20 grams in order to finance the fixed costs of the network.

B. *Possibility to reduce the cost of universal service*

1. Universal service obligations which are more onerous and costly than those required by the directive have been established in certain Member States. These can be reviewed to see if they are strictly necessary (for example a second delivery which is under-used as it only provides delivery of a very small proportion of the total mail volumes).

2. The cost of providing services to rural customers, including the maintenance of rural post offices, can be reduced by economies of scope with other services. These include for example financial services or other government services or franchising, all of which are already being pursued by universal service providers in some Member States.

3. There is the possibility of applying the uniform tariff more flexibly so as to allow tariffs to take account of the additional costs for certain new, added-value services meeting particular needs in the market-place.

CONCLUSION

The Directive 97/67 EC and the new proposed modification integrates the principles established in the Corbeau Judgement in the sense that several alternative means are considered to make it possible in each Member State to apply the most appropriate measure to ensure the financial equilibrium of the universal service provider.

The principles in the Corbeau ruling are reflected in the harmonisation achieved by the Directive. This ruling cannot be used as a valid reason for going backwards on that achievement by extending postal monopolies beyond the maximum permitted under the current Directive since the same Directive established alternative means of ensuring universal service available to Member States.

WEDNESDAY 18 OCTOBER 2000

Present:

Brooke of Alverthorpe, L. (Chairman)
Brookeborough, V.
Cavendish of Furness, L.
O'Cathain, B.
Skelmersdale, L.
Woolmer of Leeds, L.

Memorandum by the Post Office

EXECUTIVE SUMMARY

The Post Office supports the introduction of competition into the postal market, and recognises the need for a reduction in the size of the reserved (monopoly) area.

The draft European Commission Directive proposes a reduction in the scope of the reserved area of such an extent that, if implemented in 2003, it would lead to a financial impact on the Post Office that would almost certainly push it into loss. This would undermine the ability of the Post Office to continue to meet the social obligation laid down in the Postal Services Act 2000, to provide a universal service at an affordable and uniform tariff.

The Post Office would strongly prefer to reduce the reserved area limit to 150g, rather than the Commission's proposal of 50g.

The Post Office believes that the Commission's proposal of a Compensation Fund to support the Universal Service Obligation (USO) is unworkable in the postal sector.

The Commission would be prepared to see the USO relaxed or redefined in order to permit competition to be allowed to grow. In particular, the Commission questions the requirement for a uniform, affordable tariff nation-wide. This is at odds with the policy of the UK Government as recently enshrined in the Postal Services Act 2000.

The proposed new category of "special service" (including express services) would remove legal certainty from the definition of the reserved area and open up all bulk mail to competition through what would in effect be "back door" deregulation by means of court actions.

INTRODUCTION

1. The Post Office supports the view that the introduction of competition in the postal market will produce benefits in efficiency and service quality, reductions in price and increases in choice for all customers. Competition provides an opportunity to encourage innovation and increase efficiency and productivity. However, there is a large potential conflict between the introduction of competition and the Universal Service Obligation (USO) set out by Government in the Postal Services Act 2000—to provide a universal service at a uniform and affordable price. This conflict needs to be addressed by introducing competition in a gradual and controlled way to ensure that the provision of the USO is not jeopardised.

2. The draft Directive proposes that:
   — the existing weight/price limit should be reduced to 50g/2.5 times the basic weight step price for letters, including direct mail;
   — outgoing cross-border mail should be fully liberalised; and
   — "special services", including express services, should be placed outside the reserved area.

3. No firm date for full liberalisation has been proposed, but the next phase of liberalisation is scheduled to start on 1 January 2007 following a further review of the sector. If the full proposals, as currently set out in the draft Directive, come into effect in 2003, then full liberalisation in 2007 would seem to be inevitably the next step.

4. In the view of the Post Office these proposals, taken as a whole, will not provide an adequate protection for the provision of the USO. They are not supported by firm evidence or cogent reasoning and in some cases assertions are made which are contradicted by the evidence provided by the Commission's own consultants.

5. The Commission suggests that to guarantee the financing of the USO, a compensation fund would constitute an alternative mechanism to the maintenance of a reserved area. The creation of a compensation fund was presented in the 1997 Directive as an alternative solution and a complement to a reduced reserved

area, intended to guarantee the maintenance of the universal service in the context of increased competition in the postal market. There are, however, serious problems with a compensation fund in the postal sector and there are no examples of countries were it has been successfully applied.

THE UNIVERSAL SERVICE AT A UNIFORM AND AFFORDABLE PRICE

6. In the text of the Explanatory Memorandum of the Commission's draft Directive, it is argued that their proposals are consistent with the USO. However, as is made clear in a number of places, the Commission foresees substantial conflicts between the inflexible pricing regime implied by a uniform tariff requirement and competition, and indeed argues in the text that a uniform tariff and a uniformly applied service standard are not essential features of the postal service. This view sharply contradicts the policy position of the UK Government, whose commitment to universal services at uniform and affordable tariffs has only recently been enshrined in the Postal Services Act 2000, Section 4(1).

7. In section 1.3 of the Explanatory Memorandum it is stated that "Experience of deregulation of postal markets shows that there is no contradiction between the maintenance and improvement of this service and the gradual introduction of competition, provided the universal provider has the necessary commercial and pricing flexibility to respond within competition law."

8. In section 2.8 it is also stated "There is furthermore no evidence that a substantial market opening would compromise the requirement in the Postal Directive for 'affordable tariffs'. Uniform tariffs in some cases can easily evolve into a 'uniform structure of tariffs' to take account of different categories of users as is already the case for business customers". In fact there is ample evidence that competition in postal services leads to a substantial increase in the price for consumers. This is demonstrated in an economic study recently completed by the Institut d'Economie Industrielle at the University of Toulouse. Tariffs in Sweden for consumers have increased substantially since the Swedish postal market was liberalised in 1993—by a total of 59 per cent in real terms, part of which was due to the imposition of VAT. At the same time businesses mailing to towns are enjoying lower tariffs but through a complex tariff structure which offers a range of different prices dependent on the delivery area.

9. The text also says in section 2.8: "a rigidly imposed uniform tariff for all customers is not a compulsory part of the Postal Directive framework and this proposal reflects that fact." In other words the Commission is clearly stating that postal liberalisation is not compatible with the uniform tariff requirement and is prepared to see this element of the universal service relaxed to enable competition to occur. In fact, in the same section of the Explanatory Memorandum it is argued that it is not logical to agree a system of cost-based terminal dues for the delivery of cross-border mail within Europe and at the same time argue for a uniform tariff within the domestic reserved area. What the Commission seem to be asserting here is that if there is no Europe-wide uniform tariff there is no justification for a national domestic uniform tariff.

10. It is thus made clear for the first time in this draft proposal that the Commission does not support the principle of uniform, affordable tariffs nationwide and gives a higher priority to the introduction of competition.

11. In the same section, the Explanatory Memorandum also opens up the possibility of relaxing the universal service in other respects. It suggests that quality of service standards may be selectively reduced provided they exceed the minimum specified in the Postal Directive and that where a service exceeds the current universal service requirement in the Directive this could be lowered. The Commission is clearly prepared to allow deterioration in current universal service standards where they exceed the common minimum level and also to contemplate its redefinition to enable competition to occur.

REDUCTION OF THE MONOPOLY THRESHOLD TO 50GMS/TWO AND A HALF TIMES THE BASIC STANDARD TARIFF

12. The Post Office believes that to reduce the monopoly threshold to 50g whilst at the same time continuing to be bound by the USO, would push the Post Office into loss. A more sensible route would be to reduce the threshold initially to 150g. This view has been based on carefully researched evidence and the development of a sophisticated model of postal liberalisation which enables an estimate to be made of the financial cost to the Post Office of liberalisation. The model shows that a reduction in the monopoly threshold to 150g, with the USO still in place, would reduce Post Office profit levels by approximately one quarter, while a reduction to 50g would be likely to eliminate Post Office profit completely. A reduction to 150g would also allow a review to be made of its impact, enabling well-informed decisions to be taken on the future pace of further liberalisation.

13. The analysis provided in the Explanatory Memorandum does not discuss profit levels at all in this context and only quotes the market share that would become subject to competition—16 per cent. This superficial analysis fails to recognise that competitors would enter markets where their advantage is entirely a result of the high profit opportunities provided by the uniform tariff that the incumbent postal service is obliged to provide. As a result of this classic "cream-skimming", the profit impact from the loss of the market share indicated would be substantially higher than would have been expected were there no USO. Profits

currently used, through the mechanism of the uniform tariff, to cross-subsidise rural consumers would instead be taken by competitors who would have no incentive either to offer a universal service or indeed to be efficient.

SPECIAL SERVICES

14. In the draft Directive the Commission introduces for the first time the new concept of "special service" which is defined as an enhancement of the basic letter service by the addition of extra features. There are serious problems associated with this proposal:

— any additional component added to the basic letter service would make it a special service, thereby locating it outside the universal service and removing it from the reserved area, whatever the weight/price limits;

— serious legal uncertainty would result, since the list of the services described in the draft as special is not exhaustive and there is no provision for resorting to any authority to define what is a special service and what is not.

15. It is argued that the price of such services may be low and that the "unit price of a particular service may no longer be a true indicator of whether that service carries added value." However, if the unit price cannot be considered as an indicator of added value it is not possible in any situation to decide what qualities of additional services should be regarded as having "added value". The proposed amendment provides a list which is not exhaustive but is presented without any explanation as to what criteria to use to add to the list. In practice this would make it impossible in any dispute to provide legal certainty as to the boundaries of the reserved area. It would encourage the addition of "sham" features whose purpose was solely to circumvent the reserved area.

16. A letter delivery monopoly which can be circumvented by adding a arbitrary electronic or other additional feature to a delivery service to take it outside the monopoly would, in the context of current technological developments, lead to the *de facto* loss of all bulk mail to the reserved area.

17. The Commission thus deviates from the rule that it had defined (in its Green Paper in 1992) for value added services, that "the most effective method of determining the added value is to consider the additional price that the users are prepared to pay". Similarly it calls into question principles which, to ensure transparency, it had established in its Notice on the competition rules in the postal sector, on 6 February 1998 (Ref 98/C 39/02). Lastly, it sets aside provisions of the Court of Justice, in particular in the Corbeau case, which are intended to protect the economic equilibrium of the universal service provider. These provisions determine that a postal service competing with the universal service provider may be prevented if either the competing service is not dissociable from the universal service of general interest or if the provision of the competing service would jeopardise the financial equilibrium of the universal service provision.

DIRECT MAIL

18. Although the Commission has stopped short of recommending the full liberalisation of direct mail, the Explanatory Memorandum states that six member states have already opened the direct mail segment to competition. In the Netherlands, one of the six, the very tight definition of direct mail means that much of what many mailers regard as direct mail remains within the Dutch reserved area. Again in Germany, direct mail is only liberalised down to a weight step of 50g so that most direct mail is caught within the German reserved area. Some of the other countries that are quoted as having a liberalised direct mail sector have, in the past, suffered troubled financial circumstances and poor quality of service.

19. It is also asserted that liberalisation of this sector would "boost direct mail volumes and quality enabling the direct mail industry as a whole to be strengthened." However, the consultants who studied the liberalisation of direct mail in Europe on behalf of the Commission failed to find any evidence that the direct mail sector had benefited from competition in delivery where this was occurring.

20. The Explanatory Memorandum states that direct mail volumes *per capita* in Europe are less than half those in the United States, and implies that liberalisation would enable volumes to rise to this level. However, direct mail lies within the postal monopoly in the USA. The high *per capita* mail volume in the USA is almost certainly at least partially due to the low unit costs achieved in mail delivery by the USPS—arising from the high volumes achieved through the delivery monopoly. As the Commission's consultants state[1], direct mail is very sensitive to price. Because of the economies of scale of delivery, duplicating delivery networks would increase unit delivery costs overall and consequently diminish direct mail volumes.

---

[1] Study on the impact of liberalisation in the postal sector, Lot 1: Direct Mail, Arthur Andersen, 1998.

Compensation Funds

21. The draft encourages the use of Compensation Funds as a means of funding the USO. However, the draft Directive only examines the concept of a compensation fund, without studying the principles behind its design or the requirements for its application in the postal sector. There would need to be a broad agreement across the European Union on the definition of the cost and this would need to be recalculated every year. This exercise would be complex and expensive. The draft Directive proposes an *ad hoc* approach, leaving the design of the financing scheme to national authorities, with the Commission responsible for proceeding with a review of the detail of the scheme on a case by case basis. This approach reveals that the concept has not been studied or developed in a thorough way and, in these conditions, it inspires no confidence that this funding scheme could be genuine safeguard for the maintenance of the USO in a liberalised market.

22. Comprehensive identification would be needed of the operators and their services which would be required to contribute to the Fund. No criteria have been provided for the establishment of such information. This contribution base would need to be fixed so as to avoid any distortion in competition on the postal market or any competitive advantage for any operator. Contributions would vary year by year depending on the market shares of the competing operators. All operators would need to have a common cost accounting procedure to evaluate the required extent of their contribution. It would require a strict enforcement policy for the monitoring of volumes, costs and revenue for all providers—many of which may only have a short lifetime in the market. This would need to be linked to a licensing regime for operators. This would not be feasible given that there are many operators acting on the fringes of the market which has low entry (and exit) barriers.

23. This mechanism is not applicable in a competitive postal environment and would put in peril the provision of the universal service at an affordable price, and at a uniform tariff. The reserved area constitutes a simpler means to guarantee the achievement of these social objectives and its scope must be sufficient to cover the entire cost of the universal service.

Summary and Conclusions

24. The draft Directive proposes a reduction in the scope of the reserved area of such an extent that it would, if implemented in 2003, lead to a financial impact on the Post Office to a degree that would almost certainly push it into loss. This would undermine the ability of the Post Office to continue to meet the USO laid down in the Postal Services Act 2000. A less risky option is to move to 150g, and then to take stock.

25. The alternative of a Compensation Fund to support USO, which the Commission is encouraging, is unworkable in the postal sector.

26. While the Commission explicitly recognises the conflict between competition and universal service, they would prefer to see the USO relaxed or redefined in order to permit competition to be allowed to grow. In particular, the Commission questions the requirement for a uniform, affordable tariff nation-wide. This is at odds with the policy of the UK Government.

27. The new category of "special service" (including express services) would remove legal certainty from the definition of the reserved area and open up all bulk means of court actions.

September 2000

Examination of Witnesses

MR JOHN ROBERTS, Chief Executive, the Post Office, MR JERRY COPE, Group Managing Director, Strategy and Business Development, the Post Office, and MR ROBERT BISHOPP, Director, Regulation, the Post Office, called in and examined.

Chairman

66. Good morning, gentlemen. I shall start by firstly thanking you for the written evidence which you let the Committee have, which has been helpful for us in preparing, and secondly thanking you for finding the time to spend with us this morning. Perhaps I could start off by referring back to the 1996 enquiry which the House of Lords Sub-Committee undertook into liberalisation, where I think that in many respects the Post Office came out of it with flying colours, the Committee being extraordinarily supportive of what you were doing at the time. You will maybe question this, but I think it is worth observing that since that enquiry there has been some decline in the quality of service which we have had in the British Post Office by comparison with other North European post operators, and some of them have started to catch up and overtake us in terms of the quality of service performance. Moreover, I think that perhaps it could be argued that productivity, which you have been seeking, has not achieved the improvement experienced by some of the other post operators in other parts of Europe, notwithstanding the very substantial injections of capital into automation. Do you not think that a good shock from the introduction of a really good piece of competition, as proposed by the Commission, might be just what is needed now to shake the Post Office and to improve your performance?

(*Mr Roberts*) I do not think we have ever had any problem with competition. I think we were one of the

Chairman *contd.*]

first Post Offices in Europe to say that liberalisation should happen. My Lord Chairman, I think the issue for us is the way in which it is going to be done. In many cases it is interesting to me that those countries in Europe who now seem to be the firmest advocates of competition are those who have been through the kinds of changes which maybe we are now going through in the United Kingdom in terms of the relationship with their governments. So you get people who have been privatised, or corporatised or about to be privatised, who therefore have had a quite different market to operate in for some years, who are now saying, "Well of course the market should be opened up." In our case, as you know from our memorandum, while we do not have any problem with competition and we expect liberalisation to continue, what we have always argued is that competition and liberalisation should be handled in a gradual and controlled way—I take the words directly from the Directive which the Commission issued—and we do not think that a move from 350 grams to 50 grams is either gradual or controlled.

67. Given what you have just said, if in fact you are, in a sense, asking for more time and to go more slowly, does not that mean that you will fall even further behind your competitors?

(*Mr Roberts*) I was not going to pick up, first of all, the points which you make, but I do not necessarily agree with them. First of all, I think you have to define what you mean by "quality of service". In our second class service, our second class quality of service is at record levels, and probably at record levels in Europe. If you look at the first class quality of service, then I do agree with you that in fact we have seen over the past three or four years, particularly as we have gone through some of the changes with our unions which the other organisations went through some time before, that we have been affected, and our quality of service for first class has got stuck at about 91 per cent which is a couple of percentage points behind some of the other European countries. If you look at it at that relatively simplistic level, I do not think that tells the full story, because you have also got to look at the kinds of services we provide, and the issues are how many deliveries a day do we do. Many European countries only do one delivery a day. The Dutch, for example, will deliver once; they will start at eight o'clock in the morning and they will finish at five o'clock in the afternoon. So for me it is the package of services that we give, as opposed to just the headline figure. In terms of those packages of services, if you look over the same period, we have been increasing the number of business collections we make, the number of postboxes on the street. The whole thrust for us has been to put a lot more into customer satisfaction and loyalty, which is one of our key messages now, rather than saying, "Ah well, it's all about another percentage point on the number of letters that we deliver the next day", important though that is.

68. But from a customer point of view, is not the level of performance on the first class post really the one which is the yardstick which is used to judge you?

(*Mr Roberts*) I am not sure that is correct. Certainly in terms of the things that we see, people also put a lot of emphasis, for example, on the time at which they receive that delivery in the morning, and we have been putting a lot of effort into making sure that we do get back to delivering by 9.30 in the morning for first delivery virtually everywhere in town areas. They also put a lot of emphasis on the way in which they get access to our services, which is why, in some sense, there has been such a debate over the future of post offices in the country. So I do think that you are quite right that if we were suddenly saying that the overnight quality of service had slipped from 91 to 70, or something like that, there would be a major impact. However, on the research that we do, I think that more and more people are taking a basket of measures. This is something we have also been discussing with our statutory Users' Council, because they too have been moving away from just a single figure into looking at a range of services.

Baroness O'Cathain

69. I was interested to hear you talking about customer service. Do you really actually put your customer first? In saying this, may I say that I am very pro the Post Office, but my experience, which is anecdotal of course, is that I live both in the country and in London, and the London service used to be very good, I always had my London mail at 7.30 in the morning, but it now comes at 10.15, right in the middle of the City of London. My mail in Sussex comes religiously, hail, rain, snow, the lot, at 7.15 to 7.20 in the morning, it is absolutely spot on and terrific. You do not need two deliveries if you get that sort of service. Looking at liberalisation and making sure there is a level playing field in Europe, is there not something endemic here and the problem—which could very well be the unions or old Spanish practices in London or something else—you are never going to get right unless you actually tackle the underlying causes first? That is number one. My second customer point is that for the ordinary man and woman in the street buying stamps, there does not seem to be acknowledgement of what the customer wants. This is a case for Post Office Counters, so I suppose it is not really 100 per cent valid to bring it up here. Sometime ago, I suddenly hit on this wheeze of these wonderful boxes of 200 stamps where you did not have to lick the wretched thing. Yet when I went in to buy more I find you have suddenly withdrawn them. When I asked, "Why have you withdrawn them?" I was told, "I don't know. Somebody up in head office has withdrawn them." You can now get them on a great big page. Who wants that? Customers are actually walking out of the place and getting furious. There is a subsidiary point on this as well, and that is that the stamp gum is made of cow gum, and people are worried about BSE and CJD. It is a fact. The chattering classes do not know any better but that is what they are worried about, and that is why they like these stamps which you peel off. We get to a stage where that combination of withdrawing them without any notice, and then having your deliveries at 10.15, in the middle of the City of London, does not look like being customer friendly to me.

Baroness O'Cathain contd.]

(*Mr Roberts*) I think your original question was did I think we put the customer first. The honest answer to that is no, not as much as I would like. This is one of the things that we have been trying to do in the past 12 months. We have just had an enormous internal reorganisation, and one of the key elements in that is precisely your point. We cannot hope to continue to be an effective organisation if we are not delivering the kind of customer service we want. One of the things, therefore, that we are trying to do—my point about delivery by 9.30—is to put a lot of investment back into getting those deliveries done by then, and yes, one of the biggest areas is the big urban and industrial centre. The key point there, if I may come back to the Chairman's initial point about competition and everything else, is that we now, as you know, deliver mail anywhere in the country, Sussex or London, for the same price. The biggest issue for us—and this is the guts of it for us in terms of why we are not happy with what is being proposed by the Commission—is that we do not believe we would be able to continue to do that if we move down the direction that they have now got in mind. So while I do fully take your point that we have got to try to improve the services in the cities to make sure that we hit the kind of levels that you are used to in Sussex, one of the things that worries us is that the investment to do that has got to come out of our being able to maintain a sort of uniform approach to price so that people do feel that they are getting the right kind of service right across the country.

Chairman: Lord Skelmersdale has a subsidiary point on this question.

Lord Skelmersdale

70. Various things occur to me from what you have said, Mr Roberts. The first is, you mentioned business collections. Surely they are on contract and have their mail collected?

(*Mr Roberts*) We also have small businesses, where they are not on contract and do not have direct collections. We have started to put in, I think, more than 1,000 special business collection points which are not the ordinary postbox where there is a fairly narrow slot, purely for businesses who may be posting 200 letters, as opposed to the bigger contract customers who, you are quite right, would be on contract arrangements and have their post collected. One of the things we have been trying to do is to focus on SMEs. Many SMEs, particularly at the M end of SME, are people who are not in the league of the big posters but equally need something more than, as you occasionally see, simply feeding letter after letter into the postbox.

71. Fair enough. We already have a competitive parcels area in the postal service, and Parcelforce competes with TNT, Securicor and goodness knows who else. Ever since that point, it seems to me that Parcelforce has been making a loss. Why do you keep Parcelforce?

(*Mr Roberts*) Why do we keep it?

72. Yes. What is it doing there under your umbrella?

(*Mr Roberts*) One of the reasons is that we believe that the strategy for organisations like ours in Europe, over the next five to ten years, is going to be that we will see people becoming what we call complete distribution companies. From the biggest users, more and more they are coming to organisations like us and the Dutch Post office, and they have a series of activities which embrace letters, ground-based parcels, slower parcels, express parcels and more and more palletised groups of parcels, for instance. As we have looked at the future of this organisation—and it is on the assumption that the British Post Office is going to continue to be one of the perhaps four big players in Europe—we believe that to be able to provide those services you need to operate in all those four segments of the market. If you do not, then particularly the biggest users of the post, particularly multinational companies, will more and more go to any company that can provide all their needs in the one place. This whole idea of the one-stop shop is affecting postal services just as it is with others. So you see that at the moment the German Post Office has just taken a controlling stake in DHL which traditionally has been in the express parcels area; the Dutch bought TNT. These kinds of barriers between the old-style postal administrations in countries and the private consolidators and freight forwarders are coming down more and more. While we have, quite rightly, as you say, made losses in Parcelforce for some little time, the strategy that we have been following has been to improve the way in which we handle all the internal operations. We have invested in a new hub in Coventry, because we were actually batting not on an even playing field, we were trying to do it with depots spread all around the country, where it was quite clear too that to run an efficient parcel service you have one central hub, things go in there, are sorted and come out again. Also we have been putting in the technology. We have just about reached the end of that. We have a recent agreement with the unions which is now going through, which will also enable us to deliver in the evenings. So the whole approach both to the customer and to the way in which we run Parcelforce has been changing over the last five to ten years. It got stuck in the early 1990s, after the previous Government had said that it wanted to privatise Parcelforce. It went through a period where the Treasury refused to allow any investment in it whatsoever. Until that process reached an end, when the Government decided it was not going to privatise Parcelforce, we probably lost four or five years when we should have been investing in the business to bring it up to the standard of others, and it is pretty tough, when you then lose that time, suddenly to start competing again.

73. You are running from way behind, and I understand that, but now you are on profits. You say that a reduction to 50 grams would totally wipe out your profits?

(*Mr Roberts*) Yes.

74. We were told in evidence last week, by Mr Waterschoot, that the bulk of paying mail is at the 20-gram level. First of all, would you agree with that? Secondly, at what point in the weight scale—not the price scale, because I think that is rather different—do you believe that the USO (the universal service obligation) is covered?

Lord Skelmersdale *contd.*]

(*Mr Roberts*) Let me answer it in two ways, and perhaps bring one of my colleagues in as well. Here in the United Kingdom, if you go down to 50 grams, something like 30 per cent of our volume would then be opened up to competition and something like 40 per cent of our revenue. That is at 50 grams. We have a fundamental difference with the Commission over the way in which these sums have been calculated. It is very complicated. It is all to do with economic modelling. They have an approach which is called net avoided cost; in other words, they try to add up all the losses that occur on loss-making routes and say that is the cost of the universal service obligation. We believe it is fundamentally flawed, because in doing that, they make the assumption that the market will remain stable, and of course the one thing that liberalisation will do is completely destabilise the market. We therefore use a different method which is called entry pricing. It has been developed by PriceWaterhouseCoopers, and it has been used in both Holland and America. If I may, I shall ask Robert Bishopp, who has been very much involved in this, very briefly to talk about the way in which this operates, because this is very much behind the sums of money which we have talked about as being the impact on us and therefore the cost of the USO.

Chairman

75. Before you do that, could you also log down that we would like to know why you believe that liberalisation would completely destabilise the market, given that where there has been the ultimate move to a total abolition of the monopoly, this has not proved to be the case, where the major incumbents have continued to retain 85 to 90 per cent of the market?

(*Mr Roberts*) I think that is because of the way it has been done. If you look at Sweden, for example, in Sweden the market has been taken away, and for a long time the Swedish Post Office operated a predatory pricing regime, which was recognised by the people in Sweden to the extent that it then climbed, which kept competitors out. So I do not think we have actually got an example in Europe of anywhere where a market of that type has been completely freed up. Everybody always talks about Sweden. Prices in Sweden over the last six years since the market has been opened up have gone up 60 per cent in real terms. Prices in the United Kingdom have gone down 9 per cent, and that is before you add VAT in Sweden. So I do not think we have got an example anywhere in Europe where somebody can say, "Oh well, the market's been opened up and it's been fine." Where it has been opened up, the market has remained the same, because the incumbent has made damned sure that it did. I can assure you that if you take a market like this, which has operated in this way for the last goodness knows how many years, and you then open it up, you are bound to get an impact on the market which means that the stable conditions now will change. I do not think I said it will destabilise it, but it will change it, whereas the European Commission's argument is that nothing will change and that markets will remain the same, people will enter it in a sort of logical way. Our view is very clearly that they will not do that, they will enter it and they will go for those areas where they will make most profit. So that is what I meant in terms of destabilising. It will not mean entering across the piece. We are not going to get very many demands to run the USO.

76. Lord Skelmersdale's point was that most profits are made around the 20-grams level.

(*Mr Roberts*) Let me ask Robert Bishopp to answer that.

(*Mr Bishopp*) Before I answer that, could I make a supplementary point which is that the calculations we have done under the entry pricing model do actually continue to assume that the incumbent—that is, the Post Office—will continue to carry the great majority of traffic, so that the profit impact that we are talking about actually itself only results from relatively small traffic loss. We would still continue to carry at least 75 to 80 per cent—indeed, a figure in excess of that which the Commission themselves have quoted. I think the entry pricing model which we are referring to tends to focus upon the fact that when competition actually comes in, it will use the existence of the uniform tariff structure to concentrate its entry on the profitable parts of the market, so that it will look at serving geographical areas where costs are low and it will concentrate perhaps on serving particular market sectors and particular customer bases where there are in fact high margins to be made. The uniform tariff structure is a mechanism by which we actually make profit in certain areas in order to fund losses in other areas. If we continue to have to provide a universal service at a uniform tariff structure, then the competition comes in, it cherry-picks or it cream-skims. The total amount of traffic that we think we would actually lose if there were a reduction in the monopoly down to 50 grams is only about 7 or 8 per cent of the total traffic we have at the present time. It is the loss of that traffic which will then equate, in terms of loss of profits, to the ability to finance the USO, to a figure between £250 million and £300 million.

Lord Cavendish of Furness: My Lord Chairman, I think we need independent advice about the net avoided cost as opposed to entry pricing.

Lord Woolmer of Leeds

77. It would be helpful if what we have just been told orally could be conveyed in a note to us, as to the two different ways of calculation—the principles, but also of course converting that into pounds and pence.

(*Mr Roberts*) The impact, yes. Certainly.

Baroness O'Cathain

78. Really what we are talking about is cherry-picking at the margin?

(*Mr Roberts*) Yes.

Lord Woolmer of Leeds

79. You are a very well established postal operator. You have a universal customer base. Why be afraid of competition, particularly if the provision of a

Lord Woolmer of Leeds contd.]

universal service was an obligation at an agreed level of weight or otherwise? Why be afraid of that? Even with the lengths to which it might go, you are talking about conditionally only 40 per cent of your revenue. An awful lot of businesses and companies would be delighted if that were the position which they faced. So I am puzzled, from outside, as to why this apparently successful business—that is the defence you made of yourselves, that you are a successful business with a universal customer base which business wants—is afraid of competition. I would have thought you would want competition, particularly if that enables you to compete on equal terms in the markets of Europe. You have everything to gain from competition, have you not?

(*Mr Roberts*) As I said at the beginning, I do not think we are afraid of competition, I think it is the way in which you move to competition from the way these markets have been established. One of the key things we now have to do by law is to make sure that we are in a position to finance the universal service obligation. That is as recent as the Postal Services Act which was passed during the course of this year. Our view, based on all the kinds of modelling which everybody has done, is that in certain circumstances like the ones we have described, we believe that we might not be in that position. If we are wrong, then we will have lost some time, because what we are saying is by all means liberalise, but do it in stages, in the way the original Directive had in mind, do not go directly to 50 grams, go some way along that path. We believe it will probably take two years to see the impact on the market. If we are wrong, then we would have no objection to moving on to whatever the next stage was. On the other hand, if we are right and the Commission is wrong, and we do get to the position where we are unable to fund the universal service obligation, or what is more likely—and I think the Commission seems to accept this in the Directive—because of the entry of new players into the market in the way that Robert Bishopp has described, looking particularly, say, at deliveries in London or London to Birmingham to Manchester (we will not be looking at London to Wick), then we may find that the only way that we could then try to maintain that amount of money to fund the USO would be by charging the price which was nearer to the cost of the services. All the evidence from the work we did on entry pricing was that three or four things happened. First of all, business to business prices, and particularly business to business prices in urban areas, if anything, went down, prices for letters which were going to rural areas went up, and if they were consumers' letters or individual letters as opposed to bulk letters they may go up four times as much. This is why we have been interested in what has happened in Sweden as the only place in which the market has been liberalised. So our argument has been not do not let us have competition, it is about the way you get to competition against the background of the structure in this country and the statutory obligation in this country to continue to fund that USO. It is interesting that the Postal Services Regulator, set up last year, has as his prime duty to make sure that we are in a position to fund the USO. That is the whole thrust of our argument. Whenever I have talked to Commissioners I have said, "I think it is a very brave decision if you do go this far, because I think that rather than doing it in two stages or whatever, and making sure that you are right, you are prepared to say, 'No, let's go for broke and go for 50 grams', and then if there are problems, presumably that could be sorted out afterwards."

80. As I understood it, in relation to Parcelforce the argument you used was that this is the overall package. You are saying the business community in certain inter-urban area deliveries are actually paying more than they need in terms of the competitive price. That is what you are saying, is it not?
(*Mr Roberts*) Yes, they are.

81. In practice, with a lot of business communications the Internet is becoming a powerful competitive tool. Are you not making sure that the competition in alternative technology is simply going to drive away that market, and that by not in fact seeking to price to the real cost of providing to that market you are inevitably going to lose out?
(*Mr Roberts*) I think that introducing the whole technological side—and Jerry Cope will comment on this as well—is quite different. It is going to be very difficult for postal services over time to compete with the kind of prices that technology will be able to put forward. You can send a three-page fax at the moment more cheaply than a first class letter. The issue for me is what sort of communication services do you want in the country, and obviously customers are going to have a choice. We have seen probably technological substitution so far in about 1 per cent of our volume. We are still growing. Volume is still growing in the main service at $3\frac{1}{2}$ per cent; it probably averages between 4 and 5 per cent over the last 10 years per annum. All the research we have done, particularly in America with something called the Institute of the Future which has looked at a lot of this, is that technology in a funny sort of way is also creating pickup and it is creating mail, and the sorts of messages which you get on e-mail are not the sorts of messages which you traditionally send through in a letter. So in one sense, whilst I absolutely agree with you that technology will continue to impact—it is probably mobile phones which are having the biggest impact on us at the moment—I do not think we would ever be able to get the cost of physical mail down to the kinds of levels of cost of telephone calls, fax or Internet. They are two different forms of communication. The big issue for me is how many years will it be—is it five, 10 or 100 years—before physical communication will decline to a point where it is tiny compared to electronic communication.

82. My last point on that is that from what you have said, frankly, you come across—not you personally, but the Post Office—as seeking to maintain a quasi-monopoly, trying to resist competition as long as you can, regarding down to 50 grams or 60 grams as years away yet and full liberalisation as many years even further away.
(*Mr Roberts*) No.

83. The concept of an aggressive, growth-orientated European postal service company wanting to get increased market share across Europe

Lord Woolmer of Leeds *contd.*]

does not come across. You want a protected home market, do you not?

(*Mr Roberts*) No, but I do want a level playing field. I am competing at the moment—or I will be in a month—with two completely privatised large European post offices. We are not privatised, we are still controlled by the Government—slightly less so as a result of the Postal Services Act—and therefore the competition for me is on a slightly different basis. As I said earlier on, I would, please, urge the Committee not to underestimate the amount of change that has gone on in these countries where governments have not had the same kind of approach to their postal services as we have had here in the United Kingdom. The 1990s were a lost decade for the British Post Office. We are desperately trying to catch up now. We are not doing this by saying there must not be competition, we genuinely do believe that the Commission has not got this right. What I am saying is that within the next five to six years we expect there to be competition, and competition quite widely. There are nine postal administrations in Europe who are currently taking roughly the same line as we are. They are not saying there must not be competition or movement, but let us have it in a couple of stages.

Chairman

84. Some of those already have, like the Germans, 200g weight already in existence?

(*Mr Roberts*) A fairly recent change, if I may say so.

85. You did mention, in your opening remark, when I was talking about the comparison of your performance with other European countries, some of them have gone through changes in their working relationships with their unions and you were now just about to embark on that?

(*Mr Roberts*) We are going through them, yes. We are not just about to embark on them. We have been making changes throughout the 1990s. We have a major change which was negotiated 12 months ago and which we were in the middle of.

86. My understanding was that you were saying that they had gone through changes which, as yet, we have not embraced?

(*Mr Roberts*) They are ahead of us in terms of the kind of working practice changes that they have introduced, whereas we are in the middle of a major set of working practice changes now.

87. Is that because they have gone through privatisation?

(*Mr Roberts*) Yes, absolutely, and we have not.

88. You are arguing the case that change must be slower to accommodate?

(*Mr Roberts*) There is a big difference between free and privatised before competition hits you, which is what has happened to the Germans and the Dutch. The position that we are in is that we are not privatised. We have not had the outside stimulus of all that in advance of competition. Remember your point about the monopoly being reduced. Three years ago the first Directive came out, and the strongest advocates of not going too much further too much faster was the German Post Office. In the period between then and now the German Government have decided to privatise. A lot of the work has been done, and their flotation is on the 21st of next month. They have had the opportunity, with the agreement of the Government, to make a lot of the changes internally, knowing that that was coming. As a result of that they are now in a position to take advantage of a market that they would want to be as liberalised as possible. They have sales offices over here and they see the United Kingdom market—and the United Kingdom market is the second biggest export mail market in the world outside of the United States—as an ideal market to come to. My argument is that because during the 1990s these countries have made more progress in terms of their relationship as a company, they are a freer company than we have been, and they have been able to get themselves into a position where it is far better for them if the whole thing is liberalised. In spite of that, we are saying that we believe the way in which this has been done could affect the ability of us to maintain uniform prices, and hence the USO. They may have a different view, I do not know. Certainly in this country, that is what we see as the fundamental problem. There are two issues; one is getting yourself in a state that you have proved the British Post Office, which is where you started, and the second one is whatever happens to the market, how do we, here in the United Kingdom, handle the implication as opposed to the Germans or the Dutch?

89. We are all agreed that the liberalisation to change that has taken place now in certain parts of Europe certainly is a stimulus to change?

(*Mr Roberts*) It is certainly a stimulus to change. Whether all of that change has benefited the consumer I think will be a much bigger debating point.

Viscount Brookeborough

90. What proportion of the electorate would be the loss making USO areas? It is quite important, it is quite a political issue and it is, after all, the electorate. When you talk about SMEs, many of the SMEs are being encouraged to use information technology, and whatever, to form in slightly more rural areas. At what stage do you become so rural that the prices would rise for your deliveries in the future if it was liberalised in the way you say?

(*Mr Bishopp*) I have to answer that question in two parts. If you ask, what is the proportion of customers, the amount of traffic, where we make a loss? The answer is, relatively small, probably in the order of about 5 per cent. The issue that I think is more relevant is, in the context of liberalisation, what proportion of customers would, in fact, actually be faced with a competitive alternative? Once you have looked at it in that context, what would then be the price that those customers would actually face in the post liberalisation environment? Mr Roberts has already made reference to the fact that in Sweden for all customers posting single items—be that businesses or consumers—they have actually suffered 60 per cent increases in real terms in their postal charges. If you are saying; in the current

Viscount Brookeborough *contd.*]

environment, what proportion of traffic is loss making in that strict sense? It is about 5 per cent. If you are saying; in the post liberalisation environment, what proportion of customers might expect their prices to increase significantly? The answer would be all the customers who are actually posting single item letters, and we use the Swedish case as an example.

91. I live in Northern Ireland, which is very rural except for Belfast and Derry. Are you saying that a small business living in such a rural environment would have to pay higher charges?
(*Mr Bishopp*) Yes.

Baroness O'Cathain

92. Does that automatically assume that the loss makers are the rural areas, or are they the middle of the city?
(*Mr Bishopp*) It is not as simple as saying that they are all in rural areas. They are concentrated inherently in rural areas. Yes, we can think of examples of where, outside of these rural areas, there are loss making routes.

Chairman

93. What is the cost of maintaining the USO in monetary terms?
(*Mr Bishopp*) If you were to do a calculation based upon the net avoided costs, then it is something in the order of £25 million to £30 million.
Viscount Brookeborough: Your profit is much bigger than that.

Baroness O'Cathain

94. That is nothing.
(*Mr Roberts*) Let him just finish his description.
(*Mr Bishopp*) If you are saying; where we would actually stop providing services at the moment in order to recover the net losses that we make, then there is actually about £30 million of services that we would actually deny. If you go beyond that and say; in the circumstance in which competition is allowed, what is the amount of traffic that would then be lost and where we would then find those coming back to us? That would actually increase to £300 million.
(*Mr Roberts*) That is after taking account of reducing our staff, because we would assume that traffic would reduce. That is the way the calculation is done.

Chairman

95. That is based on funding a lot of redundancies, is it?
(*Mr Roberts*) We have a factor we use in terms reducing hours to work. I think it is more to do with that, rather than lots of redundancy costs.

Lord Skelmersdale

96. Is this unique to you, or does the factor of adjustment apply to other businesses?
(*Mr Roberts*) No, it is unique to us. It is the factor that we use based on the experience of running mail services of how many staff hours, ie, people, you can reduce, depending on certain levels of traffic. It is the way we calculate increase. When you look at increases in mail—and mail has been growing—there are certain things you can automate, the middle processes. We know, for example, that as housing estates increase there are more doors to go to and you need more delivery persons. You can work out how much time you need to spend and how many people you need to spend it at different parts of the process. So, just as we can work out, as mail grows, how many people we need to employ, if mail declines we can work out how much less time you need and, therefore, how many fewer people.

Lord Woolmer of Leeds

97. Under the proposed Directive, as I understand it, the intention is that individual countries can still, by regulation, insist upon universal service obligation at certain levels of postage. If that is imposed at 60g, of whatever, and if the true cost of having to meet that is £300 million, nobody is going to be able to compete with you. Who is going to get into the muddle? Either it is very large, in which case you should not fear competition, or it is not as large as you are saying it is and competition is a threat. I am trying to square the two.
(*Mr Roberts*) People are not going to want to run a national postal service. We are not going to get competitors who come in and say—

98. Exactly.
(*Mr Roberts*) What they will say is; "We want to run a postal service in those bits where the margin is best. So, we will go into Central London where we would make our profit and then use that to cross subsidise the rural service." They will compete very heavily purely in those areas.

99. At what weight?
(*Mr Roberts*) At whatever the weights are. Whatever the weight comes down to, whether it is 150g or 50g, people who enter the market will only enter the market where they can really make money.

100. Of course.
(*Mr Roberts*) As a result of that the most profitable routes we have, where we currently offset the losses on the rural routes by the profit we make in the urban areas, will be under more and more intensive competition. That competition, we believe, will be fuelled by the fact that they will be able to set prices related to their costs. Ours, at the moment, are related to a uniform affordable price. In other words, for a first class letter you pay 27 pence. A first class letter from here to Scotland probably costs £2.50 to handle. We make a loss of £2.20, roughly. In London it would probably cost, I do not know, 15 pence, so we make a profit of 12 pence. Somebody coming into the market would say, "I am very happy to go into London, I can make a profit of 12 pence." If that is

Lord Woolmer of Leeds *contd.*]

the case, they will go in and charge something like 15 or 16 pence.

Lord Woolmer of Leeds: But the proposals are not that that area of the market is going to be open for competition. In the proposals the gram limit, as I understand it, does not extend to that.

Chairman

101. It is way above the majority of the pieces of mail.

(*Mr Roberts*) I have two letters. One weighs 45g and the other weighs 50. I am very happy to hand them round. They are not marked and I will be delighted to know if you can tell which is which. The biggest problem is, how do you know? Most of the mail that you all send, in the jobs that you have, is roughly about that.

Lord Woolmer of Leeds: Is most of the mail like that?

Chairman

102. Most of the mail is 20g, not 40g.

(*Mr Roberts*) 30 per cent of our mail is above 50g. 40 per cent of our revenue is above 50g. If you then look at those areas, as we tried to describe, and you get the kind of competition, while we still continue to have a standard price, the impact on profit in those areas will be quite considerable. It is that, based on the modelling that we have done, that drives the kind of numbers that then get us to roughly equivalent to the profit that the Post Office currently makes. It is not the volume, it is where you make the margin on the mail.

Baroness O'Cathain

103. I must say, having listened to you, I think to myself the ordinary customer in Central London is being so badly served in terms of customer service, and yet we are subsidising everybody all over the place. When I consider the wonderful postal service I get in Sussex and the lousy postal service I get in London and know that I am actually subsidising— You are making so much money.

(*Mr Roberts*) You are subsidising your mail to Sussex.

Baroness O'Cathain: All of these figures are fascinating, but they do not add up.

Chairman: We will come back to that, but I think there is another area which is currently being looked at by Brussels as well, and that is the special services. Lord Cavendish would like to ask a few questions in that area.

Lord Cavendish of Furness

104. Mr Roberts, you made a case quite strongly for saying you have been disadvantaged, compared with other incumbrances, through Treasury control, but I thought you were hinting at the same time that there were other areas through your status where you were disadvantaged. Can you just enlarge on that and, perhaps, give some proportions?

(*Mr Roberts*) I can give you some examples. The major area has been investment. During the 1990s you may remember that the previous administration were taking something like £1 million pounds per day—£350 million odd per year—out of the Post Office in terms of dividend, and up to the policy of the day that carried on for something like three or four years. So over that time we contributed to the Exchequer something like £1 billion. In European post offices a lot of that money is being ploughed back into the industry and, therefore, during that time we were probably heavily under investing in things that we ought to have been, for example, very simple things like bricks and mortar. Some of the delivery offices where the postmen go out from every morning to deliver to the houses are desperately in need of repair. We are putting in programmes like that now, but, in fact, that is causing a lot of pressure. Again, if I can use a German example, in the same period the Germans probably replaced all of their major processing centres with new offices. Again, they got themselves ready for competition in a way which we have not been able to do. It has been that in particular during that period, along with the fact that until last year we were not able to go and do the kinds of things that businesses would normally do, which was to get involved in partnerships and joint ventures. Those sorts of things are relatively recent for us compared to some of our competitors in Europe.

105. Thank you. As I understand it, the Commission are proposing three clear criteria for special services. First, that they are clearly distinct from USO services. Second, that they meet specific (not all) customer needs. Third, that they have two or more value added features. Is this not a sufficiently tight definition to remove any concerns that special services could be used to circumvent the reserved area?

(*Mr Bishopp*) I think there are two points that need to be made. The question of special services was actually raised in quite a famous case, the Corbeau case, which went to the European Court of Justice. The European Court of Justice determined that the appropriate criteria for the definition of the special service was, one, the dissociability of the service with the universal service, but also the second and most important limb was the impact that it would have on the sustainability of the universal service. The issue that people have raised with the Commission is why they have elected not to carry forward the European Court of Justice's second limb. What that then brings us on to is the second part of the question, which is, of course, that there is no criteria in the Directive as to what dissociability, albeit distinct from the USO is? How significant or trivial does the feature that is added need to be? The worry that one has with the current definition of that distinction is that we have spoken already about the fact that within the universal service it is possible in certain parts of the country to actually provide the elite, better quality service—and we are thinking here of mail going very short distances or mail that goes between very distinct customers, businesses, et cetera. It would, therefore, within the overall performance of the universal service, be possible to identify particular

Lord Cavendish of Furness *contd.*]

areas of traffic, or particular customers, and then to actually offer to the universal service some species of this that might be some distant guarantee of quality which, already, 99 or 100 per cent of the traffic is already getting, or small compensation claims on the very rare occasions that that service is, perhaps, not met, in order then to disassociate it from the universal services. The view that many people have taken is that if these are meant to be added value services—then the multiple of the basic weight step, as well as the price limit should apply—and if that is the sensible way of defining reserved and non-reserved traffic, then it seems illogical then to say, "You are not going to apply that for value added services. They should not be subject to that minimum value."

106. I think I would exaggerate if I said I understood that perfectly. We may need a little note on this, I think.
(*Mr Roberts*) The value issue is complicated and it is important, so we are happy to do that.

107. We are concerned that if there were to be greater liberalisation of the postal services that might be levied on services outside the reserved area with the purpose of creating a level playing field. This does not happen with Parcelforce, but do you think there are risks in this anyway?
(*Mr Roberts*) I think there are risks.
(*Mr Cope*) It is exactly the point you make. I think the competitors who are forced to charge VAT on their services competing against a post office that does not have to charge VAT on its services would lobby very hard for the introduction of that VAT, to make a more level playing field.

Lord Skelmersdale

108. Is it happening already with Securicor and Parcelforce?
(*Mr Cope*) Yes. They have to charge VAT on their services.

109. Are they lobbying?
(*Mr Cope*) Very hard, yes.
Lord Skelmersdale: The classic case, again, is in Sweden where they have gone for complete liberalisation and the Swedish Government took the view that you had to introduce VAT on the postal services in order to have classic and fair competition. It would seem to me perverse in the extreme that consumers faced with all the confidence of competition suddenly saw 17½ per cent, or whatever, increase in their postal rates because VAT had to be introduced.

Lord Cavendish of Furness

110. What is your opinion about the perception of the public buying a stamp?
(*Mr Cope*) I do not think they know whether VAT is included or not.

111. You are talking about a 27 pence stamp going to what?
(*Mr Roberts*) About 32 pence. If VAT were levied I think we would have an outcry.

Chairman

112. VAT is only going to be levied if it is conditional on liberalisation, and from listening to what you are saying to us, this seems to be a long way down the road.
(*Mr Roberts*) In my view, yes, it would be, and at the moment we obviously have no plans here for VAT on postal services. Of course, whenever it has been debated you get into the whole debate around charities and people and posting. Depending on the level of VAT, it does not take much to put stamp prices up. I can tell you from past hard experience that if you put one penny on a stamp you can get a firm reaction. So the idea of putting 17½ per cent on would—

113. What we want to see is the price going down in some areas. I am finding it extraordinarily difficult to square your views that you are quite keen to liberalise and see more competition, yet I get the distinct feeling that it is a fair way down the road. When we have been talking about maintenance of the universal services obligation I find it very difficult to see the area in which you would be welcoming competition coming in. Can you say what your programme looks like for moving towards more liberalisation? Where would you see competitors coming in? What would the consequences be there? I think particularly you suggested that you would settle, for the time being, on 150g as it would move towards liberalisation. What would your profit level be if it was down to 100g as well as the 50g, or even down to 20g?
(*Mr Roberts*) In terms of our move, I obviously have not explained myself as well as I should have done. We do see liberalisation, but we would like to see it put in in a gradually controlled way, ie, by a number of steps. The time scale which the Commission have put out is the next move in 2003. That would take it to 150g. After that we would see another move in 2005, not necessarily waiting until 2007, which is the date that the Commission has talked about. If you reduce to 150g on the basis of the entry pricing method, we believe the impact on our profit at that stage would be something like £80 to £120 million. If you reduce it to 100g, it is about £150 million.

114. £80 to £120 million?
(*Mr Roberts*) £80 to £120 million profit reduction on 150g, £150 to £200 million profit reduction on 100g, and £250 to £300 million profit reduction on 50g.

115. If you took it down to 20g?
(*Mr Bishopp*) Because of the weight limit, if you had a 20g limit you have effectively liberalised the whole of the market.
(*Mr Roberts*) At that point, we believe, if you have full liberalisation you are probably looking at £700 million.

116. So you are looking to 2000 and?
(*Mr Roberts*) If you go to 150g in 2003, another step maybe two years later, because we think two years would show what was happening to the market. If that was continuing to show no impact, then you could still move to full liberalisation not far beyond

Chairman *contd.*]

the 2007 that the Commission has in mind. I do not personally see why there is a four year gap between 2003 and 2007. If you were going to 50g, you might as well go all the way. So, for me, perhaps the fundamental difference between some of the things we have been talking about is an approach which looks at the market to make sure that we in this country are still able to fund the universal service obligation and keep the uniform price. If it is proven that we can, then we move and the argument that we have been trying to put to you about not opposing liberalisation means that we would just do it in a different way. I think all of us here expect at some point that there will be a completely open market. From my position, having been involved in this organisation for a while, unless people want a different kind of postal service in the United Kingdom, which means that you do not have the common price everywhere, I would hate to do that by mistake and that is the real kernel of the kind of thing we are saying. I suppose we are being more cautious, but we are not being cautious purely to try and protect what we have got, we are being cautious because we genuinely believe, from the work that we have done, that there is a real risk if you get this wrong that the uniform price, and hence the ability to fund the USO, could be severely compromised.

Baroness O'Cathain

117. There is a suggestion that the USO could be funded by a compensation fund. In your submission—paragraph five—you say, "The Commission suggests that to guarantee finance for the USO a compensation fund would constitute an alternative mechanism." You say that there are, however, serious problems with the compensation fund in the postal sector and there are no examples of countries where it has been successfully applied. If that is so, I would like some evidence that there are serious problems with the compensation fund. Not necessarily now, but if you could write to us about it. If there are no examples where it has been successfully applied, why has the Commission come up with the suggestion?
(*Mr Roberts*) I think that is an extremely good question. We asked it three years ago.

118. You got no answer?
(*Mr Roberts*) We got no answer. Three years ago in the first Directive almost the same statement was made by the Commission. I can remember sitting here with previous House of Lords Committee saying, "We just do not understand how this could work." Can I just speculate for a second? We have entrants coming into the market place. It is a very low barrier to entry type of organisation. Some of them will come in and go out, maybe quite quickly. All of them, in theory, as I understand this, will be due to pay some form of compensation if they were tackling areas which effect USO. We are going to have to measure it in some way or other. They are going to have to account for it in some way or other and are going to have to pay it to somebody. In the meantime the market, because it will then be dynamic, will be changing, we will be recalculating the effect depending where we are, and I really do think we have a bureaucratic nightmare or festive period, depending on how you look at it, to try and handle this. The only examples we can give you are that it was proposed in exactly the same way in Sweden and the whole idea was dropped because nobody could make it work. Finland are finding that it is there, but it is stopping people entering the market because they do not want to get involved in this. The only other place we know of is Spain where, again, they are finding it very difficult to apply. My question is: Why have the Commission not gone and looked at that?
Baroness O'Cathain: An observation on the back of that is that that is something for the specialist adviser to look at. I got the impression from the evidence last week that Sweden was regarded as the great success story. We certainly were not told that prices had gone up in real terms by 60 per cent.
Chairman: We were. We questioned them on prices.

Baroness O'Cathain

119. If they could not make the compensation fund work, then—
(*Mr Roberts*) I happened to meet with my opposite number in the Swedish Post Office yesterday and he was telling we that they are under severe financial difficulties at the moment. So I do not think Sweden are a great success story.

Lord Brookeborough

120. You said if you put a penny on the price of a stamp you get a lot of screams. Apart from the noise, what happens in the market? Do the number of letters posted actually go down, and if you had to raise the level of the uniform tariff, which would then become a uniform tariff throughout, how many pence would you have to put on to compensate you for the loss of 150g to—
(*Mr Cope*) There is an elasticity effect on prices. If you put prices up by 1 per cent, we think that we lose about 0.2 per cent of traffic.

121. You have put prices up in previous times, so, therefore, surely you are not thinking but you actually know the effect it had over a short period of time?
(*Mr Cope*) Yes, we do. We know and we calculate it, and when we are considering a real price increase—which we have not done for a long time— we take that into account in our calculations. There is an elasticity effect in pricing.
(*Mr Roberts*) One penny increase on first and second class with consequential increases as you go up through higher weights produces about £150 million revenue after tax.

122. So if it was dropped to 150g that would be one pence and your problem would be solved, presuming you get through the screaming phase?
(*Mr Roberts*) Yes. We would be able to maintain a profit by putting the price up, but one of the things that we have been trying to do is put the price down, which we managed to successfully do in the second class service by a penny. So, again, you are then back

[*Lord Brookeborough contd.*]

into a larger deterrent effect if we were going into a series of price increases.

Chairman

123. Could I come back to the USO again? We now know what the overall cost is. Do you break this down region by region, city by city?
(*Mr Bishopp*) No, we do not.

124. Why not?
(*Mr Roberts*) Because in the normal course of activity, until now, we have not needed to do that.

125. I live in Battersea where I get a terrible service, constantly use the charter to no avail, and find increasingly that my first class post appears on the second class delivery, by 1.30 if I am lucky, and I wonder if I would be prepared to pay more to ensure that I got my post in earlier, or if I cannot get it from the post office, what freedom can I ever find to look for somebody who would get to it me on time? First of all I come back to my main point about the cost of maintaining the universal service. You know the global figure. You must break it down in some form to lower units to be able to talk about the profit that you make when you are delivering post in Battersea in comparison to delivering it to Baroness O'Cathain in Arundel? There must be some breakdown. Are we allowed to have access to that to get closer to seeing what—
(*Mr Roberts*) There is not a breakdown. From our point of view there is no point in making that kind of breakdown, because the way in which the finances are put together are by the overall total of mail we handle, the costs to employ in different areas, and the price we charge for the mail. There is no point for me, given the rules under which we currently run, of then breaking that down and saying, "Oh, well, I make a profit of X in Battersea. I want to know what the costs are in Battersea."

126. But surely you ought to, as a business, should you not?
(*Mr Roberts*) The issue for us is that because we are a monopoly, in that sense we do not need to say, "Well, the profit in X is better than Y." The issue for us too is, revenue is generated where, at the end you post it or at the end you receive it? In the historical context of where we have been so far, handling that and doing that kind of calculation has not been an aid to us in running a business. If you went and looked at the cost you would find that cost control was very tight and we understood an enormous amount about the cost implications, but the revenue implication is a standard 27 pence per item, which you then read off the scale.

127. If we are moving towards liberalisation, surely this will be needed?
(*Mr Roberts*) It will be in the sense of—

128. You need to be prepare for that.
(*Mr Roberts*) A lot of the work that we are doing now, getting at costs for regulation, is actually starting to do just that. I am sorry if this sounds like I am harping on about it, but it is these kind of changes that we are now tackling that people in Europe were tackling five or six years ago. We keep coming back to your question by saying, "We are just about to do this", because, of course, life for us has changed an enormous amount in the last 12 months. Life for many of our competitors changed five or six years ago.

Lord Woolmer of Leeds

129. Given the change in the last 12 months, do you think that framework is now adequate and appropriate for you to face the challenges of liberalisation, or do you think that if liberalisation is to come it can only be faced by the Post Office as a privatised business?
(*Mr Roberts*) That is not a decision for me.

130. I did not ask for a decision.
(*Mr Roberts*) We have always said that the issue for us is that the government of the day would need to put us in the best commercial position to compete. We have made a number of steps, I think, in the last 12 months. Whether that is sufficient, I think, only time and the market will show. If it is not, then certainly, if I am here, or my successors, ought to argue with the government of the day that further changes will be needed, because certainly at the end of all this it will be about competition and I hope that whoever is in control of the British Post Office then will feel that the issue is about putting us, as an organisation, into a position where we have the best opportunity to compete. I think that would mean whatever it took to compete in that market.

Baroness O'Cathain

131. And best customer services.
(*Mr Roberts*) That has to be right, because without that we will not compete anyway.

Lord Woolmer of Leeds

132. Do you think that the governments and the major players in each of the national markets in the EU—Germany, France and Italy—will be happy with you seeking aggressively to be competitive in their markets under your present corporate structure as opposed to being privatised?
(*Mr Roberts*) I think that we are seeing major changes in the attitude of many European post offices. A number of them are under consideration for privatisation. I think there is an acceptance that there is going to be competition in every country. We have half a dozen European post offices with sales offices already here in London, and I believe that we have probably passed through the stage which was, "Oh, well, you can't compete in my back yard." All of us have now accepted that as these changes come, the smaller post offices in particular, not only the bigger ones, will all be looking to get into the best mail market they can. The British mail market will certainly be one of the most attractive. I think we will find that everybody will start to play in everybody's back yard.

Lord Skelmersdale

133. We have covered practically every subject that we can possibly think of asking you, except for one, to which I expect I know the answer because I am a Director of a mail order firm, but other Members of the Committee, I suspect, do not. You made the particular point that the 50g reserve limit would lead to what I might describe as cheating penetration. You have your two envelopes. One might even be 51g as opposed to 50g. Surely this is not particular to the 50g limit, it must happen at the 350g limit as well?

(*Mr Roberts*) I think we are then back to the characteristics of the mail at certain levels. If you think of your own post boxes every day, a lot of the direct mail tends to be more of this end of thing than the higher weights. Once you get further up it tends to be the larger envelopes. My colleagues will correct me if I am wrong, but I think most of the direct mail that we handle is much more around this level, size and weight. We think that, while you are right, there would be an impact at any cut off point, the lower that cut off point becomes the greater the impact, because of the type of direct mail.

134. If the cost for a first class letter differs by 5p, which you suggested it might, I would be very happy the spend an extra penny on a slightly heavier envelope, because my net saving would be four pence. Why is this wrong?

(*Mr Cope*) That is precisely the form of avoidance that would happen if the monopoly was reduced to 50g. The difference between that and 350g is that you are talking about goods essentially, which are weighed anyway.

135. What you are saying is that you agree with the Commission that you actually have bigger problems the lower the limit is set?

(*Mr Cope*) Policing the monopoly would be more difficult the lower the limit.

136. Surely this would be a job for the regulator, would it not? (*Mr Cope*) It would be a job for the regulator in this country, but I think their job would be extremely difficult.

Lord Woolmer of Leeds

137. Does the technology allow you to know whether something weighs 50g or 52g?

(*Mr Roberts*) Not at the moment.

138. Does any other country in Europe?

(*Mr Roberts*) I do not think any of them do at the moment, because if we are talking about individual letters, if we are talking about bulk mail, it is the number of items, because, of course, the weight does not really impact yet because it is all fairly—

(*Mr Cope*) They will weigh something like this. So, the 350g or 150g limit is weighed as part of the posting process. Whereas that is assumed to be at the minimum price, so we do not need to weigh it.

139. So, it could be 60g and that would not be a problem?

(*Mr Roberts*) It gets worse as you come down.

Lord Brookeborough

140. When I post an A4 envelope and I go to my kitchen scales and I have trouble reading off the grams and then I have even more trouble making up the right price to put on it, you do not actually weigh that?

(*Mr Cope*) Yes, we do.

141. Every single one.

(*Mr Cope*) We will weigh ones that we think—

142. It is not done by machine?

(*Mr Cope*) They are quite expert. They can tell whether they think something is wildly—

143. I thought there was a machine that weighed it and added it up.

(*Mr Roberts*) The issue is not so much what you are going to put in, it is the American Express company or Lloyds Bank or whoever who are posting thousands and thousands of the same kind of item. For us, the difference between all of those items being 45g or $50\frac{1}{2}$ grams is where we have the problem.

Chairman

144. I think we have had a very good session this morning, and quite an extended one. I am very pleased that you have given us so much time and you have been so forthright with us. We look forward to receiving the supplementary papers which you have also undertaken to send to us. Thank you very much indeed.

(*Mr Roberts*) Thank you.

Supplementary evidence by the Post Office

THE SPECIAL SERVICES EXCEPTION

The Commission proposes to amend Article 7 of the Postal Services Directive to state that "special services" may not be reserved. Special Services are defined in an amendment to Article 2 of the Directive in the following terms:

"Special services are services clearly distinct from the universal service, which meet particular customer requirements and which offer additional service features with added-value not offered by the standard postal service. Additional added-value service features are, for example, delivery on appointment, the option to effect a change of destination or addressee in transit or if delivery to the primary destination fails, tracking and tracing, guaranteed time of delivery, more than one attempt at delivery, delivery according to the priority or sequence specified by the user."

It is not only unnecessary for the Commission to pronounce on this issue but confusing since the European Court of Justice has already established principles as to the extent to which it is possible to reserve "new services" (in the Corbeau Case). In considering whether Article 90(2) (now Article 86(2)) could be used to justify extending a postal monopoly to "new services" the court held that such an extension was not justifiable provided that (1) the new services in question were dissociable from the postal services offered by the incumbent postal administration and (2) that placing such service in the competitive area would not undermine the economic equilibrium of the incumbent postal administration in providing the postal service of general economic interest.

The definition of Special Services adopted by the Commission has many problems, the most substantial of which is the failure to acknowledge the second limb of the test in the Corbeau case, namely that the "new service" must not undermine the economic equilibrium under which the incumbent postal administration provides the service of general economic interest (in other words the Universal Service Obligation as defined in Article 3 of the Postal Services Directive). Indeed, it follows from the Commission's proposal that once a service is found to be a "special service" then it is incapable of reservation, irrespective of the effect on the universal service providers ability to provide a universal service.

It is easily possible to envisage a situation in which a "special service" with many of the additional service attributes described by the Commission was both cheaper and substitutable for the standard postal service, so that the loss of revenue to the universal service provider could be extensive. In particular any letter service which had added-value services as part of the basic offering but in which the added-value services only had to be performed in specific (and unusual) circumstances (such as change of destination in transit, redelivery on delivery failure etc) could be offered at very little additional cost to the service provider. Therefore, the addition of such "special services" would tend not to materially impact on the cost of providing the "special services" and yet would be sufficient to take the service outside the reserved area and thus allow the operator to undercut the standard uniform tariff in areas of low cost (such as city centres). Indeed, the Commission has noted that "the unit price of a particular service may no longer be a true indicator of whether that service carries added value" however, it has failed to consider the possibility that that may be so not because the provider of the "special service" was more efficient, but because they were really taking advantage of a uniform tariff in areas with low delivery costs to cream-skim.

This is not an idle fear. In recent years, when the UK Post Office has challenged delivery companies operating in the City of London at prices below the uniform first weight step and which appear to be in clear breach of the UK postal monopoly, it has been common for such companies to claim that they are offering a dissociable service within the scope of the Corbeau judgement. For example, one company which later accepted a Home Office caution in respect of its activities, provided a lengthy list dealing with the ways in which it claimed its services could be distinguished from the standard service provided by the UK Post Office. Some of the suggested differences were minor operational differences which it was difficult to imagine could offer additional value to its customers. On the other hand, some of the other alleged differences could be portrayed as genuine service enhancements that might provide some added-value for some of their customers. However, when the customers were approached and asked whether or not the "special services" were a genuine factor in deciding to use the company in question, all agreed that the only relevant factors were the fact that the price substantially undercut the public tariff. Indeed, many customers were not even aware of the existence of the "special services" which the company claimed were the hallmark of its offering to business customers.

There are a number of ways in which protection for the universal service provision could be allowed for in the text of a new Directive. By far the most satisfactory would be the inclusion of the second limb of the Corbeau test in Article 7 of the Directive to make explicit that special services are only incapable of reservation to the extent that such a liberalisation would not undermine the economic equilibrium of the USP in providing the USO. Alternatively, the definition of Special Services could be redrafted to make clear that a special service is only sufficient distinct from the standard postal service if it is not substitutable for it—ie that the standard postal service and the special service are operating in different product markets. As another alternative it could be provided that a special service is only incapable of reservation to the extent that it is offered at a price which exceeds that of the standard service for that weight step. Any of these solutions would be sufficient to prevent special services from being a "Trojan Horse", by which a provider could claim to offer a special service differentiated from the standard service as a device to enable it to cream-skim a uniform tariff in high density delivery areas.

If the current proposal for "special services" was to proceed without recognition that such services should not undermine the economic equilibrium necessary to provide the USO, then a strong case could be made for saying that the Special Service provision as drafted may conflict with Article 86(2) of the Treaty of Rome as interpreted in Corbeau. There is already established precedent for the fact that in the event of such a conflict the Court of Justice is prepared to annul part of a Directive, particularly where the scope of the Directive is ill-defined.[2]

---

[2] See French Republic v Commission (Case C-202/88) and Spain, Belgium and Italy v Commission (Cases C-271/90, C-281/90 and 289/90) paras. 29–32. See also Germany v European Parliament and Council (Case C-376/98).

18 October 2000] *[Continued*

ISSUES OF DEFINITION

This raises another concern about the Commission's draft, that is the failure to provide clear basic definitions. According to the Commission's proposals a Special service must be (inter alia):

(a) "clearly distinct from the universal service"; and

(b) "offer additional service features with added-value not offered by the standard postal service."

However, "universal service" is defined in Article 3 more in terms of a postal network capability than in terms of the type of postal service provided through a network. It would be perfectly possible to provide a Special Service (with any of the characteristics listed as examples by the Commission) by means of the universal service as defined in Article 3. Thus, to say that "special services are clearly distinct from the universal service" is contradicted by the examples provided by the Commission in their proposed text.

The inclusion by the Commission of fixed examples of what they would see as "additional added value service features" is not helpful as many of the features described are already part of the standard public postal service in one or more Member States. For example, the UK Post Office already offers without charge redirection of a letter to a second address if delivery cannot be made at the first address and more than one attempt at delivery at the request of the addressee. Of the other examples mentioned by the Commission, delivery on appointment, redirection of letters in transit, tracking and tracing and guaranteed time of delivery are optional features which a sender can elect to pay for.

Secondly as the "standard postal service" is not defined it is unclear what the baseline is which a special service should be compared to. Presumably, standard postal service is a question of fact based on the service offering of the USP in each member state at the present time. As the "standard service" in each Member State will vary considerably, it follows that the degree of liberalisation of special services permitted in each Member State will also vary considerably. This goes against the principle of harmonisation which was one of the objectives in preparing a Directive on postal services.

ASSESSING THE COSTS OF PROVIDING THE UNIVERSAL SERVICE OBLIGATION

There are two principal methods that have been used for costing the universal service obligation, the net avoided cost method and the entry pricing method. These two methods answer fundamentally different questions.

The Net Avoided Cost (NAC) method

This approach was developed for and used in the Telecommunications industry after liberalisation had occurred. In a postal context it focuses on answering the hypothetical question: "If the universal service provider could choose not to provide the universal service, by how much would its profits increase?" the idea behind the net avoided cost approach is fairly simple. There are some "routes" where the cost which could be avoided from ceasing a service is greater than the uniform price received. If free to do so, a commercially-orientated operator would withdraw such services. Adding up the difference between revenue and avoidable cost on each of these loss-making routes is the financial (net avoided) cost to the operator of having to run these services. This question is most relevant in a static market situation. If applied in the context of a continuing monopoly this method would estimate the cost of supplying universal service whilst continuing to enjoy the protection of the current reserved area.

This is the approach that was deployed by the consultants who estimated the cost of universal service for the European Commission. The method was widely criticised by many of the EU postal operators as being unsuitable because it does not address the question of market liberalisation. However, this method can be regarded as being suitable in circumstances where a stable market exists. If there is no prospect of liberalisation or other major change, then this method could be deployed.

The Entry Pricing (EP) method

This approach was explicitly developed to deal with the situation of a dynamic market; in particular where increased competition is expected (for example, through a reduction in the size of the reserved area). It addresses the question: "Under specific liberalisation assumptions by how much will the profit of the business be reduced if there remains the requirement to provide the universal service at uniform prices?" The method therefore evaluates the ability of the universal service provider to continue to provide universal service at a uniform tariff after the introduction of competition to some or all of its business. It explicitly considers the profit making items as it is these that would be lost to competitors entering the market who would undercut the uniform price required to be charged by the Universal Service Provider.

This method was developed jointly between PriceWaterhouseCoopers and the British Post Office. It is more suited to address the question of the appropriate extent of competitive entry than the NAC approach since it is looking directly at the consequences of liberalisation.

A full exposition of the two methods is set out in the attached PostEurop document. A table of financial effects on the Post Office of different scenarios is set out below:

THE FINANCIAL EFFECTS OF DIFFERENT SCENARIOS

	£ million
Cost of the USO at current monopoly level (NAC Approach)	25–30
Cost of the USO at monopoly limit of 150g (EP Approach)	80–120
Cost of the USO at monopoly limit of 100g (EP Approach)	150–200
Cost of the USO at monopoly limit of 50g (EP Approach)	250–300
Cost of the USO given total liberalisation (EP Approach)	700–1,000

October 2000

WEDNESDAY 25 OCTOBER 2000

Present:

Brooke of Alverthorpe, L. (Chairman)
Cavendish of Furness, L.
Faulkner of Worcester, L.
Paul, L.
Woolmer of Leeds, L.

Memorandum by the Communication Workers' Union/Communications Managers' Association

SUMMARY

1. The CWU and CMA are not opposed to a measure of liberalisation in the provision of postal services but, like the original Directive, we believe that such liberalisation should be "gradual and controlled" and not at the expense of universal service at uniform tariffs. We believe that the current proposals have not been validated by the flawed studies of 1998. Furthermore, we believe that the proposals do not take full account of the number and location of job losses in the postal sector. In short, in our view, the current proposals of the Commission represent too much, too soon and would, if implemented, cause serious damage to the interests of customers and to the revenues and the jobs of the universal service providers.

2. We believe that the impact of the European Commission's proposals for 2003 would be:

   (a) a substantial loss in postal operators' revenues—the Commission estimate that a further 16 per cent of revenues would be opened to competition;

   (b) a substantial loss in postal operators' profits—the British Post Office estimates a loss of £250–300 million, which would almost eliminate its profitability;

   (c) a direct threat to the uniform tariff currently operated by universal service providers—a study by Toulouse University estimates that a fully competitive market would generate highly differential prices with rural customers paying tariffs more than four times those paid by commercial customers; and

   (d) a dramatic loss in jobs—countries which have already liberalised, such as Germany, Sweden or (outside the EU) New Zealand have cut jobs in the main postal operator by up to 40 per cent.

3. Although the Commission's "draft proposal" does not say so explicitly, the whole thrust of the document is that there should be complete liberalisation in 2007. This sleight of hand is bad enough, but the tactic is even more objectionable because of the methodology proposed—a review in 2004 only one year after the next step in the liberalisation process. This is categorically not the "gradual and controlled" liberalisation process to which Member States agree in the original Directive.

INTRODUCTION

4. The Communication Workers Union (CWU) represents all the non-management grades in the Post Office. The Communication Managers Association (CMA) represents all management grades in the Post Office and is part of the Manufacturing Science and Finance (MSF) union. The CWU and CMA are totally committed to the creation of a Post Office that provides the best possible range and quality of service to all its customers, and regularly submit views to the relevant Select Committees.

HISTORIC BACKGROUND

5. The current European Commission proposals are being tabled under the terms of the original Postal Services Directive of December 1997. This required that future liberalisation should be "gradual and controlled".

6. The Commission's present proposals are apparently based on five parallel studies and one consolidated study carried out in the course of 1998. These studies have been severely criticised for their poor methodology and no specific studies have been commissioned on the impact of the proposals on uniform tariffs or employment levels.

7. During formulation of his proposals, Commissioner Bolkestein did not respond to repeated requests by Union Network International (UNI)—the international trade union body to which the CWU and CMA are affiliated—for a meeting to discuss his plans.

CWU/CMA POSITION

8. We understand the case for further liberalisation, but we believe that the method of introducing such further liberalisation should be by use of the price/weight threshold and that the timing should involve a gradual and phased implementation.

9. Therefore, we welcome the Commission's recognition that it would not be right to liberalise direct mail or incoming cross-border mail as general categories. However, we are saddened that the Commission is so far pressing ahead with the idea of liberalising so-called special services. This would have the effect of taking all mail prepared or supported by electronic communication technologies outside the reserved area. This would be very damaging to the future revenues of postal administrations and we are convinced that the delivery of physical letters within the price/weight threshold must be maintained within the reserved area of universal service at uniform tariffs is to be sustained.

10. Our principal objection to the Commission's latest proposals is that categorically they do not represent the gradual and controlled liberalisation that was mandated in the original Postal Directive. A move from 350 grams/five times the basic price step to 50 grams/two and a half times the basic price step would be a huge leap with very little understanding of the consequences for universal service, uniform tariffs and employment levels.

11. The British Post Office has considered carefully what would be the likely impact of the Commission's proposals for the UK. It believes that such a rapid and large-scale reduction in the reserved area would effectively wipe out its current level of profitability. It is that profitability—based on a reasonable size of reserved area—that funds the universal service. Yet the Commission seems to have little interest in this matter, merely suggesting different options for the funding of the universal service. In our view, the universal service is so vital to European Community services that there should be a common, assured basis of funding throughout the community and we believe that the best basis by far is an adequate reserved area.

12. Furthermore, on the basis of research carried out by the Institut d'Economie Industrielle (IDEI) at the University of Toulouse, the British Post Office believes that the uniform, affordable postal tariff could not be maintained. The current Directive does not make the uniform tariff a requirement and indeed the phraseology of the new proposals suggests that the Commission no longer takes seriously the concept of the uniform tariff.

13. Furthermore, the Commission seems to care little about the likely reductions in employment. Such evidence as we have of this scale of liberalisation—notably Sweden and New Zealand—makes us fearful of the impact on both residential customers and postal administration staff.

14. Even now, not all Member States have properly implemented the provisions of the 1997 Directive and therefore the current proposals cannot possibly take account of the implementation of that Directive.

15. Here in Britain, the UK Government has implemented the original Directive and embarked on new legislation to create a more commercial and competitive environment for the British Postal Office. This package envisages a further measure of liberalisation and the Government—having at one stage considered 150 grams as the new threshold—has referred the whole matter to the new Postal Services Commission for a thorough examination. If the European Commission was to succeed in persuading the European Parliament and the Council of Ministers of the need for a reduction to 50 grams, this would make a nonsense of the study by the UK regulator and similar examinations taking place in other EU Member States.

TOULOUSE STUDY

16. The main conclusions of the study commissioned by the British Post Office and France's La Poste from the Institut d'Economie Industrielle (IDEI) of the University of Toulouse are:

   (a) the model shows very fully that, if left to itself, the market will generate highly differentiated prices for mail. The uniform price exists, not because it emerges from the market, but only because government requires it as part of the universal service obligation;

   (b) the key features of this differentiation are twofold. Lower prices can be expected in some urban markets, where entry is likely to occur, particularly for the business-to-business market. At the same time, higher prices are in prospect for households, due to their lower price elasticity of demand and, potentially, very much higher levels in rural markets where the possibility of alternative service providers seems remote due to the relatively high level of fixed costs; and

   (c) the model suggests that, for a principal and central case, entrants' prices for the urban business market might be perhaps around half of the pre-liberalisation uniform price (and even lower in some cases) and that the incumbent would cut prices in response to entry. At the other end of the spectrum, households posting to households in rural areas would face a monopoly price perhaps four times, or more, higher than the initial price level.

IMPACT ON EMPLOYMENT

17. As far as jobs are concerned, maybe we do not need to look into a crystal ball to have a reasonable indication of the future. The "explanatory memorandum" itself concedes that—even before any liberalisation measures are taken into account—employment in the universal service providers is forecast to fall by approaching one-tenth between 1997–2007. The impact of further liberalisation is not hard to fathom. The Commission's own figures for employment in Germany and Sweden—where we have already had liberalisation beyond the original Directive—show substantial falls in the number of jobs in the main providers and new jobs in the competitors being both much fewer in number and much more likely to be part-time.

18. The timing of any further liberalisation is highly problematic for postal operators because of the likely impact of electronic communication on traditional mail volumes in the new few years. Perversely the Commission talks of "a window of opportunity" for the opening of mail markets, but to press ahead with a further excessive stage of liberalisation at the very same time as we will see unprecedented electronic substitution—and when we are not sure of the full consequences of either—seems to us to be extremely bad policy-making and a direct threat to jobs.

THE SWEDISH EXPERIENCE

19. Sweden Post was corporatised in March 1994 and the letter monopoly was abolished at the same time. Since then:

　(a) the price of posting a letter up to 20 grams has more than doubled between 1988–98 (although the imposition of VAT was a major feature, tariff rebalancing was also a factor);

　(b) there was a major fall in the profits of Sweden Post in 1995–96;

　(c) the number of jobs in Sweden Post has fallen since 1992 by 21 per cent; and

　(d) the size of Sweden Post's retail network fell between 1994 and 1998 by 24 per cent.

THE NEW ZEALAND EXPERIENCE

20. New Zealand Post was corporatised in April 1997 and the letter monopoly was abolished in April 1998. In the run up to corporatisation:

　(a) the basic price of posting a letter rose by 60 per cent;

　(b) in 1992 the rural delivery fee was doubled;

　(c) in 1995 this fee was abolished when all rural delivery was sub-contracted;

　(d) profit levels of New Zealand Post fell between 1996 and 1999 by 69 per cent; and

　(e) employment in New Zealand Post fell between 1987 and 1997 by 43 per cent.

THE WAY FORWARD

21. In accordance with our view that the process of liberalisation should be "gradual and controlled", we believe that it would be reasonable for European postal operators to see a reduction in their letter monopoly in 2003 from 350 grams/five times the basic price step to 150 grams/three times the basic price step.

22. After a couple of years' experience of this liberalisation, there should be a thorough review which looks at the impact on service levels, prices, profitability, and employment levels. Only in the light of such a review should further proposals be drawn up in respect of any further liberalisation in 2007 or some later date.

23. Meanwhile, there has been no serious consultation on the current proposals and Commissioner Bolkestein simply did not respond to the request for a meeting from the Postal Section of Union Network International. Therefore we now urge that meaningful discussions take place with—no doubt among others—postal administrations and postal unions and we earnestly hope that a more gradual, and therefore a more sensible, programme of liberalisation can be agreed.

27 September 2000

Examination of Witnesses

Mr Derek Hodgson, Communication Workers' Union, Mr Roger Darlington, Head of Research, Communication Workers' Union, and Mr John Lovelady, Communication Managers' Association, called in and examined.

Chairman

145. Apologies for keeping you waiting a little while, we were just reflecting on the evidence from the Post Office last week. A number of questions remain with us to ponder on and possibly go back to them. First of all, our thanks to you for letting us have your written submission, it has been very helpful indeed. Unless you want to open up with a statement we are quite happy to go straight into questions.

(*Mr Hodgson*) No, I think the written presentation that we put summarises it very well and the time will probably be more productively spent in trying to answer the questions that you have got rather than using up time elaborating on what you have already got.

146. We spent quite a bit of our time last week with the Post Office talking about productivity and liberalisation, as you would expect. Parcelforce interests us and we know that it now operates in competitive markets that have led to higher productivity than the Royal Mail generally. There has been a much greater change to flexible working practices than has been the case with Royal Mail and there has been much reduced industrial action. We are wondering whether you do not feel that this shows the effects liberalisation can bring and are wondering, therefore, why you are opposing the Commission's proposals for liberalisation?

(*Mr Hodgson*) We have been dealing and closely associated with the liberalisation proposals right from the Green Paper which first started off some five or six years ago and we have been reasonably consistent in our attitude. Quite honestly I thought that we shared a similar attitude to yourselves in terms of liberalisation not for liberalisation's sake. We started off the examination in Europe on the basis that we were to give good quality universal service at an affordable tariff right across the European Community and from that we developed into the liberalisation process. We have been consistent in our attitude and we thought that reflected your view, that quality universal service would not be placed at risk in the eyes of liberalisation. Indeed, we were somewhat successful in the lobbying which we did as far as the Council of Ministers were concerned to impose upon the European Commission a compromise that said there should be gradual and controlled liberalisation and not at the expense of universal service. That has remained our attitude all the way through. Coming to the differences between Parcelforce and the Post Office, first of all the Post Office has been in some difficulty for some time in knowing which direction it has been going. It has been used as a political football by successive governments with threats of privatisation, breaking up of the Post Office, all sorts of alternatives have been looked at. It was not until recently that we had a clear direction of where we are going. There has been, and I am the first to admit it, a hell of a lot of industrial unrest in the Post Office as a result of that. Productivity within the Royal Mail business—Royal Mail as distinct from Parcelforce— it has been difficult to motivate people who were not certain whether they would have a job, never mind a reasonable standard of living, in the future. What we have managed to do in recent times, however, is after long protracted negotiations we have introduced a considerable amount of change into Royal Mail that has still to feed through the system. One is the Employee Agenda which is a whole new pay and conditions package which will generate more productive ways of working. You do have some difficulty in providing the productivity you desire without the motivation being there but the motivation is now being provided. We have Agenda for Leadership with the managers and then we have had Shaping for Competition since, which was being designed hopefully against the background that the present Government were going to give the Post Office the commercial freedom it needed in order to compete with what was going on in the rest of Europe and the rest of the world. That will feed through the system and there will be greater productivity resulting from it. As far as Parcelforce is concerned, it is a particularly bad example to use in terms of liberalisation. Parcelforce has not had a monopoly. Parcelforce has had a universal service obligation without the protection of a monopoly. Parcelforce, as I am sure the Post Office told you, is almost bankrupt, it has not made a profit. Yes, there has been considerable change but that is still working through the system in terms of Coventry. Yes, there has been a tremendous cutback in jobs and what have you. I do not think Parcelforce is the best example. It is because of the unfair competition that is there that Parcelforce is in the shape it is in today. For example, competitors can undercut the Post Office, they have the universal obligations. In terms of prices they can take a complete batch of parcels right across the country, skim the cream by delivering in the urban area and then dump all the rural expensive stuff on the Post Office to deliver. I think that is a particularly bad example to make a comparison with. Having said that, there has been a change within Parcelforce. Parcelforce is necessary and Parcelforce will turn its way around. We have now got the freedom to make some major acquisitions. In terms of the long-term strategy for the Post Office of the complete distribution company, Parcelforce plays an important part in it as part of the whole. We are not comparing like with like when we talk about the Royal Mail letters with Parcelforce.

Lord Cavendish of Furness: I wondered if Mr Hodgson was under the impression that we are a Government Committee. We are not and we do not have a view yet. It is an All-Party Committee.

Chairman

147. You referred to "our view".

(*Mr Hodgson*) I thought that there were conclusions that were arrived at. It may be that I am misunderstanding the situation.

Chairman *contd.*]

148. I think you have the 1996 Report, have you not?

(*Mr Hodgson*) Yes, that is right. In the 1996 Report there was a summary of conclusions and recommendations and in order to get a lead on political thinking one tends to look at these things because if there were some things being said at that point in time, in the same way as if we gave evidence at that point in time, it would be reasonable to say to us "that was your view at a particular time", so I am expressing the same thing.

Lord Cavendish of Furness: I understand fully now.

Chairman

149. We went back to the 1996 Report as you would expect.

(*Mr Hodgson*) It does make very, very interesting reading.

150. Very interesting reading. We made the point that the Post Office must refinance. The Post Office's performance now would not be viewed in quite the same light as the Committee viewed it in 1996 on a comparable basis in productivity terms with some of the European countries.

(*Mr Hodgson*) I think that is fair comment. I was dealing with the basic underlying view in terms that the universal service is the important thing with regard to direct mail. In fact, as I read the conclusions that were arrived at at that point in time, they were very similar to the conclusions that we arrive at at this point in time.

151. They are very welcome, I am sure.

(*Mr Hodgson*) It would be interesting to know if things have dramatically changed since then that would lead to a basic change in viewpoint.

152. We have all seen quite a degree of liberalisation across the world in the intervening years and we have seen some changes in levels of performance in different countries. We have seen changes in the levels of performance of Parcelforce compared with Royal Mail, even though it may not be a straight analogous comparison but it is the nearest we can go for. We were wondering the extent to which you feel those changes have arisen through the liberalisation process.

(*Mr Hodgson*) I do not believe that those changes have arisen as a result of the liberalisation process. Those are circumstances which the different businesses face. When you talk about other European post offices, if we look at the position of the European post offices, they have been supported by government, supported by financial resource, and the extent to which this particular Post Office has been constrained by Government in terms of its finances, in terms of its ability for joint ventures, the difficulty is that we are not looking at comparable things.

153. We are aware of the money that went to the Treasury and their control over that. That point has been put to us. The Post Office and the Post Office Act has been supported by CWU and CMA as being given new wider commercial freedoms by the Government that you are about to embark upon and embrace to compete in new markets. I suppose looking across at Parcelforce, where you have talked about the competitors there, could it not be argued that as you are now being given more freedoms to compete and to move into new markets that within the market itself there should be a freedom for other competitors also to come in?

(*Mr Hodgson*) Actually the original authors of the thoughts on commercial freedom in the public sector were indeed ourselves. That was part of what we developed from the Government of the day's examination in the early 1990s of what they should do with the Post Office. When the Government of the day withdrew its proposals for privatisation in part or in whole, it was we who commissioned a report and started making the case for commercial freedom in the public sector. I think what we need to look at when we are talking about competition and whether people ought to be allowed to compete, we come back to the underlying thing that what we are talking about and what the European Commission are talking about is further liberalisation, gradual and controlled, that does not affect the universal service provision and certainly at affordable tariff rates. There is a difference between opening up the sector to areas that are in the reserved area that is purely and simply there to produce the universal service and the competitive areas. You will know that the European Commission have already said that there have got to be separate accounts for the universal service area and for the competitive area. One of the things that we believe is that with new markets opening up we should be able to be competitive in those markets but on a separate accounting basis completely from the reserved area. I believe there is every justification for saying, as the Commission has said previously, that the reserved area is there only to preserve the universal service obligation and there should not be competition in that particular area.

154. The Directive does not say that.

(*Mr Hodgson*) I am talking about the original Directive. What you are looking at is amendments to the original Directive.

155. That is what we are examining, the draft.

(*Mr Hodgson*) What we must do is go back. The Commission chooses to forget on occasions what is in original Directives and subsequently in proposals for new Directives. Clearly the commitment was to provide a reserved area. Now they are talking about something quite different, they are talking in terms of other ways of supporting the reserved area which are contrary to the way we thought in 1997 and the Committee that looked at it at that point in time thought in 1996 and subsequently the Council of Ministers in the compromise that they imposed. Clearly we still hold the view that the reserved area should not be in a competitive environment, it is there to preserve.

156. It is how we define the reserved area.

(*Mr Hodgson*) Yes, and we have been consistent in talking about price and weight. Interestingly, the Commission has already changed its position in what it has put to us at the moment. We have been closely associated with it, as I said, and the original draft that they intended to put, until there was a fair amount of

Chairman *contd.*]

pressure put on the Commission that there should be in January 2003 standard mail reduced to 50 grams and direct mail, cross-border mail, taken completely outside the reserved area in 2003 and complete liberalisation in 2007. They realised that they could not go further with that proposal because they were going to be in difficulties with it. Whilst Bolkestein himself has refused to meet us. . . . Apart from being the General Secretary of the CWU I am also the World and European President of the Councils of Post Office Unions and, therefore, via our international organisation we have tried to meet Bolkestein. Bangemann we have met on numerous occasions and although we had some pretty direct words with him in terms of policy he was always prepared to meet us but Bolkestein is not meeting us. We have met some of his civil servants and we can not understand from them exactly what the base lines for the proposals are, or where they are going, because they keep changing the ball game as we are going along. This is one of the things that we get worried about. It seems to us that it is very much like policy on the hoof.

157. What do you think of the latest figures?
(*Mr Hodgson*) The latest proposals?

158. Yes.
(*Mr Hodgson*) Too much too soon. Clearly in our view it will place the universal service provision at risk now. We are on record saying that competition has got to come. In fact, it was we who sought the Post Office to begin to face competition. The 50 grams and two and a half times the price, clearly in our view will place the universal service at risk. Then we go on to say that all new services, your expenses and whatnot, will be outside the reserved area. We keep coming back to the fact, and this is something we have said to the Commission, that the proposals are there: "tell us what justification there is for those proposals? You did five studies and then had a consolidating study. All of those five studies were flawed. All of them were criticised in various ways. Their methodologies were different and questionable. We then had a consolidating study that questioned the base lines on which the five original studies were done." Incidentally, there was a study on employment that was done that the Commission chose to lose where it talked about half a million jobs going in the postal public sector over the next five or six years.

Chairman: We have some questions on jobs which Lord Faulkner would like to put.

Lord Faulkner of Worcester

159. I wonder if I can press you on that because in your evidence you are asserting that you see significant job losses as a result of the Commission's proposal. Can you talk us through a little bit how you come to those conclusions?
(*Mr Hodgson*) The evidence that we have got to date where there has been liberalisation in places like Sweden and New Zealand. . . . Incidentally, through the social dialogue we sat with the Swedish post office and I asked for details on the success factor, because everybody talks about the Swedish post office, and it is not comparable with any of the large European groups and neither is New Zealand because they are extremely small. There have been significant job losses in New Zealand, significant job losses in Sweden. On profitability, this year is a bad year in Sweden, I do not think they are going to break even this year. The price of the universal service provision has gone for a ball of wax. What you will find in examination of these countries is that full-time job equivalents have reduced to almost half of what they were previously and then there is a lot of part-time and short-term contract casual labour associated with them. This falls in line with the study that was done for the Commission, I think it was probably asked for about three or four years ago, and conveniently not publicised too much because it talked about 500,000 jobs going in the postal sector. This was a Commission study. One of the things that we keep saying to them is "tell us and provide us with the information and the details on job losses and the impacts on jobs". There are suggestions that the job losses will be compensated in the public sector by what develops in the private sector. We have said "okay, these are assumptions but on what do you base these assumptions?" and they have not been particularly forthcoming with any concrete evidence on anything, they just say that we have got the Treaty of Rome and, therefore, we should be liberalising. When it comes to the job losses we have said "produce clear figures. You say jobs will be created" and they quote telecom. They say that with telecom there is a compensating feature. If we take, for example, telecom in this country, there is no commensurate compensating feature but that took ten years to arrive at. It is a compensating feature against a background of new services being created like mobile telephones and not the telephony that people lost their jobs in. We do not have a great deal of confidence in people telling us that there will be job creation to compensate for job losses.

160. Do you think that job losses in postal services are inevitable anyway given the extent of electronic substitution?
(*Mr Hodgson*) Sorry?

161. Given the growth of electronic mail and the fact that people are not writing letters but they are sending e-mails, is there not bound to be at best a loss in conventional postal service employment anyway?
(*Mr Hodgson*) Can I ask Roger to amplify the jobs issue.
(*Mr Darlington*) It may help you, Lord Faulkner, if I give you some figures on employers. There are very few countries, as you know, where there has been postal liberalisation. Most of them are very small countries on the periphery of their economic commerce. If we take Sweden, where the letter monopoly was abolished in 1994, 8,000 jobs have gone which represents 16 per cent. If we take New Zealand where the letter monopoly was abolished in rapid stages between 1991-1998, over that period 1,600 jobs have gone and that is a reduction of 19 per cent. We believe that the British postal market, given that it is a much, much larger market and it is much more central to the European economy, would face much stronger competition and, therefore, greater job losses. You said that electronic substitution will also result in job losses and that is almost certainly

Lord Faulkner of Worcester contd.]

true. That is an argument against introducing liberalisation too rapidly at the same time.

162. Could it not be an argument for saying that postal services will have to get their act together and make themselves more efficient in order to be able to compete?
(*Mr Darlington*) Certainly, and they will need time to do that. We are not opposed to liberalisation, what we are arguing is that it should be gradual and controlled, it should be phased. If you introduce it in too rapid a fashion with very, very little experience of the consequences—there are very few countries that have done this—and you do it simultaneously with the traumatic impact of electronic mail and business to business e-commerce, you are fundamentally threatening the revenues and profitability of a business which has a universal service obligation and a uniform tariff. That combination of introducing rapid liberalisation and rapid electronic substitution in an industry which has both a universal service obligation and a uniform tariff, in our view is unprecedented and one should proceed very, very cautiously in such an unknown environment.

Chairman

163. Has there not been some growth in jobs in the private sector in New Zealand and in Sweden?
(*Mr Darlington*) Very, very little. There are very few competitors in both of those countries and the reason is you are dealing with populations of seven, eight, nine million on the edge of Europe or on the edge of the Asian Pacific regions. Competitors, you will see, in France or Germany or the United Kingdom, if the European Commission has its way, will be much larger and much more aggressive. I think people have made the comparison with telecommunications but you have to remember that we are the prime union in telecommunications as well as the prime union in the post. In the first eight years of competition BT shed 118,000 jobs, which was 15 per cent. For the first decade there was virtually no compensating alternative employment. The alternative employment we now have is not in fixed link competitors, it is in mobile where there has always been competition. The majority of those jobs are much less secure, many are on short-term contracts.

164. In parcels has there been a growth in the private sector there? What are the numbers? Have you managed to go in there and represent people in the private sector?
(*Mr Hodgson*) Any growth in the private sector in parcels? This is where there are agreements between the TUC and Transport and General Workers' and we do not get into competitive areas for recruitment where there is a separate organisation. With the employment figures, it is very much the same as everything else that is happening with the Commission. We have sat down in front of them and said "look, give us some hard evidence on what is happening. You are not comparing like with like." Roger has said if you took Sweden and you took New Zealand those are very, very small countries in terms of population, in terms of the amount of traffic that they generate. The British Post Office delivers 77 million pieces of mail a day, which is probably more than 120 countries in the world deliver in a year. We are talking about a population of 60 million. We are talking about liberalisation in Europe but we have got some large groups appearing where we have the Dutch, the Germans, the French and the British and if that explodes and they start hitting each other there is nowhere that you can go. We sat with the Commission and said "give us some hard evidence" I do not think the approach we are adopting is unreasonable, to say "look, Commission, these are your proposals. Can you give us some substantial evidence that supports your proposals?" Admittedly we have not met Bolkestein but we have met the civil servants and they have said "we do not have to give you substantial details of why we are doing this, we are the Commission, you should be doing this".

Chairman: I think we can give an observation to the Commission of what they should be doing and I think our feeling would be probably they should be seeing you.

Lord Paul

165. I have a lot of sympathy for the job losses but what I cannot really tie up is that liberalisation alone will create those job losses. Some of the job losses will have to come because the Post Office will have to modernise and any modernisation means job losses. New jobs are being created. They are not going to be the same quality jobs, we have seen that in every industry. The quality of jobs that are coming that are new are completely different from the jobs that there were ten years ago or today. Is it not something that you will have to deal with head-on and irrespective of whether it is slow or fast it will have to be dealt with at some stage or the other?
(*Mr Hodgson*) I do not necessarily agree with the observation that job losses must inevitably come, certainly not looking at it from the view of the British Post Office. This is precisely why we sought commercial freedom, to be able to expand the industry and minimise job losses. One thing I am clear on is there are going to be about five or six major postal administrations in the world in about five or six years' time and I certainly want the British Post Office to be one of them, as I am sure you would want the British Post Office to be one of them. The projections as far as electronic mail and e-commerce are concerned vary greatly. I sat at a conference recently, to which I contributed, where I heard a representative of *Reader's Digest* telling us that whilst it was anticipated that a lot of things would to go e-mail, e-commerce and all the rest of it, *Reader's Digest*, which is one of the largest mail users, took a view to the contrary. They said they could see actual physical mail building up and probably increasing by about ten per cent over the next five years. There will be a change from two dimensional to three dimensional mail, I think that is expected. This is why it is important that we look at what we are saying comes within and what is outside the reserved area, added value and all the rest of it. There are things occurring where you order via the Internet, supermarkets and people like that, contracts are being take up. The internet is used, the Post Office

Lord Paul *contd.*]

goes along in Switzerland, for example, picks up the groceries and delivers them. There are fantastic opportunities as a result of electronic conversion and e-commerce. I do not necessarily believe that there will be job losses and there cannot be expansion of the industry if it is handled properly. This is why I talk in terms of a complete distribution company, not just Royal Mail or Parcelforce, a complete distribution company providing a service. If we can come to you and say "look, your Lordship, we can give you a fully comprehensive service that will cover everything you want: letters, parcels, logistics, banking even", if we can do that for you then the likelihood is if we can provide that service to you we will get customer loyalty, particularly if we are producing it at a price that is sensible.

166. I do not think we are disagreeing on that, that is exactly what I was saying, that there will be new job creation and you are saying the Post Office will start creating new jobs. I am not far from what you are saying.

(*Mr Hodgson*) It is a balanced judgment. The basic network is there to provide the universal service. The universal service must sustain the basic network. If you have not got the volume to sustain the universal service and the basic network then you get on a vicious spiral, and that is the problem.

Lord Cavendish of Furness

167. We do a bit of stage management with our questions and my fox has been shot once and shot again. I will see what I can do. I would just like a bit of clarification on the results of liberalisation resulting in not only job losses but part-time and casual work. We might disagree about the value of part-time work but that is for another day. Is this anecdotal, because you complain about the lack of information, or is this documented? I would like to see some information about it.

(*Mr Hodgson*) Sorry?

168. In the liberalised markets I think you talked about jobs being replaced by casual and part-time.

(*Mr Hodgson*) Yes. Documentation can be produced on this.

169. I think I would be quite interested to see some back-up on that.

(*Mr Darlington*) It is particularly true in Germany, which is not fully liberalised yet but has gone further than the United Kingdom so far, where the competition, such as it is, is very focused geographically on the larger urban areas where it is delivering and a lot of the employment there is housewives, pensioners, students, people who are able and willing to work very short hours and are willing to do it for low rates of pay and secure contracts. This is not anecdotal at all, this is hard experience based on looking at what is happening.

(*Mr Hodgson*) The Dutch and the German experiences have certain things to offer to us. We will certainly get a paper produced for you and we can provide that to you.

170. Just pressing a little bit on the compensation for jobs through creation. You presumably have done the best and the worst scenarios and, of course, there is no track record and, as you said, you cannot compare like with like. As a best case scenario would you anticipate reasonable compensation for jobs through competition?

(*Mr Hodgson*) Compensation for jobs through compensation? No. The difficulty that we have got is you have got a number of competitors moving into markets. Competitors acquiring, forming alliances, partnerships and taking over with others have tended to produce economies of scale in overheads and the biggest overhead you have got generally is the labour force. The experience of this with the partnerships, the alliances and the takeovers is to create a better economic base for a wider company and it usually results in job losses. There are a number of consequences that have occurred. In Germany, for example, I sat and listened to a presentation from the German Post Office recently and they told us that they had come down from, I think it was, around 400,000 jobs—this takes into account Eastern Germany as well which tends to cloud the picture—with between 120,000 and 140,000 job losses in Germany which have not been compensated for in alternative sectors of the postal sector.

Chairman

171. Classed as an increase in productivity?

(*Mr Hodgson*) There is the East German factor to take into consideration. It was part of the traditional politics at the time. I am not going to go into detail on that. We do anticipate, and it would be wrong of me to say that with improved technology, improved efficiency, you will not require the same number of jobs to do the same amount of work. My attitude to this for Britain is to ensure that we expand the work content and the productivity element to ensure that you have the same staff handling more work. This is precisely what the Dutch are trying to do. They have got a very small domestic base in Holland for their product and they are trying to expand, but at the same time they are not increasing jobs on a pro rata basis with what they were previously. You cannot stand still. Providing it is controlled and sensible then we can deal with those things. In London, for example, in the last decade we have closed up five major distribution centres in London and we have deployed and dealt with that situation. It is not as if change cannot be managed and we cannot adopt sensible attitudes with the employers to manage that change. Indeed, that is what we are all seeking to secure. We have not been as successful as we would like to be because of political impositions over recent times.

Lord Cavendish of Furness

172. We have heard that incumbent postal operators where the markets have been liberalised have managed to keep most of the mail traffic. First of all, do you accept that? Is there any reason why it should not be the same here providing the Post Office is efficient and gives us a good service?

(*Mr Hodgson*) Again, I do not think we are comparing like with like. Roger, you have got some details on this. Roger will give you the detail.

Lord Cavendish of Furness *contd.*]

Certainly we are not comparing like with like, we are not comparing the same type of traffic, we are not comparing the same volumes and we are not comparing the same population percentage. There is nowhere at the moment that it has happened that can give you a fair comparison because we are dealing in terms of small things rather than large things. We can give you a base line for the traffic with Germany, for example. Roger will give you the details.

173. Even without the comparison, if you cannot make a fair comparison, is there any reason why the Post Office cannot keep its traffic?

(*Mr Hodgson*) The area that we are talking about coming down to 50 grams, you are dealing in terms of 30 per cent of the volume and 40 per cent of the revenue. That is the sort of area that you are dealing in and that is the sort of area you are putting at risk. The problem that we have got with the Directive is if you go too far, and this is why I come back to the gradual and controlled. You know what our position is, we have submitted it to you, we say it should come to 150 grams at the moment and that opens up a further sector of the market and then we should look at it and if that is operational it can come down later. The problem is if you go too far and you get it wrong and the universal service is put at risk you cannot reverse the process. This is one of the things that we have said to the Commission time and time again: "If you have got it wrong, where is the escape hatch?" Again, they have been unable to tell us. I would be delighted if somebody could tell me if we go too far and open up the market, we cannot then recover the market and say "we will now restore the reserved area" because it is too late, you cannot reverse the process. Roger, you were going to give us some figures.

(*Mr Darlington*) The precise answer to your question is that in those very, very few markets that have been liberalised, so far the competitors have taken less than ten per cent. The reason for that is largely because the markets are so small that there are very few competitors.

174. How many exactly?

(*Mr Darlington*) The countries we are talking about are Sweden with nine million, Finland with five million, New Zealand with four million, the United Kingdom has got 59 million and, therefore, the competition that we would face would be far more formidable. Also the fact that this has been taking place in the last decade when mail volumes have been increasing to some extent compensates the incumbents whereas Lord Faulkner has suggested, I think with some validity, that we cannot be sure of mail volumes increasing over the next decade because of the effects of electronic substitution. You asked is there any reason why the Post Office could not compete. I think we have to keep coming back to the two unique and distinct features of the postal market as regards the incumbent. One, the universal service obligation and, two, the uniform tariffs. If you look at liberalisation of other utility industries, whether it is gas, water, electricity or telecommunications, there is no uniform tariff. If you look at what has happened in telecommunications, the only way the incumbent has survived has been by re-balancing its tariffs. There is no such thing as uniform tariffs. If the Post Office is required to face formidable competition whilst maintaining both the universal service obligation and the uniform tariff, it stands to lose significant revenue and profitability because it cannot lower its tariffs on the markets on which its margins are greatest to face its competition on those markets. The British Post Office and the French Post Office have had independent studies done by Toulouse University which have suggested that the uniform tariff would be under tremendous challenge if we had too much competition. All the evidence is that the Commission almost accepts that is the case. They are very supportive of the universal service obligation but they are very equivocal in their views on the uniform tariff. They seem to suggest that it is not the end of the world if people pay more to deliver the letters on certain routes or to certain destinations and/or have reductions in quality on certain routes or to certain destinations. We do not believe that is the position of the British Government or of the British public.

175. You have argued quite a big technical case, I want to get into your heart with this next question. Do you actually feel liberalisation and the timescale envisaged is at odds with preserving jobs and providing a universal service?

(*Mr Hodgson*) The timescale that is being proposed is, to our mind, totally unrealistic. Everything that has happened with the liberalisation of the postal service has been subject to slippage. The 1997 Directive said that there should be further proposals forthcoming from the Commission by 1998 that were to be voted on by 1999, but that did not occur. As you well know, we had the problem within the Commission and all the rest of it. So there was slippage on that. We then had a very much cobbled together and rushed set of proposals, which is those that we have got at the moment, and there were amendments and alterations being made to it literally as the damn thing was being drafted. At one stage we had three different drafts in front of us because they were redrafting that quickly. The foundation for the proposals was supposedly the studies that were done. The studies were done against the background that the Member States had not introduced the 1997 provisions to 350 grams and five times the price. So the studies were based on things occurring in Member States that they had not introduced in the 1997 phase. This was part of the reason why the studies were flawed. The Commission are diving into another proposal. The Commissioner responsible for it is on record as saying that he is going to move on the postal services where Bangemann and his predecessor could not. We believe he is motivated purely and simply by liberalisation of the market rather than a rational approach to it. Granted that the 1997 Directive said that further liberalisation should occur by January 2003, but that was to be based on proper consultation and proper consideration and that has not occurred. The proper consultation and the proper consideration has not occurred. Therefore, at this stage to say that we can go as far as he wants to go. . . . Incidentally, I have told you that the draft before the final one wanted to take all direct mail outside the reserved area and wanted to have

Lord Cavendish of Furness contd.]

complete liberalisation by 2007. If you look at those proposals closely, they are designed to make certain that in 2007 there is complete liberalisation of mail. There is no further phase that you can go to once you have gone to 50 grams. You cannot come down because that is a *fait accompli* that says the next stage has got to be complete liberalisation. Clearly the Post Office has worked on its figures and said that Post Office profitability will go up. Roger has explained to you the options that are going to be in front of the Post Office. Either it is going to lose money or it is going to increase profit. It is going to have to introduce a differential pricing policy. Clearly I would estimate that the rural area would have to pay at least five or six times more than would be paid in the urban area for the standard letter charge when they are in the reserved area. Clearly we are not ready.

Chairman

176. Would it go down in the inner cities?
(*Mr Hodgson*) Incidentally, we are in a better position than other Member States because do not forget there are at least nine or ten of the Member States in Europe who are violently against the proposal as being too quick, too soon. If we look at the people who are in favour of it, they are the people who are already geared up for the liberalisation in terms of the commercial freedom that they need. Indeed, one of the things which frightens me, and we have made representations to the Commission, is the way the German Post Office have allowed the funding of Deutches Post-AG in what they have been able to do on the basis of unfairness in the way that they are dealt with. If we go where we are being proposed at the moment in the submission it will jeopardise universal service and it will place jobs at risk as well. Jobs are not the major consideration, we can deal with jobs through the normal consultative processes and the normal negotiating processes with the employer. The problem is the universal service and if we go too quick, too soon then you cannot retrace those steps and that is the big problem.

Lord Woolmer of Leeds

177. Can I pick this up at that point. You have been eloquent in your explanation of why you do not want a 50 gram limit, at least at this point, not yet. Could you summarise for us what your proposals would be, not just reacting against what has been proposed but what would you propose as a way forward for postal services, not just in the United Kingdom but in Europe?
(*Mr Hodgson*) We have been leading a consultation process with the trade unions within Europe and we do have liaison with employers' organisations and we do operate on the basis of the social dialogue. This is why we have been able to speak to Commissioners and speak to employers. There appears to be something of a consensus amongst the trade unions, not exactly shared by the French. The French we have a problem with because they were part and parcel of the discussions, as I say, gradual and controlled liberalisation, and the French are now saying "no further liberalisation". That is grossly irresponsible in our view. The majority of the trade union organisations within the Member States can wrap around a bottom line policy of 150 grams and two or three times the price from 2003 and then further examination and further study to see where we should go from there. We are not saying the process should stop there, what we are saying is it should be taken piece by piece. We can liberalise without jeopardising the universal service provision, which was the original objective in 1997. As far as the employers' organisations are concerned, we do liaise with the employers' organisations. The majority of the employers' organisations we know share a similar view, that is at least nine of the Member States would be prepared to go along with the 150 grams from 2003 and then further examination. The rapporteur on behalf of the Transport Committee wants to speak to me about if there are possible compromises in the approach that can be sought on behalf of the European Parliament and the employers and trade unions, that is informal machinery. There are not any indications that the Commission are prepared to possibly seek another way of doing it. I know that Bolkenstein was extremely disappointed at the last Telecom Council meeting to not get the majority that he wanted but there are indications that a compromise can be found. It would appear that the compromise that the people are looking at is not dissimilar from that which we presented to you in saying it should be 150 grams and then further examination to see where we go from there.

178. You quoted the same figures as the Post Office about the proportion of revenue and the proportion of volume that would be left if you had a 50 gram limit.
(*Mr Hodgson*) Yes.

179. Which I recall was 60 per cent of revenue and 70 per cent of volume would be covered by the 50 gram situation.
(*Mr Hodgson*) Yes.

180. If the limit was 150 grams what proportion of current volume and what proportion of revenue do you estimate would remain with the Post Office?
(*Mr Hodgson*) It is not just on volume and revenue, it is where the profit margins are as well.

181. You quoted forcibly.
(*Mr Hodgson*) Yes, I did.

182. I just want to know what the answer is.
(*Mr Hodgson*) Yes, I did. You posed exactly the same questions to the Post Office and I think the responses that you probably were given was not dissimilar from the ones I am going to give you. Put *stet* under that. You did not think I would be sitting in front of you without finding out what the Post Office had to say to you, did you? In some strange way this demonstrates the integrity with which John Roberts and I approach this subject and the seriousness with which we approach the future of the Post Office, because we are very much at the crossroads. I think if I say to you that John Roberts and I enjoy understandings where we can agree to disagree you will find that on the future of the Post Office, as far as the Post Office Act is concerned—and they are non-political in terms of where ownership

Lord Woolmer of Leeds *contd.*]

lies in terms of regulator and all the rest of it, and in terms of where we believe we should be going in Europe—there is little difference between us. So you are not likely to elicit an answer that is varying from the one given by John Roberts.

183. What is the answer?
(*Mr Hodgson*) I am just looking.
(*Mr Darlington*) Can I say to the Committee I do not think there is any real argument between us, between the Post Office, between the Commission—

184. I want to know your answer.
(*Mr Darlington*) —as to what proportion of revenue would be open to competition at different thresholds of price and weight. The argument is twofold. First of all, what proportion of that revenue would not just be open to competition but would actually be taken by the competitors? Some people are saying "very little" because look what has happened in Finland or Sweden where there are very few competitors. Our argument is "No, that is not a good example, the proportion of the revenue that would be open would be much greater". The second area for debate is what would that impact be in terms of profits and there you get into different models because, traditionally, post offices have not had to worry about the profitability of different routes because of a national responsibility, a uniform service obligation and a uniform tariff. Now the Commission is using a particular model, which I think you have had described to you, based on avoided costs.

185. That is right.
(*Mr Darlington*) The French and the Germans are using a very different model, a more dynamic model, which takes account of the entry competitor's price model and that is where the difference comes in.

186. I will come to USO in a minute and all that but the argument, as I understand it, is partly about what the appropriate reserve limit is at the moment for the next stage and partly one of pace. They are the two issues. There is a subsidiary argument, what is the true cost of the USO, and I will come to that in a moment. If it is what is the appropriate limit—I will not yet come to pace—then as I consider it, the argument is 50 grams is too low because the revenue and volume we have got left to play with as a core market is not sufficient to support the USO at the uniform rate. That is the core argument.
(*Mr Darlington*) Yes.

187. The 150 grams is sufficient, that is apparently your position and the Post Office's position. I am simply seeking to ask, given you are so clear on the facts of 50 grams, what are the facts of 150? What is the proportion of revenue and the proportion of volume that is apparently, according to you as a union, sufficient?
(*Mr Darlington*) Yes.

188. You are no more able than the Post Office to give us a figure. Given that the 150 grams is so critical—you are both united on it—and you say ten other unions and operators are across Europe, yet neither you nor the post Office can tell us what the figures are.

(*Mr Darlington*) We can give you the figures but you have to appreciate we do not run the Post Office.

189. I understand that.
(*Mr Darlington*) Obviously we are dependent to a very considerable extent on the allocation of costs and revenue within the Post Office. What I think we would say is none of us know the point at which the threat to the universal service obligation, the uniform tariff, becomes critical because we have never been down this road. What we are saying, as a union, is proceed gradually in steps because this is an irreversible process. Once the genie is out of the bottle you cannot put him back in. Going too rapidly is too risky a process.
(*Mr Hodgson*) We will provide some figures to you. What I would say to you—in order that you can understand the difficulty we have and why I point it up—is the majority of the universal service providers believe that they can go to 150 grams. Now there is a lot of estimation in this as you can well imagine but, you see, the European Commission upon a broad brush basis are saying if they go down to 50 grams that opens up another 20 per cent of the market. Now that is an average across the European Community, that is a broad brush figure. Now if you look at the variants that there are in the style of traffic, the cost of the universal service provision, for example if you take a country like Greece and if you take a country like Spain with the mountainous regions and places like that as opposed to Holland, a flat country densely populated in the urban areas, then you can understand the variants that they have and the difficulties. What I can tell you is that there is a general consensus that can be found around 150 grams. The problem that I have said to you before is if you liberalise and open up the markets and then find you cannot sustain the universal service provision it is too late to try and redress it. Once the markets open up, it has gone. It is like you cannot be a little bit pregnant; if the market is opened up, that is it. This is why we are saying that it should be in line with what was adopted by the Council of Ministers, the Commission and the Parliament, gradual and controlled that does not affect universal provision.

190. One last question about the special services issue. The Commission told us there are three clear criteria for special services. You will know those as well as I.
(*Mr Hodgson*) Yes.

191. For the record, that they are clearly distinct from universal service obligations services, they have to meet specific (not all) customer needs and they have to have two or more value added features.
(*Mr Hodgson*) Yes.

192. Just a simple question on that. Is that a sufficiently tight definition to remove any concerns that special services could be used to circumvent the reserved area? If it is not sufficiently tight, could you explain what bothers you?
(*Mr Hodgson*) First of all, let me tell you, it is clearly not acceptable. I can tell you this was one of the last minute insertions into the document done on the hoof. This was not originally part of the documentation used by the Commission. It was there

Lord Woolmer of Leeds *contd.*]

to try and plug a gap when we started kicking up about it.

(*Mr Darlington*) I think the three problems we have with the proposed liberalisation of special services are that, first, it is contrary to the Commission's own approach which is that the prime focus should be on the price and weight. It did look at different categories much earlier like international mail, like direct mail and it rightly, in our view, came to the conclusion that the only way to effectively police this area was to have a very precise definition and the most precise definition would be a combination of price and weight. Secondly, in our view, it would be very difficult to define even though the three criteria we have quoted, I think, have an element of subjectivity to them. It would therefore be very difficult to enforce and either there would be lots of legal cases in order to combat attempts to breach the monopoly or the monopoly would be by default, at least to our third objection which is that this is so loose—and as Derek Hodgson, my colleague, emphasised it was a last minute addition to the thinking, it is very ill-thought out—it runs the risk of unravelling the Commission's own timetable, let alone the one we are proposing because it would be uncontrolled. You would be leaving the definition of what is a special service to competitors who would have two or more features which are pretty ill-defined in order, in their view, to justify bringing it outside the reserved area. So we think it is a deeply flawed proposal that runs the risk of introducing too much uncertainty.

193. Do you think they should have a special definition of special services or no special services?

(*Mr Darlington*) No special services.

(*Mr Hodgson*) In our view it would create a legal minefield. We would end up running back and forth to the courts all the time because people would be constantly using it to try and get round the monopoly area.

(*Mr Darlington*) If I can just add this, because it links to your first question. You were worried about the Post Office going into new markets like special services and is this not unfair if you do not allow competitors to come to the monopoly market? Of course we are not comparing the same. When the Post Office moves into new services, it is doing so on a level playing field with no special advantages. Conversely, when people move into the monopoly area they are not competing on the basis that they are going to take on universal service obligations or they are going to charge uniform tariffs, so it is not the same. When the Post Office is competing in these new areas it will have to do so fairly. If it uses anti-competitive practices, as the Germans allegedly have done, it will be taken to the European Court. We are asking for a level playing field across the monopoly reserved area.

194. If you have a protected market, with a very high proportion of volume of the market and revenue, which at the moment we do not know, 150 grams, and all the countries agreeing that any loss on USO can be compensated by cross-subsidisation of this protected market, is that not an enormous advantage as a competitive base for doing anything else in postal services? How can anybody compete with somebody who has 80 or 90 per cent of the market and the state saying "We will give you a guaranteed monopoly"?

(*Mr Hodgson*) We are talking about cross-subsidisation in the universal service provision. There is no ability to cross-subsidise in the competitive area. The Post Office currently is required to keep separate accounts for the universal service provision, which is cross-subsidised by the volume, and the competitive areas. There can not be any question of a playing field that is not level. As Roger has said, the Germans have been accused of anti-competitive behaviour and that can be taken up. You have now got a new regulatory authority in this country which is there to deal with precisely that as part of the Post Office Act.

Lord Paul

195. Mine is a little bit of a sensitive question and my Chairman, when he allocated this question, perhaps did not realise my strong views on it. It was in the evidence from the Post Office last week that they need some time to make Royal Mail a company which is able to compete in a competitive market by improving working practices, increasing quality of service and productivity before more radical competition is introduced. My own experience in running an industry has been that British workers and management are very good at productivity provided they have the same equipment. This is part of the investment which has not gone into the industry, but I do not know what investment has gone into the industry. Do you agree with what the Post Office analysis outlined, taking away the question of whether we want more time or whether we have a problem of job losses, etc, that they are fairly unprotected?

(*Mr Hodgson*) I think the Post Office needs a little more time. I think anybody in the business will recognise that it takes quite a number of years to change the basic style and structure of an industry, particularly one that has been in the public sector for a long time, which has been used, and I think people will freely accept it has been used, as a political football subjected to more inquiries, reviews, etc, etc, than anything else and has been unable to do its work. It has been starved of investment. When you consider that the EFL targets that were arbitrarily placed three years in advance, where we were required to pay £360 million a year, were not on the basis of commercial trading. Ridiculous in terms of the way to operate a business. Then we were constrained by the public sector borrowing requirement. The industry has been starved of the investment that is needed. It has been starved of the ability to expand itself and do what it needs to do. In terms of the morale of people in the industry, there has been quite a suffering in morale. John Roberts and I a couple of years ago thought we had turned it around when we started to, thankfully in my view, diminish the industrial action. I think we were operating on one tenth of the industrial action that we had been operating on hitherto prior to 1996. I am not one of those people who believes industrial action is an end product, I believe industrial action is a last

Lord Paul *contd.*]

resort. If people are prepared to come out and lose money, that means to say there is a fair amount of disenchantment. The Post Office has been successful, although it has not been allowed to invest in its future. Record profits year on year for about 20 years. The customer getting their share in terms of holding and reducing the prices. Government getting its large slice on the basis of the EFL and all the taxation, at one stage being 90 per cent of profits were going into taxation. The people that did not share in the profitability of the Post Office were the staff working there, so times have been difficult from an industrial relations point of view. I said to you at the commencement of the presentation to you that we have now secured a number of agreements in terms of management of staff in terms of the way forward. That ought to reflect itself in improvements but you do not change a large industry, such as we have got, overnight. I am confident that we are now getting there. Certainly our joint unions have produced some voluntary research which talks about where we should be going for the future in terms of investment. It might be interesting if I give you a copy of the latest piece of work that we have had done and launched recently. I will not tell you at which conference it was. I am confident that the Post Office has a tremendous future but it needs the time to do it. I am committed with John Roberts to ensuring that we realise the potential. It has not been able to reach its potential because of the political nature of things and because of the acrimony that has built up, the lack of confidence in the industry as to where its future lies. Currently Government appears to be leaning the way that inspires more confidence in the future where we can see what is happening, a five year rolling programme, the fact that we are able to compete, the fact that we are able to borrow to invest in ourselves. I believe that future is there but you do not turn a juggernaut around in a matter of weeks, it takes a little time. John Roberts I believe is right, we need a little more time.

196. You seem to be getting on very well with John Roberts and the Post Office. Is the timing expectation of John Roberts and yourself the same?
(*Mr Hodgson*) Is our time expectancy the same?

197. Yes?
(*Mr Hodgson*) A lot depends on where we are able to go in terms of the Post Office being the European and world player that I want it to be. The worrying feature for me is we were late out of the starting blocks. The Germans have spent a tremendous amount, they have bought everything that moves at the moment and a lot of it is tactical to stop other people buying. The Dutch have made acquisitions. The French have now got a five year liaison joint relationship with FedEx and the British Post Office needs to move on and acquire something equally. I think that will be the final icing on the cake that will inspire the confidence in the people to say "Yes, we have a future". They also need reassuring that any future that the Post Office has internationally has got to be on a firm domestic base. They will understand, as I understand, that we now appear to have a Government saying there is a future for the Post Office. Incidentally, the expansion of the Post Office Board to include women and the depth of the Post Office Board was part of our proposal as well. They have a regulatory authority which will concentrate the mind of the Post Office and the Board. It will certainly concentrate the mind of some of my members in terms of their attitude to industrial relations, I put it no higher than that. Certainly I believe the time is now right for it to move on. I believe that if we can get where we need to with acquisitions, if we can get to where we need to in the thinking that it does materialise the freedom that they have given us, and if we can get where we just need to with this European Directive then in five years' time we will see a Post Office in Britain and an expanded international post office which is unrecognisable from the one that we have seen in the past.

Chairman

198. What will it look like if the Commission got their way and the Directive went through?
(*Mr Hodgson*) If the Commission do this?

199. Yes.
(*Mr Hodgson*) I think we are going to be in trouble. I think we are going to be in trouble in the short term. I think that the competitive organisations that are out there, who are going to be geared up in many respects to deal with it, will move in. I see those major competitors not only looking at what is happening—and do not forget we have about six of them sat in Britain at the moment, and the reason they are sat in Britain is because we have a large domestic market—but I can also see them looking at the Asian Pacific Rim, they have spent a lot of time looking at what is happening out there. I can see the Germans and the Dutch getting there before us in terms of Europe and that expansion. We need a step into Europe, first of all, before we can get an expansion into the rest of the world. That competition has got to be on a level playing field from the British point of view more than any other Member State in Europe and it is not on a level playing field at the moment.

Lord Cavendish of Furness

200. Very quickly. We asked the Post Office—I hope I am not speaking out of turn—whether they took into account the customer, those of us who receive mail. I think it would not be an exaggeration to say they thought there was a lot of work to be done. We have talked for quite a long time and the customer has not actually come up in this conversation. Do you think there is more work to be done?
(*Mr Hodgson*) Actually, practically everything I do is based on representing the customer's point of view. Without the customers we have no Post Office, without the customers we have no jobs in the Post Office. If you recount and recall campaigns that have been led in terms of the unions which are sitting in front of you, and representing our view to Government in the European Commission, you will find that is all orientated to making certain that we keep in touch with the customer. I meet constantly with the Mail Users' Association and representatives of customers. I think we are completely in touch and

Lord Cavendish of Furness contd.]

what we say is completely in accord with the customer requirements.

Chairman

201. I am sorry but I do not want to go down that route.

(*Mr Hodgson*) I apologise, I did not make that plain from the outset. Everything that we are dealing with, we are nothing without the customer.

Lord Cavendish of Furness: It was not intended as a hostile question.

Chairman

202. I would prefer not to go any further down this route. We had quite a session last week on the customer's attitude and perception of the Post Office and services in rural areas by comparison with the perception people have who are in Central London and the current services they are getting. There is quite a mismatch between the two.

(*Mr Hodgson*) There is one hell of a difference between the rural and the urban customer. If you look at everything we have done in championing the rural cause in terms of the Crown Office, in terms of delivery and maintenance, the reason that the universal service is so important is if the universal service does not survive then the rural customer will be expected to pay a minimum of six times more than the urban customer. Then we have the other customers, we are in an industry where we have the recipient and we have the poster. It is important to us, and I do speak to representatives of the recipients as well as the posters because very often they come at it from a different perspective. As a matter of fact, only yesterday I had to remind the Chairman of the Post Office National Users' Council that there were posting customers and recipient customers and he ought to make sure he was representing the views of both of them.

Chairman: We have had a good session this morning. Thank you very much indeed.

WEDNESDAY 1 NOVEMBER 2000

Present:

Brooke of Alverthorpe, L
  (Chairman)
Brookeborough, V
Cavendish of Furness, L
O'Cathain, B
Paul, L
Skelmersdale, L
Woolmer of Leeds, L

Memorandum by the Mail Users' Association

INTRODUCTION

1.1 Throughout the Government's review of the Post Office MUA has stressed the benefits of fair competition in the postal marketplace. Not only does it offer choice to the customer and therefore provide downward pressure on prices, but it also acts as a catalyst for increased quality of service levels.

1.2 MUA continues to fully support the opening up of the UK's postal market to increased competition, believing the reserved sector of the market—Royal Mail's £1 monopoly— to be disproportionate with the sums needed to support the universal service. Indeed, postal studies indicate that the cost of maintaining the universal service obligation may be as low as 6 per cent of Royal Mail's total revenue from letter mail[1].

1.3 MUA also supports, in principle, reducing the reserved sector to a point where the universal service obligation can continue to be met with a single scale of public prices irrespective of distance, but where Royal Mail would then compete in remaining segments of the market. In order for a liberalisation scenario such as this to be successful, however, business mailers believe it is necessary to offer new entrants enough of the market in which to gain a realistic foothold.

1.4 MUA also fully recognises the importance of retaining and indeed developing a national final delivery network, and a comprehensive infrastructure of postal return-delivery options. These systems play a vital role in maintaining the social fabric of the UK, and in safeguarding the interests of the businesses within it.

1.5 MUA members are however concerned that the measures proposed by the Commission fall short of offering realistic business opportunities to companies wishing to compete with the Post Office. We therefore strongly urge further debate on the approach the UK Government takes to introducing "sustainable" competition into the postal marketplace.

THE COMMISSION'S PROPOSALS

2.1 Reducing the Existing Weight/Price Limits

2.1.1 Business mailers consider the Commission's proposal to reduce the existing weight/price limits from 350 grams/five times the basic standard tariff for letters and addressed advertising material to 50 grams/2.5 times, as being insufficient in the context of realistically introducing competition into the UK postal marketplace.

2.1.2 Industry estimates that no more than 5 per cent of the Post Office's existing market share will be de-monopolised in this way—the majority of business mail falling below 50 grams or 2.5 times the standard tariff. It is precisely these business mailstreams that potential competitors would need to buy into, if they are to realistically enter the market and compete with Royal Mail. Beyond these mail streams (which presently provide over 90 per cent of Royal Mail's annual turnover), the business case for setting up a mailing network to compete with Royal Mail holds very slim appeal, given the organisation's dominance in the market.

2.1.3 MUA therefore considers that should the European Union take this approach, it must do so only as an interim measure within a pre-agreed time-table for the introduction of further liberalisation. Were this to be the case, not only would potential competitors have a long term time-scale to work to, but also the national carrier would be aided by knowing exactly how long it had to get its house in order. The postal industry could then look forward to the emergence of sustainable competition, rather than "cream skimming"[2] operations.

---

[1] Figure taken from a 1998 study carried out by NERA on behalf of DG13 entitled "The Costing and Financing of the Universal Service Obligation in the Postal Sector in the European Union".

[2] A recognised practice where a company might set up operations in the more lucrative city centre areas, whilst leaving the national carrier (universal service provider) to deliver the more expensive rural areas.

2.2 *The Full Opening of Outbound Cross-Border Mail*

MUA members welcome the proposal to fully open to competition outward bound cross-border mail, but would note that this is likely to have very little impact on the business mailing community, given the laws governing ABA re-mailing.[3]

2.3 *The Full Opening to Competition of All Express Mail Services*

MUA believes it is necessary to seek clarification on what Express Mail Services are to be defined as. A hangover from the days when 1st class mail was sent by express train, does this definition now mean any item of mail sent by the fastest means available in any one carrier's product/service offering (ie to include Royal Mail's Same Day, Guaranteed Next Day and Time Delivery services).

IN ANSWER TO YOUR QUESTIONS

3.1 *What benefits are likely to result from the proposed liberalisation measures?*

Business Mailers

3.1.1 Business mailers see the benefits that are likely to result from the proposals as being few and far between. Whilst it is recognised that a relaxation of the monopoly is likely to see a small influx of competitors seeking niche markets in the business arena, there is concern over how sustainable this activity will be, and whether it will allow companies a robust enough platform from which to develop real competition.

3.1.2 With the proposed relaxation of monopoly thresholds, it is envisaged a few small-sized enterprises may attempt to develop bespoke final delivery services for business mail outside the new monopoly. Business customers with mail items meeting the proposal's criteria are likely to be offered mailing services in the more lucrative city centre areas, where the lower cost per item allows for greater profitability. This will be passed on to the customer in terms of lower prices. However, these services will need to be backed with high delivery performance, if they are to survive. Other than this, the majority of potential market entrants are more likely to retain a watching brief in anticipation of further liberalisation.

3.1.3 Experience gained by MUA members in the publishing sector, when attempting to develop alternative forms of magazine distribution,[4] bears out the difficulties smaller postal operators have had in breaking into the market and establishing comprehensive delivery operations, next to a dominant player with over 300 years experience.

Social Users

3.1.4 MUA considers social users will see little or no major change in the short to medium term from these proposals. Competitors to the national carrier will first need to win business confidence, and then establish networks and performance levels that will satisfy discerning customers. Additional new uniformed persons may turn up on the social user's doorstep, but having now been conditioned to this interaction with the introduction of parcel carriers, it is envisaged the proposed liberalisation will have a negligible impact on social users.

The Postal Office

3.1.5 The Post Office may at the same time stand to benefit from these proposals. With recent suggestions from Royal Mail indicating that they are considering surcharging non-machinable items over 60 grams (due to the fact that this traffic does not provide "a full contribution"), removal of this mailstream from the reserved sector may indeed be indirectly beneficial.

3.1.6 MUA members would also question the Format Pricing Strategy[5] Royal Mail is endeavouring to take forward—a strategy that is questionable, given that as the proposals suggest, Europe is looking to liberalise the market through reductions to the weight/tariff structure.

Conclusion

3.1.6 MUA considers that the proposed liberalisation measures are only firm steps in the right direction, if they are inextricably linked to a published timetable for further liberalisation. This will allow competitors clear vision with which to develop and expand sustainable operations, as liberalisation scenario unfolds.

---

[3] The practice where by a company bulk mails items to a second country for re-mailing back to the UK.
[4] Magazines already fall outside the monopoly. Further details can be made available.
[5] Royal Mail are presently considering developing a pricing structure that is based on a mail items format/size, rather than its weight.

3.2 *What problems could result from the proposed liberalisation, particularly in terms of maintenance of the universal service with an affordable and uniform tariff structure?*

3.2.1 It is extremely unlikely that any potential competitor would see feasibility in developing a national network based on the present proposals. It is far more likely that various small and medium sized competitors will "cherry pick" the more lucrative city centre locations for delivery of business mail, and the existing universal service to all postal addresses in the country, will continue to be provided by the national carrier.

3.2.2 Business customers consider that customer expectations in terms of high delivery performance from start up, allied with the cost of developing extensive final delivery infrastructures (and the monitoring procedures needed to support them), are restricting factors in the development of an alternative nation-wide postal system.

3.2.3 MUA considers the universal service will be maintained satisfactorily, but is concerned about the Post Office's future investment in infrastructure, given the heavy burdens they are being allowed to take on in terms of their international acquisitions, alliances and joint ventures.

3.2.4 Business and social customers may see increased prices in the competitive arena, ie over 50 grams, as the Post Office addresses its obligations to justify delivery on a cost per item basis. Shortfalls in automation technology investment over the past few years now leave large tranches of Royal Mail's mailbag unmachinable, and indications are that any surcharge for manually sorted mail is likely to be levied on the customer.

Conclusion

3.2.5 MUA concludes that whilst maintenance of the universal service is likely to continue in much the same fashion, sending items that fall outside postal monopoly will be likely to cost the customer more. Restrictions governing actions of a dominant player in a market will also put a break on the Post Office undercutting competition in the non-monopoly area.

3.3 *Are there any measures not identified in the Commission's proposal which would help to secure the Community's stated aims for postal services?*

3.3.1 A key issue for business mailers is that liberalisation in the market place needs to be sustainable. In the view of MUA, these proposals do not go far enough to support long-term competition in this country. Members would therefore urge more debate surrounding the way the Government chooses to implement and hone these European proposals, to meet the specific needs of UK businesses and social users.

3.3.2 Experience from the telecommunications market bears out the fact that highly successful liberalisation can be brought about by offering competitors sound business opportunities, and allowing them access to enough marketshare in order to create viable business concerns. In the case of the telecommunications market, British Telecom has consequently been forced to rise to the commercial challenges, and has developed into a global player after liberalisation took place.

3.3.3 Given the similarities between the two markets, in the same way that the telecommunications market developed by first allowing companies access to the single national telephone network to sell their own services, it is equally as feasible to offer potential postal operators access to the national carriers' distribution network "downstream"[6], and enable them to provide competitive services for all mail streams into a specific region.

3.3.4 By licencing competitors to deliver all business mailstreams into a controlled area (and monitoring their performance against the national carrier's own operations), it will be possible to analyse the effects of competition on the universal service (both financially and socially), whilst at the same time offering a competitor a viable platform from which to grow.

3.3.5 Providing that the effect of this competition does not compromise the universal service, and the licenced carrier is proficient and in a position to develop their systems further, the Postal Regulator would then be disposed to expand the controlled test bed(s) further afield.

3.3.6 The Postal Regulator has a key role to play in developing this market. In order to ensure fair play in the final delivery of both competitor and national carrier mail, the Regulator will be required to put in place tight controls for the monitoring of performance levels, and penalise the national carrier should any competitor's quality of service in a controlled area fall below that of their own services.

3.3.7 Primarily the initial impact of such a test would be on the business community, in terms of increased competitive product offerings in certain areas. However, as more of the market becomes liberalised and competitors begin to benefit from economies of scale and local delivery knowledge, the effects of liberalisation would be expected to trickle down to social users in the same way as it has done in the Telecoms market.

---

[6] "Downstream Access" is an industry term for potentially being able to inject pre-sorted business mail into the system by trunking it to the national carrier's final delivery points.

Conclusion

3.3.8 MUA believes that were the UK Government to implement a liberalisation strategy on a region by region basis, long-term maintenance of a universal service to every door in the country would continue to be assured, whilst at the same time allowing competition to firmly establish itself in the market.

3.3.9 As was the case for British Telecom in the telecommunications market, the Post Office would then be expected to rise to the commercial challenges offered by sustainable competition, in the same way as any other commercial enterprise would be expected to do.

(This Paper was prepared by a delegation of Mail Users' Association members on behalf of MUA membership. It is therefore submitted on a corporate basis).

15 September 2000

APPENDIX A

AN OVERVIEW OF MAIL USERS' ASSOCIATION

The Mail Users Association was formed in the 1970s when a number of major business mailers joined forces to fight for the restoration of postal services at a time of escalating prices and deteriorating quality of service.

The MUA is Briain's only independent association of business users concerned wholly with postal affairs. Our members are drawn from a wide range of business interests including Direct Mail, Banking and Finance, Communications, Publishing and postal related industries.

MUA'S OBJECTIVES

The MUA's primary objective is to secure a healthy and cost effective set of postal services for all domestic and business users. This not only applies to physical mail, but also includes electronic and hybrid mail areas.

We believe that this will be achieved in a mixed market, offering users a real choice between the obligatory monopoly services of Royal Mail that exist at present, and a set of competing value added options—particularly for business mailers.

In order to achieve this goal, the MUA believe it necessary to ensure that service providers are:

— customer focused in their approach to the products and services they offer;

— able to offer cost effective services at realistic prices the market can bear;

— have flexibility in their approach to customers whose needs are continually changing;

— and are able to provide reliable, high quality services on a continuing basis.

Examination of Witnesses

MR JOHN IVERS, Pitney Bowes, MR LES PUGH, Claritas, MR DAVID OLIVER, Britannia Music, MR PAUL KENNELLY, Readers Digest, and MR GEOFF PRIEST, Hays Commercial, Mail Users' Association, called in and examined.

Chairman

203. Gentlemen, welcome. Thank you for submitting written evidence to us in advance. We are hard pressed for time and, therefore, I should like to go straight into questions. Can you explain to the Sub-Committee a bit more about your organisation and whom it represents. Perhaps you will then explain your current concerns about the Commission's proposals and what you would like to see instead.

(*Mr Ivers*) The MUA was formed in about 1970 at a time when there was business mail concern about price rises and issues to do with quality of service. Today, we have reshaped the organisation so that it represents a broad spectrum of business interests, from utilities to financial institutions. I represent small to medium size enterprise. Pitney Bowes supplies equipment from very large through to very small companies. The MUA is unique in the UK in that we are a broad church of business interests. The primary focus of our attention is that our business thrives or fails on the mail service. Today, you have before you a cross-spectrum of people. I do not know whether you would like each to introduce himself and his particular company.

204. Yes, briefly.

(*Mr Ivers*) I am chairman of the Mail Users' Association which has a board. I represent Pitney Bowes which is a multi-national office equipment company. That company is a large mail user in its own right. It also provides equipment to about 200,000 UK customers. That equipment can range from small internet-type products to high volume business. I have been very much involved in the standardisation of postal services in Europe and the UK.

(*Mr Priest*) I am Geoff Priest of Hays Commercial. Hays Commercial provides a service to utilities for distribution, billing and so on. I have been very closely involved with the regulatory directive on mail in both Brussels and the UK, so I am very close to what is happening at the moment.

Chairman *contd.*]

(*Mr Pugh*) I am Les Pugh of Claritas UK Ltd, which is more commonly known as National Shoppers Surveys. We are quite big users of the mail postal service. Not only do we send out surveys but we get them back, including warranty cards. We are quite heavily involved with the Post Office. Every year we mail out about 13 million items and receive about 7.5 million.

(*Mr Oliver*) I am David Oliver from Britannia Music. We are a home shopping company which delivers mail order products—music and videos—to the homes of about 7 million individual consumers. We are the largest such organisation in Europe. We deliver about 45 million mailings a year and 16 million parcels a year. Our customers also respond through the mail.

(*Mr Kennelly*) I am Paul Kennelly and I represent Readers Digest. We are very large users of the mail in the UK. We mail over 100 million letters in the UK per annum and 10 million parcels in this country per annum. We have always been in the forefront of the move to try to modernise and push the boundaries of regulation within the Post Office, which is key to our whole market. We do more than 90 per cent of our business through direct mail, and to have a predictable, reliable and cost-efficient service is of paramount importance to us.

205. Do you constitute the majority of the members of the Mail Users' Association?

(*Mr Ivers*) We represent probably half the board. People ask me what sample of the total mail we represent. I suggest that it is about 30 per cent of all mail volumes in the UK. Our membership also includes Halifax, Abbey National, British Telecom and so on. We have a broad membership. I do not suggest that the association represents just large volumes of mail. We are also hitting many households with mail, so there is a very keen interest in maintaining a national infrastructure of household deliveries. That is another key aspect of our focus. Primarily, our interest lies in a world-class postal service in the UK, because that is the lifeblood of our businesses. We believe that competition should focus on more choice to customers overall. Our starting principle is that in general competition is healthy and will bring new services, products and improved quality of service. We believe that the proposed changes at the 50 gram or 150 gram level, whatever is the level, simply tinker with the service rather than look at the overall question of how to bring competition into the marketplace. The belief seems to be that one turns the tap and the water runs immediately. If there is no infrastructure to deliver that water, how far one turns the tap is not relevant. It is more a question of ensuring that the infrastructure is in place to bring true competition. We are a little concerned about the debate as to whether it should be 50 or 150 grams. If one takes the 50 gram level, we do not believe that it brings adequate competition into the marketplace. We tend to support the conclusions of the NERA report that about 5 per cent of competition will come into the market as a result of that change. We do not see huge changes coming about as a result. We should like to have a more concerted plan to look after customer and business interests and bring in more competition, better services and wider choice. It is irrelevant to debate weight limits and price. Without the right infrastructure, who in his right mind will provide a postal service?

Baroness O'Cathain

206. We have heard from the Post Office authorities and the unions that they are not opposed to liberalisation, but they would say that, would they not? Nevertheless, they understand that liberalisation is coming, whether or not they like it, and they must live with it. However, they look for a softly, softly and gradual approach to ensure that the universal service is available at an affordable and uniform tariff. Do you believe that that is sensible or are they trying to preserve the status quo?

(*Mr Ivers*) The world is undoubtedly changing in terms of the communications media. If one looks at what is going on with Deutsche Post and others, the international market is deregulating. If one looks at the British Telecom model, change must occur. There is a tendency to move at a pace with which the Post Office is happy; the UK is proceeding slowly in order to compete internationally. We believe that for the good of the Post Office it must be in the competitive arena. When one brings competition into the marketplace the whole dynamics of the business focus changes. One looks after customers however small or large they may be, and one ensures that there are new products and service to meet the new market needs. The current structure provides no such incentive. We are concerned that the pace of change in the UK is too slow. We also want the UK to be the centre of the world for postal services. When we look at the Dutch and German models we see that the situation is changing; they are becoming more business focused and are recruiting more customers, whereas the Post Office in the UK is moving a good deal slower. We do not believe that overnight tinkering with the weight limits will dramatically change the business of the Post Office; nor do we believe that its concern is warranted. The question is: what is it that brings new choice and competition? Weight limits will not do that.

Chairman

207. Where do you stand on the universal service?

(*Mr Ivers*) We believe that fundamentally there should be a universal service and a national network. All of us depend on every household having a mail delivery. We have met the regulator, the DTI and POUNC many times and have been pleased about their focus on the maintenance of that network. We believe that the regulator will be able to police the system to ensure that the national infrastructure ensures delivery to every household. We do not see it as an either/or question: it does not mean that the introduction of competition means the loss of the whole network. The regulator must look at what it costs to maintain that network, which we believe is probably substantially less than people say. We also believe that not many suppliers will come in to offer a limited service. Very few of our members would ever sign up to an ad hoc service which did not offer

Chairman *contd.*]

a national delivery network. Perhaps some niche products may emerge, for example delivery in so many days, but not focused on geographic limits. We do not believe that there is a huge opportunity in that area.

Lord Skelmersdale

208. I remember that during the course of the Postal Services Bill last year you successfully promoted an amendment and persuaded Lord Howie of Troon to float it in the House. Could you briefly explain the competition aspects of that amendment?
(*Mr Ivers*) That was not an amendment proposed by the MUA but the PPA, The Periodical Publishers Association, which we supported. The amendment related to magazine and periodical distribution.

209. Is it one of your members?
(*Mr Ivers*) Yes. We supported the amendment.
(*Mr Kennelly*) I suspect that you are talking about the amendment promoted by the Periodical Publishers Association. The amendment was to do with getting services within the Post Office benchmarked against relevant or equivalent services outside. For example, it was concerned with benchmarking their IT systems and transport against best in class in other companies in the UK or other postal authorities throughout Europe. I am afraid that that is as much as I know about it.

210. The threat which accompanied it was that there would be bulk post from here to, say, Germany or Holland and it would be split up and sent back, presumably at lower cost.
(*Mr Kennelly*) I am afraid that I am not fully aware of it.

211. Surely, the whole object of competition is to drive down prices. For example, we have seen this in gas and telecommunications, but you say in your submission that "business and social customers may see increased prices" as a result of the introduction of competition. Can you explain that?
(*Mr Ivers*) This is quite a complicated issue. We are saying that in the 50 gram area the regulator will come in and mandate a price minus x regime basically for the less than 50 gram service. We believe that the focus of attention is very much in the lower band 50 gram area. The effect of competition may be to focus energy into where the business is today. Those customers who are on the periphery of the service, ie above 50 gram, can suffer, because that service may arise where there may not be so much competition. We believe that there are not huge opportunities above 50 grams. Most mail today is in the 12 to 25 gram areas—certainly, it is up to 50 grams rather than beyond it. Therefore, if competition is to come about it should be in the zero to 50 gram area, with perhaps less interest in other areas. Bear in mind that that is based on a model that we do not want. We want to see a fundamentally different modal whereby lots of competition in different areas is encouraged. We see price rises in the current description of the service from zero to 50 grams, or even zero to 150 grams. Above those weights, we believe that there will be less attention to the area so that the price may go up.

Lord Woolmer of Leeds

212. You said in your submission that if potential competitors had a long timescale to work to it would lead to the emergence of sustainable competition in which cream-skimming would happen. In business terms one would be silly if one did not do that. There is a good deal of cross-subsidisation in the postal service, is there not?
(*Mr Ivers*) I answer these questions with two models in my mind. One is the model that we want to see and the other is that which is described here.

213. Describe the two models.
(*Mr Ivers*) If one looks at cream-skimming, that is quite an unpalatable term. If one thinks about postal services today where one sends out many millions of letters, it is difficult to believe that customers will use a limited network, for example services only from London to Birmingham or London to Manchester. I think it is more likely that there will be niche products and therefore growth areas. That will not take business away from the Post Office but it will develop products to meet service needs that are not met today. One may have a post-eight o'clock delivery or home shopping service. Bespoke services may be created. It would be unpalatable for someone to say that he could offer only a London to Birmingham service, and someone else could offer only a London to Manchester or London to Liverpool service. Even if one went down to very small volumes, to split up the mail into different networks would result in a very unwieldy service. There are entry rules into this game which are not about weight limits but are to do with infrastructure. I do not know whether any members of the Sub-Committee have visited a sorting office and seen the level of investment in technology. That is the entry level one needs to play in the game. We focus more on having an available infrastructure whereby suppliers compete in terms of the products and services that they offer to end users and senders and receivers with a network in the middle that is provided to all. We would hate to find that 15 different suppliers had to build sorting offices in London to deliver mail. We believe that infrastructure cost, not weight, is the determinant of competition. Given the choice, I think that most competitors would want to provide a national service, but the infrastructure costs would prohibit them from doing that. For that reason we need to focus our efforts on how to give the infrastructure network more competition.

214. You propose a Railtrack-type solution?
(*Mr Ivers*) I see the telecommunications model as the one to turn to. We see the communications media as the model to which we should work. Capacity is provided in the network for many users to access, perhaps initially through subsidised competition to get people in so that it is a sustainable model. One then allows them all to compete equally in the marketplace. But to expect someone today to come in and to provide the infrastructure would be a waste of resources. We do not want to have duplication of a huge infrastructure. A good deal of capacity is being

Lord Woolmer of Leeds contd.]

built into the automation plans of the Post Office. Why not utilise that capacity? I would hate to use Railtrack as a model. I am sure that there is a good deal more involved in the Railtrack model than we are considering here.

Chairman

215. The Post Office argues that its problem is under-capitalisation of the infrastructure. It has had to pay over too much to the Treasury which would otherwise have been reinvested in the infrastructure. Who meets the deficit?
(*Mr Ivers*) We support the Post Office in that regard. We believe that there is greater focus on international acquisitions than the building of the infrastructure and automation plans in the UK.

216. Under your model where should the investment come from?
(*Mr Priest*) The opportunity for funding will arise under the licence regime. Anybody who comes into the market, or gets involved in the universal service, or reaches a large part of it, will have to be licensed. There will be an opportunity to charge for the licence, which will then go back into the universal service provider to support the service.

217. Who pays for the licence at the end of the day—the consumer?
(*Mr Ivers*) If new entrants knew that they would be adding to capacity rather than building it from zero up it would make it a more sustainable model. If I was a competitor and I knew that I had to add capacity to the existing network so that I could play in it that might be a model which would allow me as my contribution to pay for the licence rather than build a whole system.

Baroness O'Cathain

218. Is capacity the real problem, or is it a question of customers not getting a proper service?
(*Mr Ivers*) We believe that there is an issue about quality of service in terms of service performance. Some of that is driven by the failure of the workforce and management to work together. There has been a lack of investment in some of the automation plans of the Post Office. We have worked very closely with the Post Office and have designed systems collaboratively with it. Those projects have recently been put on the back burner.

219. You are not talking about lack of capacity but bringing existing capacity up to standards that are applicable elsewhere?
(*Mr Ivers*) Essentially, that is true.
(*Mr Oliver*) There may be an opportunity in terms of the physical capacity. But all of that is being crammed into a short time window. That may mean a double win here, in terms of utilising the capacity outside normal hours and offering an improved or another service, for example evening deliveries.

220. Perhaps we need a definition of "capacity".
(*Mr Oliver*) If one says that there is a capacity here it does not mean building more sorting offices or physical resources but utilising the existing resources over a larger window. That is all about efficiency. There are people involved in home shopping and e-retailers who look for deliveries in the evening. That service is not currently available.
(*Mr Ivers*) It is much more related to getting more out of what we have—productivity—than building more capacity into the system. Direct mail is the growth area today, but volumes in the consumer area are declining.

Lord Cavendish of Furness

221. You ask whether we have visited a sorting office. To my shame I have not. If I were to go what would I find? How far under-invested is it? The Post Office claims that it has been starved of investment over 10 or 12 years and its management second-guessed by the Treasury, which is familiar territory. How far under-invested is the Post Office?
(*Mr Ivers*) That is a difficult matter to analyse. I believe that there has been a haphazard series of investments. For example, if one goes into the Post Office one sees lots of new technology, but one also sees different working practices being negotiated between management and unions. We also work closely with the unions. We discuss with them how they can build working practices to work together with management. One is not dealing with a totally unautomated process. Some investment has been made, but it should have been made on a five or 10-year basis. The first steps have been taken but next time further development is required it is not done. One has various stages of investment which do not result in a fully automated process. One has different working practices. As between regions the situation is very sporadic. One goes to certain areas which have wildcat strike action where the model is different from the others. One has models of automation which differ by location; it is not an integrated network. It is also not very much in tune with what users do today. We try to work as close to local areas as we can so that we get our mail through. We find that a lot more can be done in that area.

222. As to investment, slightly to our surprise there were some Post Office operations the cost of which was unknown. The Post Office did not seem to be all that interested in it. Is it difficult to invest on that basis?
(*Mr Ivers*) We often see the regulator about the costs of certain decisions which have been made. We often get the rebound effect, which is price increases. We often ask where the investment is and what is the return on it, which should mean prices coming down or something in return. We find it incredibly difficult to get that investment information out of the Post Office. It seems as if the decision to invest has been made, but what has happened to the return? Both POUNC (now CCPS) and the regulator are already beginning to ask those questions. We have said that we want to see a concerted effort to achieve a return on the investment based on reduced prices or new features or services. We do not see any linkage.
(*Mr Kennelly*) I can give an example. The Post Office installed IMPS machines which sort and stamp mail. The Post Office then told us that we would get 6 mm thick packages through the machines. When it

Lord Cavendish of Furness contd.]

began to run the machines it discovered that at speed they could handle only 5 mm packages. Instead of going back to the manufacturers, which any company in the private sector would do, the Post Office went back to the customer and said that it must change the size to 5 mm. The Post Office could have gone back to the manufacturers and changed the specification so that the machines could take 6 mm, but it did not.

(*Mr Ivers*) We have had worse than that. When it comes to the next round of price increases there is a premium price for services which are over a certain weight. The price is based on where the process is today rather than the demand by the customer, which is quite unusual. The Post Office is being driven by lack of automation in some respects.

223. You acknowledge in your evidence that the initial benefit of liberalisation will go to business mailers, but you go on to say that in time the benefits of liberalisation will trickle down to the social users. Is there a case for saying that the Swedish experience contradicts that?

(*Mr Ivers*) Sweden is a quite an unusual case and is not the role model that some people believe it to be. I spent a good bit of time in Sweden watching what went on there with City Mail and Swedish Post. Sweden is not an open competitive model. Officially, Swedish Post has been privatised and given some freedom. City Mail is not a directly competing service. Mail is received within three or four days. The system is driven by consolidation and it combines different mail streams. City Mail provides a different product from Swedish Post. It has found it immensely difficult to get the network and infrastructure up and running. A month ago it talked about investing to build a network further out from the major cities. It has only now started to look at an expansion of the service out of the major cities where it started and has lost a lot of money in building infrastructure. One returns to our situation. It is nigh impossible for somebody to try to compete properly by building his own network. As far as City Mail is concerned, one sees retired people on bicycles delivering the mail across town. That competes against van drivers and electronic mail. It is not a similar service and so is not a role model.

Chairman

224. Do you have unions in the areas in which your members operate?
(*Mr Ivers*) Yes.

225. Not the CWU?
(*Mr Ivers*) Yes. We have quarterly meetings with the CWU to understand its perspective and where it sees liberalisation and what changes it envisages. I have been very heartened by its progressive stance and our communication with that union. It has been very forward thinking in our meetings about the inevitability of liberalisation and employees working with management to try to build a way forward. We do not want to take either management's or union's side; we want them to collaborate to build a better platform for their customers. Our meetings so far have been heartening. There is some frustration on their part that things are not working as fast as they would like. They are concerned but open-minded about the future.

Lord Woolmer of Leeds

226. But your model would have substantial trade union and industrial relations implications, if one split up the infrastructure -the Railtrack model- from service delivery. Have you discussed that with the trade unions; if so, what have they said about it?
(*Mr Ivers*) We have not gone into the details of that model. They have seen a copy of our proposals, but we have not specifically sat down with them to discuss the model.

227. Perhaps you should do so because it has enormous trade union implications.
(*Mr Ivers*) We are not coming at it from the perspective of a trade union model. We believe that the model we have in mind will create more jobs in the industry and that, therefore, there is an untapped opportunity for new services and products. We believe that by bringing the private sector into the market with more competition there will be new products and services. The issue as far as the unions are concerned has been loss of jobs. We do not see a loss but an increase. If one talks to the major users, they want a lot of products and services which are not now being offered. We believe that greater choice can be provided.

Chairman

228. Presumably, Deutsche Post could be a partner in the scenario which you describe?
(*Mr Ivers*) Many different players could be involved in the network, and Deutsche Post would be one. I am sure that there are many others. However, it is a matter of creating the right environment. One does not want to create an environment where only someone who can invest heavily enters the market. One wants to create opportunities for flexible, nimble companies to play as well.

229. You are saying in effect that we could open up on a Europewide, if not a global, basis?
(*Mr Ivers*) Yes. What is happening now is happening both in Europe and the world. The last bastion is probably USPS in the USA which is not open today. Communications is a European and international business. People want to send mail internationally and they need an international network. We want the UK market to be healthy and successful, with as many businesses in it as possible.

Lord Paul

230. While I am all for privatisation and believe that in general government should not be in business, experience of privatisation of other industries has not been very good. Have you done any work from your perspective on the current deficiencies in the quality of service provided by the Post Office? How do you think that it can be improved? From some of the evidence we have heard, in Europe the UK Post Office is fairly high up in the quality of its service.

Lord Paul contd.]

(*Mr Ivers*) The quality of service is a major issue to us as users. Almost all major users, including the association, do their own independent surveys of the quality of service. We work in close collaboration with the Post Office. We have regular meetings. All of us here have individual accounts managers to deal with it. We continually work with the Post Office on the basis that its figures are lower than ours, and its figures are always lower than the standard targets that are being set. Why are our figures always different? We have the statistical answer that the Post Office takes a bigger sample. That may or may not be true. However, as customers when we monitor our own mail we do not have the same level of service that is published by the Post Office. When we look at the Post Office's published figures, even they are lower than the performance that it has set as a target. If one considers it on an international or European basis, one must look at lots of criteria. One is not comparing apples with apples. Germany may be at 98 per cent and the UK at 97 per cent, but in some countries it is nigh on impossible to get across the country, for example, northern Sweden. It is for that reason that e-mail is so popular in that country. One must look at continual improvement country by country. We want to work with the Post Office to drive up improvement and perhaps in future introduce compensation for non-delivery to a particular standard. We hope that in that way our figures and theirs will move up.

(*Mr Kennelly*) We look for a predictable service from the Post Office. The latest research figures provided by the Post Office show that for first class and second class post, Mailsort I and II and Press Stream I and II the service is roughly three percentage points below the Post Office's own targets. Readers Digest also does its own research. Our figures for Press Stream II, which is the service that we use for one of our products, show that the service is six percentage points below the PO's own figures. We do not believe that the Post Office figures are representative of the market. When we present our figures to the Post Office they are discounted as being unscientific and not based on factual evidence, unlike its own figures. As to predictability, the whole direct mail industry works on the basis that a customer will receive a package on a certain day. Most direct mail companies operate on the basis that a customer plans to receive a direct mail package the subsequent day. If there is a delay in the first package it means that it clashes with the second and the opportunity to purchase is lost. One of our main concerns about the service is the tail. Let us say that the service has a five-day delivery window. We are supposed to get 98.5 per cent of our mail delivered within that period, and the remainder a day or two afterwards. Our research shows that sometimes it extends beyond that period. When I looked at it nine months ago I found one case in which the period was 17 days. Some of the mail is delivered way outside the window that we are purchasing. We want the service that we are paying for, and we believe that the way to do it is to introduce a competitor. If we receive a bad service we can turn to the competitor and ask what he can do for us.

Chairman

231. Have you proposed to the regulator that there should be an independent assessment of the service?

(*Mr Ivers*) On Friday I met the Council for Consumer Protection of Postal Services (CCPS), formerly the Post Office Users National Council (POUNC). That body seeks to put a proposal to the regulator about the establishment of an independent audit of the performance figures. It is likely that it will still use the measures now used by the Post Office but they will be audited independently. Apparently, the auditors are the same as those used now by the Post Office. We have a very collaborative arrangement with the Post Office. We do not simply raise these matters today; we have been discussing them for many years with the Post Office, user associations, the industry, unions and so on to try to find a model.

Lord Paul

232. Have you done any work on how competition will improve the service that you need?

(*Mr Ivers*) A couple of years ago we looked at how a competing service could be run. We wanted to consider how infrastructure could be provided to do that. It is very difficult to look at quality of service. We have worked with the Royal Mail in this matter. It is doing about 50 things to try to improve it. We believe that it is trying to do too much and that it should focus on two or three improvements. The Royal Mail believes that it is a regional problem. Certainly, we believe that it can be improved. It also believes that a good deal of the problem is to do with wildcat strike action and automation problems. We believe that in a competing world that would be ironed out; it would not be allowed to exist as a problem for three or four years. If any of us had a problem today which meant that we could not deliver products it would be fixed immediately; otherwise, there would be no customers.

Viscount Brookeborough

233. At the conclusion of your paper you refer in paragraph 3.3.8 to liberalisation region by region. How do you see that?

(*Mr Ivers*) We are still thinking through the complex process of achieving full liberalisation in the marketplace. We believe that fundamentally there should be a national infrastructure. We need to be assured that in each region there is a full delivery infrastructure. We do not believe that there should be regional licences. We believe that there should be a central infrastructure for the sorting of mail but that the regulator should ensure that in each region—in addition, the CCPS has proposed a regional network—the quality of service is overseen. Operators can work on a national basis. We do not believe that they must be regional operators.

Lord Skelmersdale

234. Parcelforce is to an extent regionalised, is it not?

(*Mr Ivers*) It also operates on a national basis. According to our model, it would be able to do both. We do not believe that the model for competition should be based on regional licensing. There should be regulation to ensure that regional infrastructure for postal services is maintained. We believe that there should be national and regional operators. However, we are more interested in the maintenance of the national infrastructure, which is our primary focus. Perhaps the best way to start looking at it is to take a region as a microcosm and ensure that it is working. If one is to test it, rather than go national one should look first at it on a regional basis. However, we are at a very early stage in our thoughts. We are more concerned about having a national infrastructure than a regional licensing system.

Viscount Brookeborough

235. If one has a national infrastructure surely it is better to have national regulation. Why does one suddenly split it up in this way?

(*Mr Ivers*) The CCPS has a national board. Our concern is that we need to maintain in Scotland, Wales and wherever the national infrastructure. One has a national board and underneath it regional regulatory councils which seek to maintain the infrastructure. Within that competitors will be national, and there will be niche competitors for special products. There will be all manner of different competitors. We do not see the competition being necessarily controlled by region, but the CCPS will oversee regulation nationwide through the regulator. The regulator will set national and regional targets. Therefore, there will still be a national regulator, but there will be some consumer and business overview per region to ensure that the structure is maintained.

236. I live in Northern Ireland. I have always been very impressed by the delivery of mail order products, but what matters to the customer is the period between the point of order and the point of delivery. The customer is not interested in how that is divided up. I believe that it is much more a question of how soon items are sent from your particular location. What are you doing to improve that?

(*Mr Ivers*) From our point of view, when we send out product that is our delivery time to the customer, and it represents our lifeblood. For most of us here today, primarily our job is to improve the logistics; that is, to try to trim back the time between the receipt of an order and its delivery. I do not know whether the Sub-Committee would like to hear what we are doing in that area.

Chairman

237. I do not think so. I am afraid that we are well over time. We thank you for your answers and a stimulating session. We would be interested to receive any information that you might have about some of the niche services and new types of services which you have explored with the Post Office so that your customers can exercise choice, although that may be a little wide of the scope of the European directive.

(*Mr Ivers*) We are doing two things of interest. We are taking further our thinking on how to operate in a liberalised market. At the moment we are working through the mechanics of that. That may be of interest in the context of maintaining the national infrastructure. The other matter is the model of compensation on which we are working.

Chairman: As to that, we would be interested to see any further documentation that you might have. Thank you very much.

Memorandum by the Direct Marketing Association (UK) Limited

Examination of Witness

MR DAVID ROBOTTOM, Director of Development, Direct Marketing Association, called in and examined.

Chairman

238. Mr Robottom, thank you for coming and for your written submission. Perhaps you would explain to the Sub-Committee a bit more about the organisation you represent and then go on to explain your concerns about the Commission's proposals and what you would like to see instead.

(*Mr Robottom*) Thank you for giving the Direct Marketing Association the opportunity to speak to the Sub-Committee. The DMA was created about 10 years ago because of the increased focus on direct marketing and the need for an overarching trade association to represent the needs of both users and suppliers. It is the trade association for all companies involved in direct marketing, whether they be advertisers or those who wish to market products and services, or suppliers within the industry. I give the example of advertisers, home shopping companies, e-retailers, charities and voluntary services. In terms of down-market suppliers, we have companies such as database companies, list owners, printers, mailing houses, agencies and telemarketing bureaux. We now represent over 850 companies and makes us the largest trade association in the communications sector. We consider direct marketing to be one-to-one communication with potential customers in terms of acquisition and retention, using a range of media, including direct mail, telemarketing, radio and the Internet. In 1998 our industry spent over £8 billion, which equates to a turnover of about £24 to 25 billion, or 3 per cent of gross domestic product. We are considered as one of the major success stories of the 'nineties. That growth continues. As to the draft directive, in the domestic and international context we are part of the global economy. It is essential that for the benefit of industry and consumers the UK takes all the

[*Chairman contd.*]

opportunities that that gives us, especially in terms of e-commerce. As to the current structure, which is a monopoly of postal services—the last bastion of monopoly industries—effectively it is a barrier to trade in the context of the existing market. We should like to see a realisation that postal services must meet the challenge of various technological developments. They need to grow and develop now, and the most effective way to do that is through liberalisation and competition. The existing proposal does not go far enough and will probably open up about 5 per cent of the existing reserved area. That is too small to open up competition; it will not be attractive to other operators and will have minimal benefit to users. We believe that direct mail should be fully liberalised by 2003, as outlined in the first directive. We welcome the liberalisation of outward cross-border mail, but to make sense inward cross-border mail should also be liberalised. As to letters, we believe that some timetable should be set for the liberalisation of letters. The effect is too little, too late. It is essential that postal services take advantage of the opportunities presented to them by globalisation, in particular SMEs. I do not need to remind the Sub-Committee that basically SMEs are the engines of growth in the economy and it is essential that they are given as much encouragement as possible.

Baroness O'Cathain

239. We have heard from the UK Post Office and the unions that they are not opposed to liberalisation. I suppose that they would say that, would they not? However, they say that it should be gradual because one does not want to throw the baby out with the bath water. Do you think that their gradual approach to liberalisation is too cautious and, to use your own words, is too little, too late?

(*Mr Robottom*) The reality is that it continues to be cautious. If one goes back 20 years, the telecommunications and postal legislation of 1982 created exemptions with regard to the postal monopoly. We started this 18 years ago. Therefore, it is cautious and controlled. I always recommend caution and minimal risk, but the case for liberalisation, particularly in the field of direct mail, is clear. The effect on the universal service obligation is minimal. Do you want me to deal also with the universal service obligation?

240. The DMA does not necessarily need universal service provision, does it?

(*Mr Robottom*) Yes. Basically, 100 per cent of industry is behind the universal service obligation. It is a fundamental part of the structure of the economy in both business and social terms. As to liberalisation, there is an obvious link between the reserved area and the universal service. Article 7 of the first directive stated that reserved areas should be kept to the extent necessary to ensure provision of the universal service. But the key point of that directive is that the postal operator must prove the necessity by the provision of accounts which show the potential damage to the universal service obligation in terms of keeping the reserved area. Therefore, there is a need to determine the level of reserved area that is required. The European Commission had the commonsense to commission some studies 18 months ago. The NERA study which was commissioned by DGXV looked at the economic viability of the public post office service across the EU in terms of the reserved area and the USO. It concluded that the economic viability of any postal operator, including the UK, would not be seriously affected by the abolition of the reserved area. It also showed that for most Member States, including the UK, the cost of the universal service was not a financial burden. There are examples within the Commonwealth. In Australia it is calculated that the cost of its universal service obligation per capita is A$1.85. The figure for New Zealand is NZ$1. One tends to forget that the universal service provider, with its universal service obligation, effectively has a competitive edge. The organisations which we represent need a universal service and access to a comprehensive network. Therefore, the universal service obligation is not a burden for the incumbent operator.

Lord Woolmer of Leeds

241. Therefore, you do not agree with the Post Office that the cost of the universal service obligation is in the order of £350 million?

(*Mr Robottom*) I am not privy to the cost and the Post Office accounts.

242. The effect of your answer is that the cost of the universal service obligation is very modest. The Post Office estimate of the cost is £350 million. Given that there is a big gap, if this matter is important to you as an association surely you have asked the Post Office about it?

(*Mr Robottom*) We have asked the Post Office many questions.

243. Have you asked about the £350 million estimate?

(*Mr Robottom*) The Post Office has not been forthcoming about the cost of the universal service obligation. But the Post Office must prove the cost of the USO to both the Government and regulator. Under the first directive there is provision for the production of accounts. I am not privy to those costs. All we can do is constantly ask the Post Office for as much transparency as possible to develop relevant products that are geared to cost. We also look at examples like the DGXV study which was commissioned by the European Commission to look at the impacts of liberalisation and examples of other countries, where possible. I do not know whether the figure of £350 million has been submitted to and agreed with the regulator. However, I am aware that all incumbent postal operators had to provide complete transparency of accounts to meet the requirements of the first directive by February of this year. I believe that they were sent to the DTI but not the regulator.

244. One's impression is that if one does a sweep around the European Union, starting with Greece and working in this direction, one will find enormous resistance by postal operators to the proposals. Do you suggest that Britain should go it alone if the rest of Europe rejects the move to 50 grams?

Lord Woolmer of Leeds *contd.*]

(*Mr Robottom*) There is an opportunity for the UK to liberalise out of Europe. We have a key opportunity to do that because of the state of the economy and our aspiration to make it the e-commerce centre by 2002.

245. We should go it alone?

(*Mr Robottom*) We can liberalise ahead of Europe because our Post Office is one of the best in the world, and everyone in business wants UK plc to be a very successful operation. We have a very competitive infrastructure in terms of the supply side, and we have a burgeoning direct marketing industry. I believe that we can do it.

Lord Skelmersdale

246. Mr Robottom, you represent a very hawkish organisation in this field. You describe the proposal as cautious. You have said that the proposal will open up 5 per cent. Five per cent of what?

(*Mr Robottom*) It is 5 per cent of volume.

247. You are hawkish and you would really like full liberalisation?

(*Mr Robottom*) It is the first time that I have been described as "hawkish". The case for the liberalisation of direct mail is very clear. I hark back to the studies carried out by the Commission. The Arthur Andersen study, which looked at the impact of liberalisation, and the PricewaterhouseCoopers study, which looked at the case for cross-border direct mail, indicate that the case for liberalisation is there. As to letters, I am slightly more cautious. We can liberalise direct mail quite easily. The economic case is there and all one wants is the political will.

248. Does that mean that you would not go lower than 50 grams?

(*Mr Robottom*) I would fully liberalise direct mail by 2003. I would fully liberalise inward cross-border mail. There is no justification for keeping that within the reserved area.

249. I thought that it was not.

(*Mr Robottom*) Inward cross-border mail is still a reserved area. The European Court decision in *Citicorp v Deutsche Post* basically allowed Deutsche Post to charge a differential, known as ABA REIMS. There is also the REIMS II agreement which makes the reservation of inward cross-border mail ridiculous. There is no need for it. As to letters, I would be slightly more cautious. As to that, I would agree that there should be a gradual liberalisation.

250. Would that not benefit you at the expense of ordinary mail users such as myself?

(*Mr Robottom*) At the moment, there are cross-subsidies within the system. Nobody wants cross-subsidies. We want the real cost to be identified by the Post Office so that it can price accordingly. We have been asking for a transparent system so that the Post Office can develop products and prices which reflect the true cost. We have been consistent in our belief that there should be no cross-subsidies between reserved and non-reserved areas. Business mail users effectively pay net lower prices than consumers. Eighty-five per cent of all mail is business mail anyway. Therefore, to a large extent business has been subsidising the consumer for many years. The reason why we achieve that price is that we work very hard with the Post Office to try to get the cost savings. We do not automatically get it; we have to do something as business users to generate cost savings to the Post Office.

251. I do not understand how the universal service obligation can be maintained without cross-subsidy.

(*Mr Robottom*) The Post Office has the reserved area which it can use to the necessary degree to protect the USO.

Baroness O'Cathain

252. It can put up the prices in the reserved area and subsidise services elsewhere?

(*Mr Robottom*) It tries to keep the standard tariff. It is more a matter of how necessary it is to maintain the reserved area to protect USO. The whole debate, whether it is in the UK, Holland, or Brussels, is about the cost of USO. That is why people like myself who are heavily involved in domestic and European postal affairs say that all the evidence they have obtained as business users shows that if it is not a financial burden and the cost is relatively low there is a competitive advantage. Therefore, *de facto* one should not have such a large reserved area.

Lord Cavendish of Furness

253. You say that you support full liberalisation. I am a great enthusiast for competition. However, as time goes by and services become liberalised more and more of us are sensitive to the nature of universal service provision, which you support. Given the huge political and social impact of universal social provision, I wonder whether you underestimate the risks of jeopardising the universal service. It is hard to put a value on it, but for people it is obviously hugely important. I am not convinced that sufficient attention has been given to the issue.

(*Mr Robottom*) As an industry we have always supported USO. We pushed for USO in the original Post Office review, because it is fundamental to business.

Chairman

254. There is also a link between that and cost. Everybody says that they support USO but they do not say anything about a uniform low tariff.

(*Mr Robottom*) We support a uniform tariff and USO.

255. You support a low tariff?

(*Mr Robottom*) We come back to the debate about "affordable". What is affordable to a consumer may not be affordable to business.

Viscount Brookeborough

256. If it is a low tariff it will be a loss-making business. Who is to fund that loss-making business? You made reference to Australia. I do not know how the universal service operates in Australia. I very much doubt that it means daily deliveries to every

[*Viscount Brookeborough contd.*]

ranch, some of which are hundreds of miles from anywhere. In this country we have daily deliveries to every single house in the land, which is a loss-making operation at present prices?

(*Mr Robottom*) According to the Post Office.

257. I do not think there can be any doubt about that. One may well argue about the extent of the loss, but most people agree that it is a loss-making enterprise on its own.

(*Mr Robottom*) I do not believe that that is so in the reserved area.

258. Do you believe that it is profitable?

(*Mr Robottom*) I believe that in the current reserved area it is profitable. Let us not confuse the reserved area with the USO. The USO goes up to 20 kilograms. I do not believe that we have underestimated the risk. We have been heavily involved in this area for four or five years. To allay your concerns, if there was ever a stage when the USO was at risk we would be the first to shout. As far as we are concerned, there will always be a universal service in the Post Office.

Lord Cavendish of Furness

259. From your perspective, can you explain the current deficiencies as you see them in the quality of service which you receive from the UK Post Office? How do you think that that could be improved by liberalisation?

(*Mr Robottom*) In the past two or three years the quality of service targets set by the Post Office, in consultation with CCPS, on all the business mail products, of which there are about 10—Mailsort, Press Stream, stamped, metered and so on—have not been met.

260. If one has ambitious targets one may find that they are not achievable. Perhaps you think that the targets are not high enough.

(*Mr Robottom*) I believe that there are problems with the network and how it is managed. I receive monthly performance statistics from the Post Office. On a monthly basis it has hardly achieved those targets in the past three years. Perhaps it has been achieved once or twice in that period over the whole range of products. Users want reliable, predictable and measurable services. Predictability is key to it. For example, users want to know that 95 per cent will be delivered within, say, six days. The key aspect is that for many mailers the tail will last for only four or five days. If one can imagine the shape of the mailing, the bulk of it drops off within a short time of despatch, say, four or five days. However, in a number of instances the tail can run for 20 to 30 days. Users want that tail to be three days, for the reason that they want to generate business and serve customers. They need predictability. In addition, they need a reduction in the number of lost and mislaid items. One finds that the Post Office will not give figures for lost items. However, CCPS recently did some research to show that the Post Office lost 1 million items a week. That is a huge concern. Further, there is a huge range of products being pushed through the post, particularly off the back of e-commerce. Direct mail plays a key role in the fulfilment of e-commerce. It is fundamental to confidence in the new media that the back end also works. Why do I think that competition is a good thing for quality of service? If one looks at the evidence from any of the markets which have been liberalised and brought in competition, there has always been a beneficial effect in the overall efficiency of service. A monopoly has no pressure without competition. Short of people like myself saying that it must improve, there is no direct impact to bring about improvement.

Chairman

261. We have come to the end of our questions. Is there anything else that you want to say in conclusion?

(*Mr Robottom*) In the context of the UK economy and the growth of e-commerce, this matter cannot be viewed in isolation; one must look at it in relation to other media. We must ensure that we have an infrastructure which works for both business and consumers. The way to do that is to introduce competition.

262. In conclusion, perhaps you will provide the Sub-Committee with any information that you may have obtained from the Post Office, extending over the past four years, say, about the number of lost items? Thank you very much for coming.

WEDNESDAY 8 NOVEMBER 2000

Present:

Brookeborough, V.
Faulkner of Worcester, L.
Woolmer of Leeds, L.

O'Cathain, B. (Chairman)
Paul, L.
Skelmersdale, L.

Examination of Witness

MR NANNO AUKES, TNT Group N.V., called in and examined

Chairman

263. Good morning, Mr Aukes, and welcome. Thank you for making the great effort to come over especially for this Committee. Thank you also for the submission that you gave for the evidence and also for the overview of the TNT Post Group N.V. Could you explain briefly to all of us in simple words what TNT is? I say that because I have an idea that it is an Australian company. I think it is now a stock limited (public limited) Dutch company.

A. (*Mr Aukes*) I will try to explain. TPG is the TNT Post Group, a company which has three divisions: mail, express and logistics. The mail part is done by PTT Post. In express and logistics we work under the brand name of TNT. That is why you recognised TNT, which was originally an Australian company we acquired some years ago. We work in three activities, mail, express and logistics, with the two brand names, PTT Post and TNT.

264. So in fact TNT is not really the post side of it. It is the express company. The post side is not known as TNT, is it?

A. No, mostly not.

265. When you say "TNT Post Group N.V.", that is another company?

A. That is the holding company which owns PTT Post and TNT. The listing of the shares is as TPG shares, and these obviously are shares in the holding company. They are listed on the big stock markets around the world.

266. The Netherlands Government owns some of the stock?

A. It owns about 44 per cent of TPG stock.

267. Do you have operations in other countries? Obviously TNT is well known throughout the world.

A. Yes. We operate in other countries and also in the three areas of activities: logistics, express and mail. You will already know about the express business in other countries under the brand name TNT, but we have smaller operations in mail activities in Europe, for instance, in Belgium and Italy.

268. Therefore you are in a good position to be able to inform us as to how you feel about the whole European focus of mail. You are not just inside the borders of the Netherlands?

A. No.

Lord Faulkner of Worcester

269. You have given us a very powerful document calling for further liberalisation. For the benefit of the Committee, could you summarise that and tell us what you regard as the priorities for the liberalisation programme?

A. Yes. You already have our submission. I can shortly summarise our point of view. I gave evidence before this Committee four years ago, in 1996. What I said then could be summarised in the following way. The proposals of the European Commission are too little and too late. With recent developments, we feel more strongly about that now. If you are asking me what should be done now, I think there should be a firm end date for total liberalisation of the postal market. We would like to see that in 2005, and realistically that might be too soon, but at the latest in 2007. We think that there should be liberalisation of the direct mail market as soon as possible around Europe and hence liberalisation of cross-border mail, and that there should be a good definition of special services, so that innovation does not stop. Those are the main points on our view as to liberalisation within the time schedule.

270. You would like to see the market liberalised at all levels, from the smallest package and piece of post up to parcels?

A. Yes.

271. Is that the sort of market that already exists in the Netherlands?

A. No. As you already know from what we wrote in our paper, in the Netherlands we have a relatively small monopoly consisting of a reserve area that can best be described as letters up to 100 grams, where direct mail is excluded from letters. So, direct mail is free from competition. That makes it an open market. We estimate 75 per cent of the postal market is open for competition in Holland, whereas in big countries like France and the UK we estimate the figure may be 15 or 20 per cent.

272. Given that you are such a major player in the Netherlands and such ardent enthusiasts for liberalisation, do you not think there is a bit of a paradox between your company's stance Europe-wide and what goes on in your own country?

A. I understand the question very well, as I have been asked it before. The point is that in an already quite open market in the Netherlands, companies like Deutsche Post and Royal Mail have activities which they are building up. From our point of view, we do not have the same possibilities as in the UK and German markets. We would like to be ahead of

Lord Faulkner of Worcester *contd.*]

the rest because we are in favour of competition. We want to be in the front line of discussions but we do not want to go alone totally along the road to liberalisation, for instance like the Swedes did, because we think that the situation is very unbalanced for a company like TPG compared with Royal Mail and Deutsche Post.

Lord Paul

273. The Dutch Government holds 44 per cent of the shares. How far can one talk about liberalisation in that situation? If there is liberalisation and competition, would the competitors not be a little more afraid with a government shareholding of 44 per cent?
A. If liberalisation goes ahead at the same pace, the Dutch Government will sell off its remaining shares. They have already said that they are going to do that in the telecommunication sector. I expect them to follow the same policy in the postal market. If there is a totally liberalised situation, of course they will get rid of their shares. There is no argument for a government to be an operator in a liberalised situation.

274. It is not a catch-22 situation: competition will not happen when the government is such a dominant shareholder and at the same time the government will come out if there is competition?
A. If the regulation changes, if we could agree in Europe that we will liberalise the market in 2005, for instance, or 2007, then the other steps will be prepared for selling off the shares eventually. Then a normal market situation will be achieved step-by-step.

275. You are a strong spokesman for liberalisation. Why have you not told the government to get off your backs?
A. That is not only TPG policy but government policy as well. The government is also aiming for liberalisation of the postal market and they support that view in the European Union. Perhaps they are more cautious about these sorts of things than we are.

Chairman

276. Could it be, following Lord Paul's point, that they are just a bit scared—as you say cautious—because, if they pulled out, they are afraid that the costs might be too high for the consumers?
A. Ownership does not regulate prices. In Holland we have a total separation between the normal postal regulation, which has a price regulatory system, and the ownership of the company.

277. As the government is such a big shareholder in your company, they must have some influence on the situation?
A. That is relatively little in Holland. As you might know, shareholder power in Holland is not very big. Shareholders do not interfere with policy issues in Dutch companies.

278. On a different matter, for clarification, may I ask you this? You said that direct mail was free from competition. Did you give a figure of 75 per cent for mail being direct mail?
A. No. When you talk about the traditional postal market, that includes parcels, cross-border mail and document exchange.

279. What proportion of the total then is actually open to competition?
A. I said that from the total postal market, which I described in the traditional sense, 75 per cent is open for competition.

Lord Skelmersdale

280. Would it be accurate to summarise what you have just said as the Commission being feeble or, as we in this country say, wet? In other words, they are not going nearly far enough by reducing that to the 50 gram level?
A. We say that they do not go far enough. That is correct.

281. You would like to see a total liberalisation by 2003?
A. We argued for that a few years ago. We are realistic enough to see that 2003 is not achievable any longer. If a directive were introduced now, it would take some time to implement that in every country. I do not see 2003 as a realistic date at this moment. 2005 is the earliest possibility but I do not expect the European Commission and the Council of Ministers to take that decision. From listening to discussions in Brussels, most of the talks are about how to weaken the proposal of the European Commission even further. From our point of view, that is not a very nice thing to see.

282. You will have noticed, I am sure, in your discussions with other postal companies across Europe that the British Post Office is very worried even by such a minor step in your view as a reduction to 50 grams because it does not believe that at this level of competition, and therefore reducing income, it will be able to support the universal service obligation. You obviously feel that you can do this at home very happily and why should not we. Is that your attitude?
A. I read in an English newspaper that Mr Roberts from the post Office said that he was afraid to lose £100 million in the financial results of the company per year because of the proposal by Mr Bolkestein for 50 grams.

283. We were told the figure was higher at £300 million.
A. That is what I read. The argument was that the Royal Mail would lose all the volume which was included in that proposal, which is of course, from my point of view, unbelievable. If you look at the percentage of market share which postal operators have in the liberalised sectors, in Holland we have more than 90 per cent of the direct mail market because we think we have a very good service there, which is open to competition. If you say that direct mail will be open for competition in the UK, that does not mean that all the direct mail will be lost from the revenues of the Royal Mail. That is what they argue. I find that unbelievable because we expect the incumbent operator will have a very high percentage

Lord Skelmersdale contd.]

of the market, if a specific part of the postal service is being liberalised.

284. The Commission have produced in a document an alternative or several alternative ways of keeping the universal service obligation. One is direct subsidy. The other is to make competition open to the USO. Would you accept either of those propositions?
A. Open competition for the USO?

285. Yes. In other words, if TNT is competing with German Post or ourselves, it would be subject to the same USO that we have in our own country, and indeed vice-versa: if we were competing with you.
A. You can think about taking that road. If you look at what happens in the market when competitors enter that market, and they all start as niche players, they start with a certain specific service for a certain client group. It is easy to see that we do not duplicate the postal system of the Royal Mail in the UK or Deutsche Post will not copy the Dutch postal system in the Netherlands. They are going to work for specific sorts of clients where they can design their organisation on the specific service they have to deliver. I do not think it is easy to promote competition in that way, but of course you could imagine that with a licence system you will put some specific conditions on the licence to enter a specific part of the market. You could have all kinds of graduations of the service obligation, together with specific sorts of licence. I know that the Postal Service Commission here in the UK is thinking along those lines to open up parts of the UK postal market.

286. Indeed, they are thinking of a regionalised service obligation, for example in the West Country or in Scotland.
A. If you have that sort of service obligation, you have to balance the opening of the market with obligations, and that is feasible.

287. So you are not in favour of subsidy?
A. No. I think it is very difficult to establish the cost of a universal service. I have read many studies by all kinds of experts and they come to quite different conclusions in France, the UK and many other countries. There is no generally accepted way of establishing the costs of the universal service.

288. Every country seems to use a slightly different economic model to establish the costs, and sometimes that is very different?
A. Yes. It is very difficult to base regulations on this kind of information. I think the other route is probably better.

Chairman

289. Before I ask Viscount Brookeborough to come in, it is easy to provide the universal service in a country like the Netherlands by comparison with the situation we have in this country, just on the geography?
A. It is a common belief that there is a very big difference between countries as to the difficulty and the cost involved. You know that Sweden has a universal service and the country is sparsely populated. They have many fewer people per square kilometre than in the UK. Of course, we have islands too in the Netherlands. I know that a common argument in other countries is that there are islands which create extra costs. In practice there are ferries to islands to supply the island community with everything they need, such as food. In addition to that, a small amount of mail is sent. The ferry does not operate only for the mail but for supplies as well. The only extra cost involved is that of the ferry service. The Netherlands has islands in the north and the service is done in that way. I know that the same is true for islands in Denmark and the UK. It is a common belief that it is very difficult to render that service and it is very expensive but in practice I do not think that is the case.

Chairman: I am going to ask Lord Brookeborough because he actually lives on an island.

Viscount Brookeborough

290. I live on a big island, in Northern Ireland. Following on from the Chairman's remarks, your definition of universal service maybe slightly different to the way we see it in this country. For instance, in paragraph 18 of your submission to us, you would "allow delivery to local collection points rather than addresses—everyone needs to buy food yet there is no universal service obligation to sell bread to every address". People in outlying communities have deep freezes. They do not go to the shops every day. I do not live on the top of a heathery hill like many people do in Scotland. Even where I live, people do not shop every day. Some of them go to the shops only once a week. In the more remote areas, once a week a mobile shop may come round. If one followed your course for what you seem to consider to be universal service collection points, once a week delivery would not be enough.
A. What we have in Holland and what I expect to continue in a liberalised situation is daily delivery of mail to every address in the country. That is not because the organisations are charity organisations but because the big clients of the postal organisation have a demand for nationwide delivery and that is what we sell. A big client in Holland expects us to deliver to every household in the Netherlands. That is what they pay for.

291. But you have actually promoted allowing delivery to local collection points?
A. Yes, but that depends on the service level and what is agreed with our clients. Up until now they have demanded delivery to the household. If you are going to create a liberalised situation, there might be innovations in the service which say that maybe big clients find it acceptable for their clients to have that service done differently.

292. Your geographical situation is obviously different from ours. Where delivery is required to individual houses outside a certain area of population, this is going to cost a lot of money. Since much of that is in a reserved area, who is going to pay for it, or are prices going to have to rise? The small user will be the one who suffers.
A. I do not expect the USO to change that dramatically. As I said, the big clients expect a service to be rendered of a certain quality.

Viscount Brookeborough *contd.*]

293. Can you define a big client? Are we talking about big businesses?
A. Yes.

294. These are individuals?
A. Yes, but they are the clients of those big clients. Various big financial institutions send very large amounts of financial statements nowadays.

295. Therefore, they will have to pay extra to get that mail delivered and you will charge the receiver of that who wishes to reply extra in order to reply. Therefore the costs is going to escalate for the small businesses and for the individual living in the community?
A. What happens now? If postal operators lose their big clients, then there will be a problem because then the individuals, who also want to send letters, cannot lift with the big volume of the bigger customers. The thing that makes it acceptable in terms of service and price is the big volume from big customers who really fill the postal system. Only 5 or 6 per cent of the mail is paid for by individuals. If the postal system loses a large amount of volume of business mail, then in the end the private consumer will pay. That is why we say that postal services have to be competitive for the larger volumes, for the large business customers. If they are not, then there will be trouble anyway.

296. So you do not mind if the price rises for extreme rural areas. You have just said that the price will rise.
A. In practice the big customers have a volume of mail, say a few millions of items a year. They say that is the amount of mail that they want delivered and they want one price for that. You have to decide on a price and there are cost difference already at present.

297. That is fine where it is a big business which is making millions of pounds, say in insurance or whatever. It is not so good when there is a little old lady living half-way up a hill who wishes to write letters because she is not IT capable. She is the one who will suffer. That is why we have a uniform and affordable price.
A. Yes, but if the USO is in place in a liberalised situation, with a price-capped system, you can regulate prices for the small user and for the private consumer, which is already the case now. We expect that to continue because we understand that society will not be happy about a big difference in price. I do not believe that will occur. You will face a cost of complexity within your organisation if you have different prices for consumers with a small amount of mail. Many kinds of complexities are involved in that. It can be regulated, so I do not see the problem.

Lord Woolmer of Leeds

298. I understood that in Sweden following liberalisation the price of domestic mail increased very substantially.
A. Yes.

299. So in practice, despite your honeyed words, the customer in Sweden is actually faced with a substantial increase.

A. I do not know if your information is correct. You should ask the Swedish Post about this. I know that part of the problem lies in the fact that they have VAT at 25 per cent applied on the postal services, whereas in all other countries that is not the case. I know that there has been some increase in price, which has to be compared with other increases in prices for other postal operators, and they have also increased their prices. To counteract the effects on the consumer, there is a special discount programme for small users. If they buy a certain limited amount of stamps, they get a discount. In real terms the price increase in Sweden is not as big as you suggest.

300. If you have a fully liberalised service of all forms of post and mail, you would inevitably have to put VAT on, would you not?
A. That is another issue which in Brussels is separate from the liberalisation discretion.

301. I am asking you. If it is fully liberalised, you should have a level playing field.
A. In my opinion the normal situation should be that in the end VAT will be imposed on the postal service as well because it is logical that, if a service is competing with other communication services which are subject to VAT, the playing field should be level.

Lord Skelmersdale

302. It does not happen at the moment because in this country you, TNT, are competing with Parcel Post for packets and parcels over 350 grams. You are paying VAT and the British Post Office is not. Presumably you are complaining like mad.
A. In Holland we have the same situation but the other way round. The Dutch Government said then that it would change the universal service obligation. They have defined a large amount of direct mail and parcels as being outside the universal service, so VAT is applicable there. We have a level playing field in that area now. They have got around the problem of the VAT issue because that is linked to the universal service obligation on the European level.

303. Except, as you pointed out, in the Commission it is not linked at all. It just happens to have the same Commissioner. That is the only link.
A. That is a strange thing. In the end the Commission will realise that, if they liberalise the postal market, then they will have to accept that VAT will be applicable. That is the only sensible conclusion.

Chairman

304. May I ask for clarification? You are talking about universal service provision. I get the impression, and I want to know how true it is, that really the little customer, the person who lives half-way up the hill, as Lord Brookeborough said, and the little old lady writing personal letters really does not come into the thoughts of the major postal organisations in Europe. I get the same message from other people who are running services like the Royal Mail, that the person who writes a couple of letters a week really does not come into their thinking because you are talking about big financial companies with

Chairman *contd.*]

many millions and they can send out these circulars, and they actually send out millions of items of mail a year. The problem is, of course, that governments have to think about the customers because that is where the voice is. It is not necessarily so in the financial field.

A. I understand that perfectly.

305. Therefore, surely, any provider of these services has got to be aware, and they would be very stupid if they are not, of what the man or woman in the street, as we use that expression in this country, is thinking and how they will react. I am sure they would react extremely nastily towards VAT on their mail, despite what you think is the best situation.

A. Then I will have to elaborate on these issues as to what I mean by the imposition of VAT being applicable to the larger customers. In Holland VAT is not applicable to individual persons who send parcels and printed matter but it is applicable to business users. The same situation applies further along the road in that specially defined universal service for the consumer where we can still have exemption from VAT. If you have an obligation in that specific service, it is still possible to have that situation. That is up to the government.

Lord Paul

306. New technology—e-mails, et cetera-- has brought a lot of competition to the postal services. As I understand it, they are preparing themselves by struggling to innovate and be competitive. Would not imposing liberalisation at the same time be putting just too much pressure on at one go?

A. I understand your question. I think innovation does not spring from one party in the market. What I call the competitive dynamics in the market will create innovation. The situation is that you have the traditional postal operator which looks to the future and says maybe all kinds of bad things are going to happen with e-mails. There is a large amount of unpredictability in that market now. It has become more and more unclear what is going to happen and when it is going to happen. I think the best way to start innovation in the postal market is to introduce competition now. That innovation will not spring from one operator acting in that market but from the interaction between the different operators and the new entrants in the market. If there is no possibility for competition, then the new entrants are not going to invest in innovation. There will be no activity to create innovation in the market.

307. That was not my question. There is competition from e-mails, et cetera. In order to face that competition, they are innovating and modernising. To add another complication at the same time on the top of that would be too much, would it not?

A. I do not think it would be too much. I question your statement that all the postal operators are innovating now at a sufficient pace. I do not think they are. More should be done and you can look at what is happening around in the world of communications, which will affect the postal world in the coming years in a very serious way.

308. You are really saying that, if you push them hard enough, they will move and that will be better for them or else they will drop off?

A. There is no guarantee that everyone will be successful in the future. Do not ask me that question because I cannot give you that guarantee. If you ask what will be best for the postal sector as a whole, I think liberalising the market is the best way to go for the sector as a whole.

309. That brings me to my next question. From your experience in liberalisation, what will stimulate innovation and improve customer service?

A. I think in the end the pressure put on organisations by the possibility that they will lose clients—a very basic idea—is really pushing innovation. If a client has specific demands and wants a differently shaped service or has other inquiries or wants something else, he will be tempted by another competitor who can make his service better or cheaper, or whatever, that is really pushing the company.

310. Coming back to my colleague Lord Brookeborough's question, would it not be the poor man or the ordinary person living half-way up a hill who will suffer and not big business?

A. I think you have to separate that from a regulatory point of view. You can have guarantees for the private consumers and price regulation but that must be based on sound business economics. That is only possible when they have the drive to satisfy the needs of the big customers. If they do not do that, in the end the private consumer will end up worse off anyway.

311. When you start regulating, then the industry cries out that there is too much regulation.

A. Of course industry will always cry out that there is too much regulation. In the telecommunications world, the incumbent operator still has an obligation to install the basic telephone services for every consumer in the Netherlands but they do not have any reserved area because they are the incumbent operator. They have such a strong market position in the country that they can handle that obligation. That is the case in Sweden, a difficult country, so I do not see why it cannot happen in the UK where there can be guarantees for the private consumer and for an extra guarantee you can have a licence system which states that, if too much of the market is opened up, a new entrant also has obligations, if that is thought necessary.

Chairman

312. Can I just support what Lord Paul has said and take that one step further? If there is complete liberalisation, is it not only human nature that the companies will go for those areas of activity which are going to be of least problem and most return, and we use this expression, cherry-picking. Because nobody will be prepared to supply the service, we still will not be able to look after the people, even if there is this help to subsidise the man or woman living half-way up the hill?

A. If you have regulations to deliver the mail to every household in the UK, and if you establish the

Chairman *contd.*]

fact that it is possible for the incumbent operator to fulfil that obligation, why should he not do that?

Viscount Brookeborough

313. But let us say you have a business in the United Kingdom and you compete in the areas where you are profitable and you do not want to go into the reserved area because you do not think it is profitable or into the universal service on a low cost base. You do not necessarily want to go into that because it is not very profitable because of the outlying areas. Who is going to pick it up? You cannot have a regulation which says, "You will form a company to give a universal service at a loss".

A. I said that you have two lines of securing that service. The simplest way is to give the incumbent operator which has such a strong market position the obligation to render that service to every consumer in the UK. Secondly, you can have a licence system where you say that new entrants, on a balance of possibilities, can enter the market and set out the obligations that they have to fulfil if they want to keep their licence. Maybe in some areas they will have to deliver to all addresses. That is up to specific research on how you are going to do this in a particular country. I expect that in Holland in the end we will end up with a universal service obligation, with a price-capped system and an obligation to deliver to every household in the Netherlands in the liberalised market where others are going to do whatever they want to do in that market. I still think we have a very good position because we have what in more commercial terms is a unique proposition, that we deliver to every household in the Netherlands and we want to be perhaps not the cheapest but the best and most respected in the market.

Chairman: I must say that it sounds very complex.

Lord Woolmer of Leeds

314. Presumably you would feel that the lack of organisation means that postal services, for example in the UK and elsewhere in Europe, are at a higher cost than they really need be if there is competition, certainly in the business mail but not in rural mail.

A. But also in business mail.

315. One of the effects of liberalisation, if it came in at the pace you would like to see it, would be a lot of pressure very quickly on costs and that would mean almost certainly significant job losses, employment losses, in the existing postal services?

A. Yes, I know that is a widely-used argument.

316. That may or may not be a deciding factor but it would be inevitable?

A. Yes, in a way. If I can look back to what we have been going through over the last ten years, about ten years ago corporatisation took place and that was a new starting point for the company. If you compare this with that situation, there were losses in jobs because of automated sorting. We introduced a whole new system with six new sorting centres in Holland and about 5,000 jobs were lost. The end result was that for the traditional mail sectors we have more people working now than five years ago because of growth in other areas in new services. It is true that by trying to become more efficient and by introducing new technology, jobs will be lost but that is a normal situation in industry where human labour can be replaced by machines—new information technology and automated sorting. That makes the service cheaper and contributes to growth in volume.

Lord Skelmersdale

317. That has nothing to do with competition. Lord Woolmer was talking specifically about competition?

A. But of course competition will enforce this process because everybody has to become very efficient and fast. I have tried to tell you what we encountered in trying to become more efficient in that period. Jobs will be lost on one side of the business and new jobs will be created on the other.

Lord Woolmer of Leeds

318. What have been the new services that have actually over a number of years resulted in more employment now, as you have told us? What are the new services?

A. Before I come to the new services, there has been growth in volume and that has been created by having low costs and relatively low prices. That may create more volume; for instance, in direct mail there is quite strong growth. That is thanks to low costs and low prices. We have developed services like print and mail services where you take the whole chain from a company which sends a lot of bills, like a big telecommunication industry such as BT. You probably all received bills from a telecommunication company. These companies create a large amount of mail. Doing the whole process is not a core activity for those companies. The data for producing bills is created at the end of their computer system. They actually do not create the bills themselves but send us the data and we create the bills, put them in the envelopes and provide the whole service. That is an additional thing we do. We are in the business of data services. We can help companies with large data collections from customers with the right addresses and mailings and advise them on how to go about direct mail. We stimulate that medium.

319. Some of that is hybrid mail?
A. Yes.

320. Could I just turn to that area? In your document, and I am asking you to repeat it to get it on the record a little more directly, you argue that things like hybrid mail, in-bound border mail and direct mail should be completely liberalised and that fears about liberalisation by content are not justified. Could you talk us through that?

A. Yes. That is one of the services where innovation takes place and it should be free for competition. Innovation should go as fast as possible and then other market entrants will get their chance of a piece of that business. What is happening now is more our concern, that in Europe, through the implementation of the last postal Directive, re-monopolisation is taking place in certain countries

Lord Woolmer of Leeds *contd.*]

where hybrid mail was already liberalised. For instance, in Italy they tried to re-monopolise that hybrid mail by so-called implementation of the Directive, which of course in our opinion is contrary to the intention of the last directive.

321. It is certainly my impression, and it may be the impression of other members of the Committee, that, rather than your aspiration for complete liberalisation to take place as a result of the current discussions, it is possible that the proposals put forward currently in Brussels may not even get as far as that. Where do you think the Brussels proposals are likely to get within Europe? Which countries and which services are likely to be most resistant to the change? In the UK there is resistance and that is to go more slowly over the longer time. Which other countries in Europe in your experience are likely to resist the move for liberalisation of postal services?

A. It is quite clear that the whole of the south of Europe is not enthusiastic about liberalising postal markets. France is the biggest defender of keeping the monopoly as long as possible. What I would like to add to this discussion is that in my opinion it is a pity that the UK has not a very specific point of view in the European discussion now because discussions are still going on within the UK as to how you would like to go ahead with further liberalisation. It would be a pity if, by the end of this year, a political compromise of any sort were to be reached which, in our opinion, would generate a standstill situation in the European Union and then perhaps a few months later you will come along with your more pronounced view as to how to go about liberalisation in the UK. That will probably affect your opinion about how it should be done in the whole of Europe as well. It is very sad that this sequence of events is going to take place. There might be the possibility that you will try to get more time from Europe to get your real view over on how to establish the future of the postal market.

Chairman

322. That is a very interesting point but I think Lord Brookeborough put one before that. The old saying "politics is the art of the possible" occurs to me. As you say, for example France was pretty well intransigent about liberalisation. By "other southern European countries" I take it you mean Spain, Italy and Portugal. What are the chances of getting this? You opened up the session by saying that, if you could sum it up, you think that the European Union is dragging its feet, that it is being delayed, and that your personal view and that or your organisation is that you want us to get through this as soon as possible and certainly to have liberalisation by 2005 and at the latest 2007. What do you think, in view of all the points and concerns that you yourself have raised, is the likelihood is of getting it by 2005?

A. 2005 may be a bit optimistic. It largely depends on the views of the UK and Germany in the political discussion in the European Union as to what is really going to happen. We have our point of view, as has the Dutch Government. Countries like Finland, Sweden and Denmark have their views. In the end, the discussion in Brussels is very strongly influenced, of course, by the decision of the bigger countries. The points of view of the UK and Germany are critical in the next period because, in the end, that will decide what is going to happen. Other countries are really already committed to a certain point of view, which is not going to change very much.

Viscount Brookeborough

323. In Holland do you as TNT deliver the mail to the door or do you use a local delivery service?
A. We deliver to every household, to the door.

324. The postman is a TNT postman?
A. Yes, but he works under the brand name PTT Post.

325. Is he the only postman who will call at the house or are there other people delivering the same type of mail to the house?
A. Yes.

326. So there are lots of postmen going along the street?
A. There are not a lot of postmen but there are delivery services, for instance from direct competitors, which have direct mail and that is open to competition. They deliver that direct mail to the household.

327. Would you see that if you got into the British market, that your postal service van would deliver to every remote farmhouse, or would you want to see a regional delivery of services? If you had them, would this not slow down the whole process and therefore targets might not be achieved, by transferring men to local delivery services? How are you going to deliver to outlying areas?
A. That depends on what kind of licensing system you are going to develop in the UK. If you have a balanced situation and you say that one part of the market is open but there is that sort of obligation if you have a licence for this amount of mail, then we will have to see whether that is a viable business.

328. So you might use local delivery services rather than having thousands of your own employees?
A. Yes, of course; you are not coming here with your own people. That would not be feasible.

329. You say in your executive summary: "There is a race against time to liberalise postal services." What is this timescale? Is that because you have got an advantage and wish to compete ahead of other people? Normally a race against time means disaster if one goes outside that timescale.
A. We mean that in the end the postal sector will be worse off if you do not liberalise the postal market because of the lack of innovation and competitiveness of the postal service compared to other means of communication. It is very important that we have been able to go through a lot of changes in the organisation without forced redundancies. That is because we took the time to change the organisation. The earlier you set clear goals for the postal organisations, the earlier they will get through the changes. That will diminish the possibility that there will be some kind of big bang in the future. Whether by very severe substitution or by suddenly opening the markets, you will have more social

8 November 2000]   Mr Nanno Aukes   *[Continued*

Viscount Brookeborough *contd.*]

problems than you have if you do it in a more gradual way.

Lord Faulkner of Worcester

330. Following on from Lord Brookeborough's question, you have painted a picture of more than one person coming to the door delivering post in a liberalised market. What arrangements do you see would be in place for the collection of post? Would you see, as in New Zealand, more than one postbox on the street corner, so that there is a red one and a blue one and you choose which postal company to use?

A. That is a possibility but I do not see it as a very desirable situation because of the lack of clarity for the public in general. Most of us want to have a very simple system. In Holland and here you have the red box and you put your mail in there.

331. You can have a liberalised system and one red box. How can I, as a customer, choose for you to deliver my mail rather than somebody else?

A. Of course you can have a universal service obligation with the incumbent operator and say that others can collect in another way. They can collect, for instance, within a shop or within a gas station. Then they do not have the publicly recognised red boxes but another system which is sufficiently clearly separate for the public. I think that is what you want to establish.

Chairman

332. That has been a very useful session. Thank you very much indeed. Before you go, is there anything you would like to say, in view of our questions? You may think we are probably barking up the wrong tree. There may be confusion about the issues?

A. The main point that I would like to stress again is that the kind of view put forward by the UK in the European discussions is very important. It would be a pity if you do not have a specific view now and accept what is happening in Europe, while you are concluding studies in the near future and perhaps reach another point of view. That would cause delay in the progress of the European Union because you are one of the key players there.

333. That is a novel description of our role in Europe, is it not!

A. If you analyse the political situation, you will come to the same conclusion.

334. Thank you very much indeed. We particularly thank you for coming all this way. It has been a most interesting session and you have been very kind in answering our questions.

A. Thank you very much. I feel honoured to be here.

WEDNESDAY 15 NOVEMBER 2000

Present:

Brooke L. (Chairman)
Brookeborough, V.
Paul, L.
Woolmer, L.

Memorandum by the Department of Trade and Industry

SUMMARY

The Government supports further liberalisation of the European postal market consistent with the universal service. In the UK we are in the process of putting in place a new regulatory framework for posts including the establishment of a new postal regulator, the Postal Services Commission. PostComm has a mandate to introduce more competition into the market and to come forward with proposals for liberalisation consistent with maintaining the universal service. The Government therefore wants to take account of PostComm's work before taking a final view on the detail of the scope and timing of future European liberalisation.

THE CURRENT EUROPEAN POSTAL SERVICES DIRECTIVE

1. Directive 97/67/EC of the European Parliament and Council of 15 December 1997 established a harmonised regulatory framework for the Community postal sector. The Directive defined the universal postal service and limited the area that could be reserved to items of domestic correspondence price at less than five times the public tariff in the first weight step of the fastest standard category provided the weight is less than 350 grams. It was estimated that the impact of these measures was to open around 3 per cent of the European postal market to competition.

2. The Directive also set in train a process of future liberalisation by providing for the European Parliament and the Council to decide on further steps to take effect with effect from 1 January 2003 and for the Commission to bring forward an enabling proposal by 31 December 1998. The Commission proposal was delayed mainly by the resignation of the previous Commission and the need for the new Commission to re-examine the issue. In March 2000 the European Council of the Heads of State and Government, meeting in Lisbon, gave impetus to the process through a commitment to speeding up utility liberalisation in Europe including postal services.

THE COMMISSION PROPOSALS

3. The measures contained in the current proposal provide for further and continuing opening of the Community postal markets in a step by step approach contemplated by Article 7 of the current Postal Services Directive. The draft directive provides for further opening of the European postal services market in at least two further stages.

4. The first stage aims to reduce, from 1 January 2003, the current weight and price limit of the reserved area to 50 grams (or two and a half times the fastest standard tariff for the first weight step) for all ordinary domestic correspondence including incoming cross-border correspondence and direct mail. Outgoing cross-border mail and some express mail would be excluded from the reserved area. The Commission has estimated that the effect of this stage will be to open up around 16 per cent of current market share to competition. The next stage would then be a further review leading to further proposals from the Commission and decisions by the Council and the Parliament about the further steps to be applied with effect from 1 January 2007.

5. The Draft Directive also provides that:

— the principles of non-discrimination and transparency be applied whenever universal services providers apply special tariffs;

— rules be adopted by regulatory authorities to ensure that there is no subsidisation of services outside the reserved area from revenues from services in the reserved area except to the extent to which it is shown to be strictly necessary to fulfil specific universal service obligations in the competitive area;

— the procedures for dealing with users' complaints are applied to postal services outside the universal service;

The current situation in the United Kingdom

6. The British Post Office monopoly has been set at £1 since 1981. This limit was modified slightly last year, to also limit the weight to 350 grams in line with the last Postal Service Directive.

7. Legislation has recently been adopted (The Postal Services Act 2000) to establish a new regulatory framework and a regulator, the Postal Services Commission (PostComm), with responsibility for ensuring the universal service. Under this new framework, the Post Office will no longer have a monopoly but will be licensed to operate in a "reserved area". This reserved area, which is broadly similar in scope to the Post Office monopoly area will be regulated by PostComm who will be able to license other players in the market consistent with its universal service obligations.

8. PostComm has a mandate to introduce more competition into the postal services market and to come forward with proposals on the future liberalisation of the market. It is not constrained in what it can consider. However, in making recommendations it has an over-riding priority to ensure that the universal service is maintained. It will also look at the costs of maintaining the universal service.

9. PostComm is expected to come forward with recommendations around the spring of next year once it has had an opportunity to consult with interested parties and do the necessary analysis. Clearly there is a need to correlate the results of the Postal Service Commission's work with decisions in Europe. PostComm's full recommendations will not be available until well into 2001, whilst discussions on the draft Directive will begin at Ministerial level at the October meeting of the Telecommunications Council. This process has been made clear to both the European Commission and the Presidency.

QUESTIONS RAISED BY THE COMMITTEE: PRELIMINARY REMARKS

What benefits are likely to result from the proposed liberalisation measures?

10. The Government strongly supports liberalisation consistent with the universal service. In general terms liberalisation promotes competition and greater choice and keener pricing for consumers. That is why the Government has given a mandate to the Postal Services Commission to look at how to introduce more competition into the postal services market in the UK.

11. However, whilst individual countries may liberalise unilaterally, in an increasing international postal market it is important that there is a coherent and co-ordinataed approach to liberalisation across Europe to ensure a level playing field so that markets are not distorted.

12. Liberalisation encourages greater innovation, productivity and growth of post office business. This is particularly significant as the Post Office positions itself to compete in the global market place. It is vital to the future of the Post Office that it repositions itself as a major player in the global distribution market.

Analysis shows that it is only by developing internationally, to address the needs of its business customers, that the Post Office can continue to maintain a strong domestic network. The pressures imposed by competition will help to prepare the Post Office for that challenge and the liberalisation in other European markets can provide opportunities to which a competitive Post Office will be well-placed to respond.

13. It is important that for both the Post Office, and for other postal companies, that there is a level of certainty and predictability in the market. That is why the Government welcomes the overall framework proposed by the European Commission to make a simple reduction in the price/weight threshold to apply from 2003 and to then set a timetable for further decision-making shortly thereafter. We believe it is critical for the definition of the reserved area to be "clear-cut" and easily understood so that it can be simply implemented and monitored and for there to be an agreed timetable for decision-making.

14. It is also imperative for consumers that the universal postal service at a uniform tariff is maintained. We have asked the Postal Services Commission to make recommendations how best to liberalise the market in order to deliver the benefits of liberalisation whilst maintaining the universal service at a uniform tariff.

15. The postal sector differs in some important respects from other utilities. We all now understand how to liberalise monopolies with high cost infrastructures that can be separated out and made a platform for competition. But liberalising posts while ensuring the universal service is maintained, is much less well-charted territory. That is why we welcome the European Commission's step by step approach, and a further review of the sector in 2004 before deciding how to proceed to the next stage. This provides a necessary control to ensure that the benefits of liberalisation can be measured and assured.

16. The Commission proposal allows for direct mail to continue to be reserved at the same limits as all other correspondence. Whilst there are arguments in favour of freeing such mail to competition, liberalisation by content would introduce additional monitoring requirements and greater legal uncertainty. We therefore welcome the Commission's proposal on this aspect.

17. The proposal to liberalise out-going cross-border mail is, so far as the United Kingdom is concerned, simply regularising a *de facto* situation and is therefore establishing a greater level of legal certainty.

Conversely in-coming cross-border mail remains within the scope of the reserved area and avoids practical difficulties of regulation that would be associated with verifying origin.

What problems could result from the proposed liberalisation, particularly in terms of maintenance of a universal service with an affordable and uniform tariff structure?

18. The Directive proposes to introduce a new definition of "special services" which represent "added value" enhancements to postal services, which are then to be taken outside the reserved area. Express services are specifically targeted in the current proposal. It is clear that further work needs to be undertaken to the definition of such services to ensure that this element does not put at risk the legal certainty provided by the weight/price definition of the reserved area nor used as a device to render the reserved area void. (In the UK, any postal service which costs more than £1 or weighs more than 350gms is outside the reserved area, and such a service whether express or not can be offered by any competitor).

19. Whilst the proposal to continue to define the reserved area by price/weight is consistent with the current UK situation the levels proposed do not correspond with the current tariff structure of the Post Office. In the UK the first weight step for letters is 60 grams for which consumers pay 27 pence (much lower than the sixty-seven pence allowed for 50 grams in the European proposal). Most other European countries have a 20 gram first step with a next step of 50 grams and in many countries postage is much more expensive than it is in the UK.

20. Concerns have been expressed that the proposal is too rapid a reduction in the reserved area (the European Commission proposals are estimated to open some 16 per cent of the European market to competition). The Post Office has told us it believes there is a risk that the impact on its profits will be significant as competitors move quickly into the more profitable end of the markets and that the resulting pressure will impact on its ability to maintain a uniform tariff. The CWU has also expressed the concern that the proposals pose a threat to the Post Office network and to jobs. These are issues that the Postal Services Commission must address in its analysis.

Are there any measures not identified in the Commission's proposals which will help to secure the Community's stated aims for postal services?

21. The Postal Services Commission will want to look at whether the EU proposals will lead to equivalence across the member states. In the UK postal services outside the reserved area operate in a completely open market. It is only when operators want to offer services within the reserved area that they are subject to regulation. EU legislation allows for licensing regimes outside the reserved area and there should be consistency between the two approaches.

22. It has also been suggested that Compensation Funds could be introduced to support the universal service and current European legislation provides for this. the Government is not convinced about the practicality of such schemes in the postal sector. The new Postal Services Act 2000 makes no provision for extended licensing outside the reserved area or for compensation schemes.

September 2000

Examination of Witness

MR ALAN JOHNSON, a Member of the House of Commons, Minister for Competitiveness, DTI, called in and examined

Chairman

335. Good morning, Minister. Thank you for finding the time to come personally before us and thank you also for the two papers* that we have had from the Department. If I may, I would like to open up with a question which does pick up on the two papers. Could you summarise the Government's views about the Commission's proposals on the liberalisation of postal services, as there appears to have been some change between the original written submission to this Committee, which said the Government was awaiting the outcome of the review of liberalisation by the Postal Services next year, and more recent views which have been generally more hostile to the Commission's proposals. We did notice the difference.

(*Mr Johnson*) First of all, good morning. It is good to be back in front of your noble Lords. I was here about six years ago in a different capacity. Derek Davis is with me, who heads up the department dealing with the issue at the DTI. We support the phased liberalisation of postal services consistent with retaining a universal service at a uniform tariff. We think there are all kinds of opportunities and enhancements for customers through liberalisation. That is the route we want to go down but we do not want to jeopardise universal service at uniform tariff. In terms of your point about the Postal Services

---

*Explanatory Memorandum 10544/00 dated 9 October 2000, attached to COM(2000) 319 final: A proposed European Parliament and Council Directive COM(2000) of 30 May 2000 amending Directive 97/67/EC with regard to the furrher opening to competition of Community postal services.

Chairman *contd.*]

Commission, the regulator, we have of course domestically asked the regulator to look at what is now called the reserved area, a limit to the reserved area, and that is a piece of work that we do not expect to finish until around the spring of 2001. It would obviously be sensible to take their views on this whole issue and we were rather hoping that they might have completed their work by the time we came to a crunch decision on the Commission's proposals. That might still be the case. However, it became obvious to us as things moved along—there is an orientation debate on this on 22 December at the Telecommunications Council—that we actually could be required to deal with this in advance of the regulator completing the very substantial piece of work that they are doing for the domestic reserved area. We will probably need—in fact, we will need, and we have asked the regulator to give us—an indicative feel for this. You say our position has changed. The only thing that has changed is there was a debate going on—the Post Office, the NFPC and CWU, all the interested parties, were generating about this—and we tended to agree that a move down to 150 grams we did not feel would jeopardise the universal service at uniform tariff; indeed we were proposing to do that domestically last year. So there has been a fair bit of research and work on what effect that would have. All we have done in that respect is to say that we have to consider it in the context of the whole of the package, and we want to take PSC's advice on whether we could go further, but our view is that a move to 150 grams would meet our objectives; that is, would not damage universal service at uniform tariff. We agree the overall framework as acceptable as a basis for discussion. We agree that the reserved area ought to be defined by price and weight. One of the major issues I was dealing with before this committee a few years back, was whether it was possible to define it by content and there were all kinds of problems with that, so we think the Commission is right to suggest that the reserved area should be defined by price and weight and not by content. We are concerned about the proposals on special services—and I am sure we will talk about that some more. We think it is appropriate to take the first step in 2003, then to have a good look at the effects of that, before moving to the next phase in 2007. That encapsulates our general approach, and, with all due respect, I do not think it has changed. Perhaps we have clarified one particular issue, which, in response to the debate, was: did we think a move to 150 grams—which is what the Post Office has suggested—would damage the universal service at uniform tariff? No, we do not.

336. We felt it had changed. We felt that the DTI position was quite open in the first instance and broadly supportive of what the Commission was seeking. Maybe we misunderstood that. Certainly we would like to get our hands on as much information as we could about what would lead to real problems in maintaining the universal service. Are you saying that 50 grams would damage the universal service?

A. We would like to see some evidence on this. Our major approach to this is that no-one has actually looked at this with any proper analysis. Given that our absolute prime concern is to maintain universal service at a uniform tariff, there is a big difference there. Telecom has had a universal service with no uniform tariff. It is very difficult to find an equivalent area which has been liberalised where they had this, we think, crucial issue for the British public—one which we have just recently enshrined in law for the first time. Universal service at uniform tariff is now in the Postal Services Act. It is called the Rowland Hill principle. We exported it to the rest of the world, because it came in in 1840 with the Penny Post, and it had the biggest effect on making postal services accessible and affordable for millions of people. We will not damage that. The argument to move to 50 grams. We believe that we are moving towards complete liberalisation in the postal market but we have to do it very carefully, we have to do it in a phased way and we have to be sure at each step along the road that we do not make it more expensive for people to post or receive letters in rural and remote areas in this country. When you ask about 50 grams, the Postal Services Commission for the first time are there—you know, rather than people stick fingers in the air and take guesses at this—to carry out a proper analysis. We hope they can give us some indication of their very broad thinking on this before we go to the Telecommunications Council in December, but we certainly think that when they have completed their body of work next spring we will have a far better feel for how the limit of the reserved area can be set whilst protecting the universal service at uniform tariff.

337. I think the Committee would share all your concerns about protecting the universal service and the price of it as well. This Committee, however, did a review four years ago, when the first proposals for liberalisation came out of the Commission, and we wrote a very glowing report of the performance of the British Royal Mail by comparison with some competitors in Europe.

A. Yes.

338. The evidence we have been taking seems to indicate that there is now not quite the same satisfaction with the performance of the Post Office, notwithstanding some very substantial amounts of investment, capital investments, which have taken place. There is a view around that, whilst we have to protect rural areas without any question, the performance particularly in the major cities, some of the major cities, is far lower than one would expect of the Royal Mail and targets have not been hit. The view has been expressed by some of the people giving evidence to us that competition is the only way in which performance and efficiency will be raised within the Post Office and that the 50 gram weight limit, whilst it may create some problems, is the price which ought to be paid to raise the level of performance. How would you respond to that?

A. I remember 1996 very well. That was when I appeared before you in a different capacity. Although I am here now as a minister, I can be absolutely consistent with what I said then. As I remember it, it was that the UK Post Office did have a good quality of service. We were at the forefront. The British Post Office introduced not just quality of service targets, but independently measured before anybody else was doing it. We had a 150 gram monopoly limit when the Dutch had 500 grams and

Chairman contd.]

the Germans had six tonnes or something—I cannot remember, but something extraordinary. I jest. It was about 750 grams.

339. They are now down to 200 grams.

A. Yes. And quality of service was good. But what I said in 1996 and what I say now is that the UK Post Office fell behind because there was an absolute dead hand placed upon any movement at all for almost 10 years. The previous government announced in around 1991 that there would be a review of the Post Office. They put forward proposals in a Green Paper; those proposals disappeared. There were commitments to introduce a regulator in 1992; it did not happen. There were pleas by the Post Office for government to allow them to enter into joint ventures; those requests were rejected, even though they were allowed under the legislation at the time. There was a period of hiatus. Nothing happened, apart from the Post Office having to pay back, in external finance limits, £1 billion in three years in the mid-nineties. And then nothing happened again when we came into government, because we needed to review the situation and look at all the options and not rule anything out, so we went through a process of review again, that ended with the Postal Services Act. That has now gone through the House. At last we have the prospect of genuine commercial financial freedom for the Post Office. But look at what has happened to everyone else in the meantime. The Germans have come straight from a kind of civil service to complete liberalisation in a very short period of time. Lack of investment problems, the problems created by that period, have meant that the Post Office had fallen behind on quality of service. But it is a fair point; it is not central to this issue. This issue here is: if we went to Brussels and agreed to reduce the monopoly level—a huge step (you know, the basic step rate for a 27p first class letter, or a 19p second class letter, is 60 grams, to bring it down to 50 grams) on the basis of no proper analysis as to how that would affect the universal service at a uniform tariff, would be foolhardy. So we are being very cautious here. We think it needs to be phased. We will take advice from the Commission. That is their job now and we are very pleased that the Commission has been set up, the regulator has been set up, but we will not take any risks with something that we believe the public in this country, and the public in lots of other parts of Europe, really cherish; that is the fact that you pay the same price whether you are posting from Islington to Westminster or from Penzance to Glasgow.

Lord Woolmer of Leeds

340. You said that there had been a fair bit of research done on the effect of a move to 150 grams. I would like to discuss that a little bit more, if I may, but, first of all, has there been equivalent research done by your department on a move to 50 grams? In other words, you said there is an awful lot of analysis done, but have we done it in this country?

A. No. The analysis that was done on moving to 150 grams, in the end we decided we should not move ahead on, because we were appointing the regulator. Why bring down a monopoly level from a pound just as you appoint a regulator to advise us on where the monopoly level should be? We had done some research and the research put through a couple of models as to how it would affect traffic—and we are talking about the domestic situation, we are not talking about Europe, of course, we are talking purely about in the UK—and that led us to believe that bringing the monopoly limit down to 150 grams would not damage universal services at a uniform tariff. In terms of the work that has been done on 50 grams, that of course is the work that the Commission are doing. Unlike most other regulators, where their principal task is to encourage competition, in the Postal Services Act that is one of the Commissions' duties, but their principal, number one duty is to protect the universal service at uniform tariff. That is precisely the work that they are doing. I think it would be wrong of us to duplicate their work in the DTI.

Chairman

341. We are talking about the Postal Services Commission as distinct from the Brussels' Commission?

A. Sorry, yes. Perhaps it would help if I called them PostComm, which is their shortened title.

Lord Woolmer of Leeds

342. If, as you have expressed it today, you are very clear that the move to 50 grams would threaten universal services obligation at a uniform tariff structure, that is a very clear view—

A. To 150 grams?

343. Down to 50 grams. You said 150 grams would not threaten it, as I understood it, but the move to 50 grams would. In effect, you put two points to us. One was that it would be premature to move to 50 grams rather than 150 grams because of the PostComm position, but at other times I heard words from you which implied that, whatever PostComm said, in your view a move to 50 grams would be premature and would be threatening. That is the impression I gained.

A. Let me try to correct the impression. My duty is to ensure that we maintain universal service at uniform tariff. I simply do not know, I am cautious, about going below 150 grams. We are relaxed about going to 150 grams; we are extremely cautious about going beyond that because no evidence exists. We have asked the Commission for advice. Their advice may be that 50 grams is fine and that will very much inform our approach to this whole issue.

Chairman

344. This is PostComm?

A. This is PostComm. If PostComm say, "We have looked at this and our indicative view is that you can be quite relaxed about a move to 50 grams," that will be the most important input into our discussion.

15 November 2000] MR ALAN JOHNSON, MP *[Continued*

Lord Woolmer of Leeds

345. Effectively, the analysis of the impact in this country of a move to 50 grams, from the Government's perspective now, is best known by PostComm, and that we will look forward to at a very early stage. What is the Department's estimate of the cost of the universal service obligation?
A. The cost of it?

346. Yes. There must be a view in the department.
A. I am not sure that we have a view of what the cost is, in the sense that if it did not exist ... I think to calculate the cost of it you would have to be able confidently to predict what tariffs Royal Mail would charge if they were free to introduce zonal pricing. You would have to know, if the universal service at uniform tariff went, that it would cost £10 to send a letter from London to Aberdeen or that Royal Mail would only charge 6p for a delivery across London. We do not know. We do not have that kind of information. The Post Office probably could make a stab at it, but ...
Chairman: They have. They say their current profits of £300 million will disappear. Based on that is, presumably, the cost of maintaining the universal service and the tariff at the present rate.

Lord Woolmer of Leeds

347. When the Commission were before us they gave an estimate of £50 million.
A. With respect, I think that is a slightly different thing. What the Royal Mail is saying is that if you went to 50 grams and they were to maintain a universal service at a uniform tariff, that would be their profits gone. The question was: What is the cost to them of universal service at a uniform tariff? I think that could only be gauged by some very rough and ready figures as to how they could react to that by moving into zonal pricing which would show the true cost of operating a uniform tariff.

348. Presumably a view on the cost of the universal service obligation with a uniform tariff structure would be pretty central ultimately to a judgment about the degree of liberalisation and so on, because, in the face of competition, anybody being obliged to provide the universal service obligation effectively and quite properly—and I totally agree with you—is providing effectively a cross-subsidy somewhere along the line to ensure that we have got the proper universal mail that we all want and support.
A. Yes.

349. So, in a sense, it is not a hostile thing to say to the postal service or to the Department that there is a cost. Being clear what that is, is very important, because, the further liberalisation goes, the more explicit and transparent a view has to be on that because someone has to meet that cost eventually: any competition coming in presumably could well have some obligations put upon them. I just wonder whether the Department has done any work on this, because the two estimates we have been given before us on this inquiry—and it was for the cost of the USO—are £300 million by the Post Office and £50 million by the Commission. That is so big that it must be central to the difference about where the degree of liberalisation might properly fall.

A. Yes.

350. That is my point.
A. That is for PostComm to assess. That is the major piece of work they are undertaking. I know from talking to Graham Corbett last week that they are commissioning a major piece of research on this whole area—and it will be very welcome because there has been an absence of that so far. Within that they will assess the costs. The only other point I would make on that is that there have been many debates over the years about competition. I think the one thing it is fair to say is that there are not many people, if any, willing to move into competing with the Post Office on universal service, John O'Groats to Lands End. TNT made a suggestion some years back that there should be a duopoly: provided they were guaranteed half the volume, then they could manage it. Everyone else who I think this committee have met, and a committee in Another Place have met, has said: no, it is not commercially viable. So I think we know that much.

351. Linking that to something you said to us earlier in this committee, where you said that you believe we are, by implication, eventually moving to complete liberalisation.
A. Yes.

352. How do you think in your mind complete liberalisation could ever be consistent with universal service obligation at a uniform tariff? I hear you say that the Government does see that eventually complete liberalisation is likely to happen. How can that be consistent with universal service obligation at a uniform tariff? You have just said you cannot see anybody actually wanting to compete with and provide that as well as the Royal Mail. How can you get competition?
A. People argued that they would need a monopoly of 500 grams otherwise the postal service would collapse. It has moved down from 500 grams and it has not collapsed. I have always argued (in my previous capacity and in this capacity) that no-one is interested in a monopoly. What they want, what the public wants, is universal service at a uniform tariff. Any monopoly limit should only be enough, just sufficient, to protect that. I think if you move gradually down this route, if at every step of the way you have a good look around and the Post Office and the major postal operators in Europe have a chance to adapt to the new situation, there are new opportunities that are opened up by liberalisation, but they take a time, for them to be able to get into those kind of markets and take full advantage of them. So I think if it is approached gradually, just as gradually we have come down from ... You know, I joked, but some people would have put a seven tonne limit on monopoly if you had given them the chance a few years ago. But gradually postal operators are coming to terms with this liberalisation, but it does have to be a gradual process and it does need to ensure that you do not move too far too quickly, simply because, as President Nixon said, once the toothpaste is out of the tube, you cannot put it back in again. You cannot move to 50 grams and then say, "Oh, we have damaged the universal service. We could do that in five years time, but let us go back up to ..." Impossible. Once you do it, there is no going back.

Chairman

353. So what you call complete liberalisation would actually be lowering the limit until such point as there would still be a monopoly at some level but the monopoly was sufficiently protected to be able to say fund the universal service obligation—
A. We might move to no monopoly. We could well move to no monopoly at all. I think liberalisation is moving in that area. Domestically, we have said that the Postal Services Commission should continue to look at bringing the reserved area level down.

Viscount Brookeborough

354. Good morning, Mr Johnson. I welcome the fact that you put at the top of your priorities the protection of the customer. I live in a rather outlying area in Northern Ireland, so I appreciate that. You talk about full liberalisation, the Post Office does, and so does Patricia Hewitt in a letter she wrote to Lord Tordoff: "... with several Member States calling for a target date for full liberalisation ..." and you are now talking about there being no monopoly. Are you saying that full liberalisation is with the 50 gram reserve rate or are you saying with no monopoly whatsoever?
A. I am saying eventually. I agree with the Post Office and most other analysts on this that we will move to full liberalisation (that is, no reserved area) eventually, down the road. It is how quickly we move to that position. The fear is that if you try to move to that position too quickly, then the whole thing would fall apart, you would regret the decisions that you had taken. So we are in favour of phased, gradual liberalisation. On the move to 50 grams, as I say, if the advice of the Postal Services Commission to us is that there is no problem with that, that will be the most important input into our deliberations because that is what we set up PostComm to do. That is why we looked very carefully at the composition of it— you know, it is not one single regulator, as with Telecom, etc, because there was some criticism when the regulation in other sectors was reviewed that one person just becomes a focal point, that it is better to have a committee. So we are in new ground here and there is no point setting up the commission up and ignoring their advice.

355. Obviously you are well aware of the state of affairs in the Netherlands and Sweden, because they have produced their information on it. Again Patricia Hewitt says that "joint discussions with Member States were divided". Who are the others who are sympathetic towards what we believe and what you believe and to what extent are they so?
A. The first point about the evidence from places like Sweden, New Zealand and the Netherlands, if the argument is that that proves that you can actually liberalise completely and keep a uniform tariff, it does not, I am afraid. When the Postal Services Commission have looked at this in detail, we will get it chapter and verse, but I know from my previous experience that in New Zealand, once the changes started, people living in outlying rural areas had to pay $80 a year to get mail delivered to their door. In Sweden they do not have a uniform tariff any more; they have zonal pricing. In some other countries the moves towards liberalisation have meant an increase in tariffs. I think the Post Office make the point about the Swedish Post Office. In New Zealand there was an initial huge increase in tariffs. In Canada there was a change of government—it was one of the major issues about liberalisation leading to the closure of rural post offices. And yet there are other countries ... I mean, in Holland, the Netherlands, that is something that we ought to watch and admire. It depends what postal service you want. In this country we have two deliveries. There is nowhere else outside Central Paris that has two deliveries. In Sweden they do not deliver on Saturdays, they deliver Monday to Friday. In Holland, if your front door is more than 30 metres from the street, you have to pay to provide a postbox because they will not come and deliver to your door. It has to be a proper analysis of what we define as universal service, which is to the door. That is the first point. In terms of where the different member states stand, I do not think I am really equipped to do that. It is moving all the time, there are working groups going on all the time. Broadly, when this started, the Dutch and the Germans, the Finns and the Swedes (Finland, of course, is another liberalising country) were in favour of liberalisation.; the French and the Italians were not. We feel that actually we should take a very moderate view on this. We could actually be conciliators here. We were in the forefront of liberalisation, we have a very good record on these issues, and so we are careful not to fall into camps, but that was generally where it stood at the start of this. How that is developing through the working groups, I am not too sure. (*Note received*) Helpfully, a note has arrived, delivered first class, that tells me the up-to-date scores in the Eurovision contest! Pro liberalisation are Finland, Sweden, Denmark, Germany, Netherlands and Austria. Anti—and that is probably not anti liberalisation, that is anti 50 grams—are France, Greece, Luxembourg, Spain, Portugal and Italy. And in mid position are Ireland, UK and Belgium.

356. Can I ask a quick question about the price of stamps. In Sweden and the other countries which are liberalised, either their performance has gone down or they have increased price rather dramatically. When we had the Post Office here I think they indicated, first of all, that if we increased the price by a penny (which after all is not 25 or 30 per cent), although initially it would cause a lot of screaming and yelling, the use of the postal service would continue to rise and that would actually generate somewhere around £150 million, which is midway between what Brussels says it would cost to keep the universal services package and what the Post Office says it would cost. What is your view to having ultimately to have a compromise and working out what the cost will be of producing an increase?
A. It sounds messy to me, but, returning again to PostComm, their role under the legislation in this country is to deal with tariffs. They will in future set the tariff structure. The Government will have nothing to do with it whatsoever. It is very difficult, of course, for the Post Office to raise the price of a stamp by less than a penny—that is one of their dilemmas. But that, thank you very much, is an arm's length relationship now and PostComm will decide on the tariff structure. I have absolutely no doubt that, in looking at the advice they are going to give to

Viscount Brookeborough contd.]

us about this proposal from the European Commission, as opposed to what they are doing domestically, they will also look at this question of what impact it is likely to have on tariffs.

Chairman

357. If I may pick up on one of your earlier answers. You said you have to look at the totality of the service which is provided in this country and you mentioned the second class mail. We questioned the Post Office about the extent to which the consumer appeared in their order of priorities. The chief executive conceded that perhaps the consumer's interest was not as high as he would wish it to be and they were striving towards making sure it went to the top of the list. Are you sure, is the Post Office sure, or will it be the responsibility of PostComm to assess the total package and gauge the views of the consumer—for example, on whether they want a second class post or whether they would not prefer to see better performance by resources being focused solely on first class mail, one mail only? Is that your responsibility or the Post Office's or would it be PostComm's?

A. It is certainly not my responsibility. It is a combination of the Post Office's responsibility, obviously, but it is PostComm and, of course, the new revamped consumer body that we have set up, the CCPS. POUNC* have done a good job with very limited resources since 1969 when the Post Office became a corporation—but it has been very limited resources. We are replacing POUNC with the Consumer Council for Postal Services (CCPS) from next year, it comes in with the Act, and they will have a much more rigorous role there. There are references to their role throughout the legislation and they will have better resources to deal with their task.

358. Will there be greater opportunities for the consumer's voice to be heard?

A. Yes, absolutely. That is the whole point of setting up CCPS. That is not to say that POUNC did a bad job, but with limited resources it was very difficult for them to really dedicate the time and effort required to get a proper feel for consumer concerns. We think the CCPS will be able to do that. We have appointed a chief executive already and he is confident that they will be able to perform a much better role on behalf of consumers.

Lord Paul

359. First of all, it is very nice to see a minister who is so knowledgeable about the industry.

A. I looked behind me then!

360. One question, not relevant to this inquiry but just for my own knowledge: What is the role of Minister of Competitiveness?

A. That is a good question. It is a generic title that was dreamed up for me. My responsibilities are the Post Office, employment relations, and large chunks of British industry (aerospace, bio-technology, chemicals, automotive). My job consists of jobs that two different ministers were doing before that were pushed into one, and then, because no-one could think of a title that married up those three different areas, Minister for Competitiveness came out. It is difficult to say and it also makes it seem as if I am responsible for almost everything in British industry, because everything is about competitiveness.

361. Thank you very much. Because competitiveness is the most talked about programme nowadays, I was wondering about that. The UK has, over 20 years, been in the forefront of liberalisation, privatisation, etc, but one gets the feeling that in the Post Office we are dragging our feet. Do you believe that?

A. Yes, to a certain extent. I think it is part of this hiatus I was talking about. This is not particularly a party-political point, it is just fact that in the 1992 manifesto of the party that came into government, two things were mentioned about the Post Office: we will introduce a regulator and we will reduce the monopoly limit to closer to the price of a first class stamp. Neither of those two things happened. Issues that were not in the manifesto were pursued but not the two actual issues, the concrete proposals, that were contained in the manifesto. So nothing happened. The regulator could have been set up a while ago, the monopoly limit could have been looked at much sooner, and, perhaps more importantly, the Post Office could have had the commercial freedom and financial freedom that it was crying out for when five of its major competitors in Europe were camped out in offices within a mile of this building, picking up UK postings and taking them overseas—and not just posted but printed overseas. So, yes, we have fallen behind. The other point, as my officials reminded me this morning, is that liberalisation in every other area, whether Telecom, gas, electricity or energy, has always been approached very, very carefully, with a great deal of analysis and thought about each step along the way. I think that reinforces my message that that has to be our approach to this issue as well.

362. The Government has given the Post Office the freedom to compete outside its traditional areas. Is it only fair that the competition should be allowed to compete in the Post Office's core market?

A. Yes. Absolutely. That is absolutely true. Of course the Post Office do have obligations that do not apply to the other, I think, 4,000 postal operators/couriers in this country; that is, the Post Office have to deliver 27 million addresses six days a week. We have just enshrined that in the legislation as well. They have to do that at a uniform tariff. Whereas other parcel couriers can decide whether they want to go to the Shetland Islands or not, the Post Office cannot, they have to. That is part of their universal service obligation. Anything up to 20 kilograms they have to deliver anywhere in the country. So that has to be borne in mind, and that of course is what the reserved area is about and that is what some of the other issues, like VAT exemption, are about. Having said that, there is no reason why the Post Office should not face competition for the benefit of the consumer, for the benefit of the industry, and that is why, of course, the Postal Services Act requires operators within the reserved area to seek a licence.

---

*Post Office Users' National Council.

[*Lord Paul contd.*]

The Post Office will have to seek a licence, but PostComm can grant licences to other operators within that reserved area if they feel that is necessary. So the whole premise of the Postal Services Act is based on very healthy competition but protection for the parts of the Post Office that the British public really do—and this is not an exaggeration—cherish. It is protection of those aspects. In a way it is the British public seeing change but not change—you know, lots of changes going on commercially but to them it is the same, reliable, consistent Post Office on the corner and deliveries coming through the door, twice a day in most areas.

363. The unions, in their evidence, expressed concern that with liberalisation they have job losses. One has sympathy for that view but if you are creating competitors they will create new jobs.

A. Yes. The unions obviously have a concern about jobs. There are something like 1.3 million people in Europe employed in the postal sector, but the evidence shows there has been a slight reduction. I think it is in the evidence that we have submitted that there has been a slight reduction in the overall number of jobs in Europe: some reduction in Germany, some reduction in Sweden. In Holland, 412,000 extra staff in the postal service. I think actually there are huge opportunities here, you are quite right: moving into other areas will develop new areas of work. My view is that there is a core workforce which you really you cannot go much below. You might send lots of messages by E-mail—new technology is going to impact upon postal services—but, as long as you are delivering to 27 million addresses every day, it is difficult to think of any way to do that other than physically—you know, there is a hard core of jobs there, and I think the postal services are much better off in that sense. It is a labour intensive industry in terms of delivery and there is very little prospect of that changing.

Chairman

364. I will conclude with a couple of final points, one linking to the unions' evidence to us. Where we have seen liberalisation taking place in other industries and, indeed, in the public service, where we have seen more modern management techniques being introduced and changes, for example, in the civil service, we have seen a very significant shift towards more casual staff and part-time staff being engaged. But there was very strong resistance from the postal unions, when they gave evidence to us, to any move in that direction taking place, even in the context of liberalisation. Do you not agree that as part of the move towards liberalisation there will have to be more flexibility in this area than has been shown so far?—especially if the second post disappeared.

A. Can I say, first of all, there is no evidence at all about the second delivery disappearing. There is nothing that I have seen that suggests that the Post Office are interested in moving down that route.

365. I was suggesting about consumer needs as distinct from the Post Office.

A. In 32 years in the business I have never heard consumer representatives say that. It is quite the opposite: consumer representatives want to hang on to the second delivery rather than get rid of it. But, leaving that aside, I really do not want to get into the area of industrial relations in the Post Office or the staffing levels of the Post Office. It is very tempting for me to do so—given my previous background, I would probably never shut up and we would be here for the next hour and a half—but it is genuinely a matter for the Post Office and the unions to work out. Maybe five years ago, or whenever it was you had your last report, four years ago, ministers might have been tempted down that route. Now that we have established an Act that says there is going to be an arm's length relationship, I think it would be wrong of me to get involved in those kind of areas.

366. Finally, coming back to the core of our inquiry, which is the proposal from Brussels, you have indicated that you think there may be some changes in December, when decisions may be reached. Would you care to speculate on where we might end up in December?

A. I think it is doubtful that there will be decisions. There is an orientation debate, but there is a working party going on constantly, looking at the sort of technical aspects of this, so I think it has become more unlikely that there will actually be any decisions made. I would not like to speculate, other than to say that I think the broad parameter of the proposals particularly ... I know it is something we have not talked about in great depth, but particularly the acceptance that the monopoly should be defined by price and weight—which was a big issue over the last five/six years—I think they have come up with an acceptable proposal. I know it is a big issue—and there are one or two issues on the side (like special services, etc)—but I think it will come down to, yes, we should liberalise. There is no-one arguing against liberalisation. It is what level we go to. It will be that which causes the major debates, not the other issues like incoming cross-border mail, like direct mail, etc. There is going to be a very healthy focus on this one particular issue.

367. Thank you for coming in and giving us your time. I think you will be comforted to know that much of the evidence we have heard so far, both from the Post Office and from the unions, is right in accord with what the Government has been advocating too. What our committee will come up with, I do not know.

A. I am not sure if I am pleased about that or worried. Thank you very much.

Memorandum by the Free and Fair Post Initiative (FFPI)

1. Summary

The FFPI is a voluntary, independent, not-for-profit initiative. Membership is open to all persons and entities that agree to the terms of reference. The terms of reference set out that the FFPI strives to promote liberalisation of postal services and fair competition in the postal sector.

The postal sector, like other delivery services, is increasingly recognised as a key industry for the internal market in Europe. When the EU leaders met in Lisbon earlier this year they agreed to speed up liberalisation in post, gas, electricity and transport.

The FFPI believes that the EC and the EU Member States within their respective spheres should set the postal industry's growth potential free through full liberalisation. Increased economic freedom in the postal sector will spur innovation, increase choice for consumers and lead to more jobs. Without liberalisation, outdated economic structures will remain and the Industry will not be modernised. The FFPI will seek to ensure that the EU carries out its pledge and creates a liberalised internal market for postal services in 2007 at the latest where customer's interests are put first.

FFPI believes that the USO should be maintained and should be continuously reviewed at Member State level in order to correspond to evolving consumer preference. The FFPI also believes that it is not necessary to maintain letter monopolies in order to perform the USO. The USO should not be used incorrectly as argument against liberalisation in the debate.

The FFPI supports, as a first step towards liberalisation, the Commission proposal to lower the monopoly for the reserved area to 50 grams, which would in fact only open up 23 per cent of the postal market revenues to competition. Should a 150 grams limit be retained, as proposed by some opponents to the Commission proposal, this would only open up less than 10 per cent of the postal market revenues and would not create the necessary dynamics to modernise and improve postal services.

The European Commission has rightly concluded that the developments in the market for postal services in recent years has lead to increased competition concerns and to increased distortions of the internal market. Certain postal operators have moved significantly to make acquisitions and to expand internationally in competitive sectors.

Current EC rules for the Postal Industry are insufficient and unclear and make the infringement of EC competition and internal market rules a possibly lucrative alternative for postal operators. New rules on liberalisation must be accompanied by clearer and more stringent rules on what the Member States and postal operators can and cannot do.

The FFPI believes that the increased competition concerns in the postal sector need to be tackled at European level and if the EC fails to do so, we risk a situation where public postal monopolies will have been replaced with private postal monopolies. Liberalisation will have failed if such a scenario becomes reality.

2. About the FFPI

The FFPI was officially launched on 23 October 2000 in Brussels. FFPI is a voluntary, independent, not-for-profit, initiative and does not receive any subsidies from any governmental body and it relies on membership dues and user fees to cover its operating expenses.

The current membership is composed of European and national business associations and individual companies from several EU Member States and industries. The members of FFPI mainly represent users of postal services although some members are active in the postal or neighbouring sectors.

The FFPI strives to promote liberalisation of Postal services and fair competition in the Postal sector. To this end, FFPI identifies and seeks to shed light on potential breaches of EU Internal market rules and anomalies on the market. The sphere of the FFPI's interests also includes services that are ancilliary to Postal services, such as communication, transport and logistic. The initiative recognises that the USO is vital in order to guarantee the supply of postal services for the benefit of consumers.

Membership in FFPI is open to all persons and entities that agree to the terms of reference.

3. Postal Services—The Ugly Duckling of EC Liberalisation

Regulators in Europe have repeatedly been forced to consider whether so called natural monopolies are the best way to serve consumers and society as a whole.

Natural monopolies were created when governments assumed responsibility for infrastructure that was essential for the build up of the modern welfare state, such as electricty, telecommunications, airlines and postal services. EU members regulated these natural monopolies nationally through restrictions to entry for competitors, rules on pricing and profit limitations. The idea was that protected monopolies in these sectors would ensure the provision of the social goal of universal service at an affordable price for all.

A combination of consumer demand, political vision, technological evolution and market forces however has set a process of rapid EU wide deregulation of most of the natural monopolies in motion that has lead to benefits to society that exceed most predictions. Initial resistance to EC liberalisation in some countries, caused by doubt surrounding the scrapping of familiar utilities in favour in favour of an environment with multiple suppliers and diversified services, has disappeared. Few question the enormous benefits of EC liberalisation and calls to re-monopolise deregulated industries are unheard of. Past fears of job losses in liberalised industries have been replaced by general recognition of their potential as job creators.

Several former natural monopolies are now growth industries and constitute the corner stones on which the future European economy is being built on. This means that the market openings created by EC liberalisation can lead to results that go far beyond what could be envisaged at the time when deregulation measures were first put in place. Consequently, the numerous success stories of EC liberalisation in recent years should be enough for regulators and politicians to make sure that opportunities to achieve the same results in other sectors of the economy are not wasted. This is unfortunately, however, not what has happened in the postal sector that has an 80 billion Euro turnover.

FFPI believes that the EC should pave the way for economic growth and improved services by tearing down the mental and regulatory barriers that still surround the postal sector.

4. A Slow and Insecure Liberalisation Should be Avoided

The postal sector is undergoing a dramatic modernisation that is driven by three converging factors; changing consumer preference, technological improvements and increased market concentration. It is essential that EC measures to liberalise reflect these rapidly evolving market conditions.

The EC Commission describes the current situation well in its proposal for a new directive on postal services:

> "If the EU's postal services are inefficient, goods and services will not flow optimally throughout the Union—damaging economic growth and jobs. The benefits of electronic commerce will also not be fully realised if the EU's postal services—at the heart of business to business and home delivery in Europe—are not top class. There are therefore strong consumer and business interests in ensuring that a wide range of high quality postal services and products are available. Moreover, the postal market does not exist in isolation but interfaces and competes with other forms of communication, making it doubly important that it keeps pace with modernisation and technological advances, attracting investment and innovation". (COM 2000(319) final)

It is however important to recognise that transformation of the postal sector will take place whether the EC regulates the market or not. The contents of the rules in place will however be decisive to determine if the transformation will be successful. Without appropriate EC rules, the potential of the ongoing process in terms of growth, consumer choice, competitive prices and new jobs will be missed. In addition, the increase in market distortions in the EC will not be tackled in an effective way. It is therefore crucial that appropriate EC rules are in place to regulate the conditions for the modernisation of the postal sector.

One main reason so far for liberalising the postal sector at a snail's pace has been that there must be sufficient time and room for manoeuvre for postal operators to adapt to the new environment in a "gradual and controlled way". The FFPI believes, however, that if EC liberalisation of the postal sector continues at minimal speed, both regulators and the postal operators soon will be overtaken by market developments. For instance, more and more people seem to recognise that the EU risks seeing its public monopolies replaced with private ones unless the market is regulated and policed more efficiently. In a scenario where the liberalisation is too slow, the transition of the postal sector will suddenly accelerate due to market changes and, eventually, be brutal. It will therefore not be, as intended, gradual and controlled, since the rules that regulate the market will be out of tune with reality. This is to a certain degree already the case.

The FFPI believes that the EC must adopt new rules that provide all those concerned with clear messages at least on a minimum of issues. For instance, postal users, potential competitors and the postal operators have a legitimate interest in knowing at what date the market for postal operators will be open for competition.

FFPI believes that it is only if a final date for liberalisation is adopted that a real incentive exists to improve services. In addition it is only if a final date exists that potential investors and potential competitiors have sufficient incentive to invest and to innovate. Public monopolies should not be replaced with private monopolies. The FFPI therefore believes that the EC should decide that an internal market for postal services with full competition should be put in place by 2007.

5. The Social Obligations Linked to Postal Services will Benefit from Deregulation

The FFPI's term of reference clearly state that the USO should be maintained. Postal services constitute an important feature of our societies and the FFPI believes that the EU Member States' governments, according to the principle of subsidiarity, should be allowed to define the scope and the contents of the USO provided to their citizens.

The USO is however often used as an argument against liberalisation. It is argued that the USO require the postal operators to maintain a reserved area, a monopoly, for the vast majority of letter services in order for them to be able to finance the USO. This argument is however not correct. Other possible solutions exist that do not block the benefits of liberalisation as the reserved area currently does.

The EC Directive provides the Member States with the right to set up a compensation fund. Another way to finance the USO is to finance it through the state budget, as a direct subsidy from the state to a postal operator, as is done in one European country today. By doing so, flexible mechanisms can be created that allow for the scope and content of the USO to be constantly reviewed and geared to consumer preference.

In accordance with the subsidiary principle, it is up to each Member State to define the content and the extent of the USO provided that the minimum requirements of the EC Directive are complied with. Consequently, each Member State can evaluate, debate and decide on the cost level of the USO as well as on financing mechanisms' options. One method to arrive at the most efficient solution for the provision of services is to go through public procurement procedure. This method could be applied to the postal sector.

It is interesting to note that in Sweden where postal services were fully deregulated in 1993, the Swedish independent postal authority, PTS, recently concluded that "the Swedish legislation is founded on the notion that the universal service can be provided on a strictly commercial basis, which has proved to be correct,"

To conclude, there is no contradiction between a universal service and deregulation. The Member States have a large freedom to organise and finance the universal service obligation as they wish, provided that the EC rules on competition are respected.

The FFPI believes that the USO should be reviewed and benchmarked constantly and that it should not be used as pretext to oppose liberalisation and potentially as a tool for cross-subsidisation that distorts competition.

6. Liberalisation will Fail Unless the Increasing Competition Concerns are Tackled Effectively and Soon

The EC Commission has been unable to police the market in a satisfactory way. This has contributed to distortions of the market and widespread uncertainty for companies and consumers.

Most of the postal monopolies in the EU continue to benefit from large domestic monopolies. Consequently, most incumbents continue to benefit from the advantages linked to legal monopolies: experience, network, economics of scale, know-how, brand image, customer loyalty which are difficult for any competitor to acquire quickly.

In addition the existing letter monopoly constitutes a valuable asset to them in an increasingly competitive environment. Recent reports in the media with regard to the flotation of the Deutsche Post World Net show that the market valuation of the German Postal Operator seems to be significantly affected by the duration and the scope of the letter monopoly. This, combined with the fact that Germany has the highest stamp prices in Europe and that legal action has been taken against the stamp prices in Germany, seems to indicate that consumers, at least in Germany, are paying more for their stamps than what is required with regard to the USO. The arguments put forward by the postal operators, and by their owners, that a maintained reserved area is a condition for the functioning of the USO need therefore to be assessed in a critical way.

It is often not recognised that postal monopolies have the freedom to expand into new business areas in competitive sectors as all other European businesses under the EC rules. All but one postal monopoly is now breaking even and, for some of them, the financial strength they have built up is being used to expand rapidly and massively into neighbouring markets, often through acquistions of companies in the logistics, transport, express and parcel sectors. They also use their financial muscles to enter new markets, providing their portfolio of consumers with services in the e-commerce, banking, insurance sectors, etc... The postal monopolies' expansion is taking place both domestically and abroad.

The Commission's failure to police the postal market thus has repercussions across borders and far beyond the market for postal services.

7. FFPI Program Points on Free and Fair Post

1. The EC should set a date for full liberalisation of the postal sector in Europe, which should be 2007 at the latest. The EC should accelerate the gradual opening of the market for postal services prior to full liberalisation. That will provide the necessary dynamics for innovation and competition.

2. The FFPI believes that the USO should be reviewed and benchmarked constantly. It should not be used as pretext to oppose liberalisation and potentially as a tool for cross-subsidisation that distorts competition.

3. The EU members should be encouraged to apply the EC Directive on postal services that is in force correctly, which is currently not the case. The EC Commission should be encouraged to take action more swiftly against member states that fail to apply the rules.

4. It is forbidden for postal monopolies that provide universal services to cross-subsidise the competitive activities with resources from the reserved, monopolistic, area. Complaints about illegal cross-subsidies are however freqent and it is therefore essential that the Commission finalises its pending investigations without further unnecessary delay to set up clear guidelines on what is and what is not allowed.

5. Full implementation of the provisions on separation of accounts between reserved and non-reserved area market segments has to be a priority action for the EC. Without transparent accounting, there can be no level playing field.

Examination of Witnesses

SENATOR PHILIPPE BODSON and MR AXEL RINDBORG of Free and Fair Post, called in and examined.

Chairman

368. Good Morning, Senator, and welcome. I trust you had a pleasant journey across.
(*Senator Bodson*) Absolutely, thank you very much.

369. You were listening to the Minister as well. I apologise for starting a little late. We can run on a little longer in our session to make sure we cover all of the questions. Lord Paul is going to have to leave a little early. Could you open up and explain to the Committee the objectives and membership of your organisation, if you can just give us a quick general overview?
(*Senator Bodson*) May I suggest that my English sometimes will not be understood, my English is not totally proper. I would like to suggest that you would come in and say I should repeat what I am trying to explain. The Free and Fair Post initiative is, in fact, an independent, voluntary and a non-profit initiative. We are trying to, in fact, create a counter-weight to show those who oppose the liberalisation in Europe. We feel that those who oppose it are much better organised and for the political world it is very hard to fight against one lobby if there is not a counter-lobby on the other side. Therefore, a lot of people who are in favour of creating that counter-weight came to me. We could talk about the reasons why they came to me and I agreed to try and get involved in a start-up. It is really a start-up operation because we are a brand new organisation and at this stage of the game we are starting to get new members. Basically what we want to be and what we are is mainly a user organisation. We are speaking, we are looking, we are analysing the postal sector from the point of view of the user. It does not mean that competitors of the traditional operators will not be part of our membership because we are in favour of liberalisation and they are also in favour of liberalisation. We would like to approach the whole question from the point of view of the consumers, the customers, as a matter of fact. This is a word which is never used in the postal sector, as in any other monopoly in the world, that is basically what we are talking about, the customers. At this stage of the game our operation is something like six weeks old. We have had a chance to talk to a lot of people, and we are very honoured we have been asked to come and justify it in front of this Committee. As our most famous we have Euro Commerce, that is the European Retailers' Association. They represent 4.7 million companies in Europe. They have 22.5 million employees. We have the MIDF(?) in France, which is the Employers' Organisation in France, as you have the comparable British industry in the CBI in England. We have the FEB in Belgium, but I would not consider that as a very important member, having been the Chairman of that organisation before, one could immediately say it is because of my previous relationship. We have competitors, UPS, which is a well known company in America, ZEBLER(?) in Belgium, but it is also very important to say that a lot of people have agreed with the purposes and the objectives we are pursuing but they do not want their names to be mentioned, for two reasons. It is very interesting when you talk to them, some of them have privileges with the Post Office and they do not want to appear in the group to be going to the side of liberalisation because they would be afraid of losing their privileges. Some of them, in fact, have very low prices, which gives them an advantage in front of their competition. Therefore, for different reasons a lot of people do not want their names to be mentioned. The last thing I would like to say, there was a very important organisation in Brussels name BEUC, Bureau Europeen des Unions de Consomateurs, it is the European Consumers' Organisation, it is a very large organisation. As a matter of fact the members of the BEUC in the United Kingdom are the Consumers' Association, the National Consumers' Council and the Consumers in Europe Group. The BEUC has really publicly stated its options and it options are very much in line with what we are trying to defend, although they are not a member of our initiative *per se*.

Lord Paul

370. Chairman, thank you very much for explaining that I have to go, I do not want the witness to think after listening to the answers I walked out on him. Could you summarise for this Committee the programme of liberalisation that you would like to see in Europe?
(*Senator Bodson*) It will not surprise you if I start, having heard and having listened very carefully to the previous testimony, with the fact that being a

Lord Paul *contd.*]

consumer organisation we are giving a lot of importance to the Universal Service Obligation. For us there is absolutely no question that this has to be maintained. I was very interested to hear that on that item there is total agreement from everybody. As a matter of fact I have not heard anybody saying that the Universal Service Obligation can disappear. Therefore, this is definitely something we will be shooting for. We believe that we are not alone in that. We believe that the service, in terms of the quality of the service and the price, will improve only if there is competition. I must come back to my previous life. I was the head of a very large electricity company and gas company in Belgium. We had a monopoly, although we were a private company. When you are concerned, and rightly so, with the attitude of those monopolies vis-a-vis the customers you must understand that this attitude is made of the attitude of every person in the company. It is not because the top of the companies are really concerned about the consumers, and they are, that the rest of the company is following. There must be a psychological change, this is reason why we feel that a very strong signal has to be given in order to make sure that every individual in the postal sector is now realising that it is the end of a period, the period where they could do whatever they wanted and nothing would happen. Now, if they do not act properly, if they do not go in the direction of the customer, they will lose the customer. This is the only way you can help the bosses of those monopolies to really turn around their operation and make it a customer sensitive operation. Therefore, the first priority is Universal Service Obligation, the second priority is to change the minds in order to improve the services. In order to do that we need a signal. The signal for us, is that there should be a date for full liberalisation. It is a question of compromise. I do not want at this stage of our organisation, where we have not had a chance to discuss that in detail with our members, because we are very new, to give you a date. What is important to understand is the psychological value of a date, whether it is 2007, or 2010, whatever the date, it is going to show and it is going to give a signal to everybody that at some point in time the whole of the game will be totally different from what they were. That is going to help change and turn around the organisation. Therefore, this is exactly what we are shooting for.

371. If you achieve that what do you think will be the benefits?

(*Senator Bodson*) The benefits will be enormous. The benefits will be that the Post Office will be more efficient. The service will be better. If you allow me to, maybe, jump forward and try and tell you the way I would look at the postal sector in 2020 or 2030, I do not know. This is important, because what we are talking about right now is a transition period. We are talking about a transition period without really knowing how we will organise ourselves when this transition is going to be over. I am going to dream. I am not aiming to tell you right now what is going to happen. This is a possible model. In 2020 I could well imagine that there would be absolutely no monopoly, no reserved area, as the Minister said, but each Government would define what they want in terms of Public Service Obligation and Universal Service Obligations, how many deliveries a day, the price, and everything. If I retire in the mountains I want my mail to be delivered. As a person I want that and I do not want to compromise on that. I would also think that, for example, when we are talking about uniform price sometimes we forget to say affordable price. Because if it is a uniform price which is much too high, this is of no interest to us. A uniform and affordable price might be zero. Why? If you look at the value right now being exchanged you realise that consumer-to-consumer represents only five per cent of the mail traffic, business-to-consumer is around 80 per cent, business-to-business is twenty per cent. Why should we not say in the future that all letters sent by you and me as private people would be free, without charge and the rest would be paid by the companies? Each time you receive a letter from a company you would receive a prepaid envelope for your answer, and between companies they would pay. That would be totally competitive and as a person we would not have anything to pay any more. As far as the Public Service Obligation is concerned it would be a tender. Every three years or every five years the Government would say, "We want somebody to take over the organisation, to deliver the mail in every part of the country. We want so many Post Offices". It is up to the Government to decide what the content of the Universal Service Obligation is and then you make a tender. Then you will not have any complaints from any competitor. The tender is a negative tender, I will do that service obligation if the Government gives me two billion, or it depends on what currency you are talking about. Therefore there is no way to complain any more because everyone would have been able to bid for it and that is it. Therefore, each country will be able to adapt its Public Service Obligation to the culture. It is also going to be interesting to see. For example, if you were in Switzerland and you go to small villages in Switzerland you take a bus, that is the post bus, the post bus is also used to transport people who want to go and walk in the mountains. Therefore, there is a lot of ways you can combine those services instead of rendering those services alone. That is exactly the way I look at it.

Lord Paul: It sounds very interesting, the best of luck.

Lord Woolmer of Leeds

372. Good afternoon, Senator. You will have gathered that the Post Office is opposed to the Commission's proposal to reduce the weight to 50 grams and for the liberalisation of special services. The Post Office in this country is saying, this would threaten their ability to deliver a uniform service at an affordable tariff. You obviously think their fears are misplaced, why do you think so? How would you seek to persuade the Post Office that they are wrong in their fears?

(*Senator Bodson*) Let me put it this way, when you talk to the people of the Post Office they have a very hard time combining their opinion that 50 grams is too low to be able to maintain the Universal Service Obligation. I will not always repeat what it means,

Lord Woolmer of Leeds contd.]

the number of deliveries per day, price, affordable, uniform and so on. They have a hard time to maintain that with the fact that they are not opposed to liberalisation, even to the point where there would be no reserved area. When you put the two things together they are pulling back and they say, "Well, it is a question of making sure that everything is going to be progressive and controlled". My question to them is, do you really think that an opening of 3 per cent, because opening up to 150 grams would be opening up 3 per cent of the market, in the time frame of three years, do you really think this is an opening? I agree this is controlled and this is progressive but do you not think that 3 per cent every three years is a little bit too low? Do you think it is going to give the impact we want this decision to have? I do not think so. To specifically answer your question, I believe that the Universal Service Obligation does not depend on maintaining a certain level of reserved area. I think this is consistent with what the Minister just said, he said, "Maybe in the future we will be able to reach total liberalisation", which means in his own mind there is no definite argument which says that a universal service operation is necessarily linked to a certain size of a reserved area. Why 50 grams? Because it is a further opening of 20 per cent. We think it would give a very strong indication of the direction we are moving in. It would still leave the postal sector, the incumbents, with a big amount of reserved area. I have been in the electricity sector, as I told you, and I have lived that experience of liberalising a sector, that is what I call this famous transition period. All kinds of models have been developed. You know, the models are always correct. You can organise the models in such a way that they tell you what you want them to tell you, it depends on the parameters. You adjust them there and then. For example, nobody—and you can even take the telecom sector in your country, where you have very, very important players in the world today, and I admire a lot of them very much—has anticipated how much the customers of the old monopolies would remain the customers of the old monopolies. There is enormous inertia. You play a little bit with that inertia factor, you can demonstrate anything you want in terms of the postal sector. It is going to be very hard for me to give scientific evidence. As far as the financing of it is concerned, the Government has the possibility to do it many ways either through tender, through tax, through the budget or just to a minimum price for each stamp or for each piece of mail.

373. In your document you touch on Universal Service Obligations. You say that you as an organisation are supportive of them, but you also say that this should not be used as a tool for cross-subsidisation that distorts competition. Listening carefully to your explanation and how you deal with the Universal Service Obligation you said very clearly that your model would be that every few years businesses would tender in the negative sense to say to the Government, "This is what we need you, the Government, to pay us to fund the Universal Service Obligation", whereas your view as an organisation is, that Universal Service Obligation should not be funded by cross-subsidisation of different postal users but it should be paid for by the Government of the country recognising what the cost is of the USO. That is your model. There are two ways of paying for Universal Service Obligation, one is some postal uses pay a higher charge. For example, business users in this country allegedly pay more than they need do because they are paying for the cost. The model you have given to us, as a Committee, is that the Government should explicitly recognise that it is a cost and the Government of the day should meet the costs, pay for it. That is your model. That was what you told us. In the Commission's papers they do explicitly make the point that there are different ways of paying for Universal Service Obligation. That is one of the issues under discussion. Nobody before us in this country in evidence, nobody, has suggested that we in this country should move to the Government picking up the cost for the general taxpayer of the USO. Your model is, in fact, that.

(*Senator Bodson*) Maybe I was not clear enough.

374. You were very clear. You called it a negative tender.

(*Senator Bodson*) I spoke about the negative tender in my final phase, when we would be out of the transition period. I said that this negative tender could result in the winner asking for some money. I said that that money could come either from the budget, that means from the Government, or from a tax which would be imposed on any piece of mail which would fly around the country, which would mean an indirect subsidisation. When we are talking about cross-subsidisation it is very important to understand what we are talking about. Today there is cross-subsidisation, this is absolutely obvious. What we are afraid is that because we will get out of the monopoly system, those who are subsidising that are losing a portion of their business. For the big users, maybe their prices will go down and, therefore, the company who is forced to maintain that Universal Service Obligation has the route you spot yourself, about £300 million. The question is whether that £300 million is realistic or not. Therefore, the first thing we have to have is analytical counting, which would be defined in a very clear way, and there will always be discussions and instead of discussions of 50 to 300 the discussions would narrow down with the quality of the analytical accounting. It does not mean there would not be any discussion, I do not dream, I know that for a fact. Instead of having such big range we do see that very much. Secondly, that is also very important, what we do not want is to avoid that under the pretext of having to give that Universal Service Obligation to some companies in Europe, and there are a lot, it imposes very high prices for everything, for their normal service, and those high prices generate enormous profits.

375. As you liberalise is it not inevitable that new businesses coming in will go to customers who are under the cross-subsidy process? That is what happens at the moment, there is cross-subsidisation, certainly in the British Postal Service, businesses probably pay more for their post than it really is costing, and people in the country areas get their postal service much more cheaply than the true cost. In liberalisation it must be the case that people coming for new business would go to businesses who

Lord Woolmer of Leeds contd.]

are paying more than they need and say, "We can do it cheaper". Liberalising must drive down the cost for businesses who are currently overcharged, so that must mean that there would be a threat eventually to how you fund the Universal Service Obligation. Is that not inevitable? After all, what do you want to do with liberalisation? You want to bring down the costs and prices where they are being cross-subsidised and you want to have more competition.

(*Senator Bodson*) I agree entirely with your reasoning. The only thing I have to say is, I think competition would improve the efficiency of the sector as a whole and, therefore, the cost of the sector would go down, which means globally for the economy it would be a more efficient sector, less costly. The second thing, within the sector there would be definitely movement if we liberalise a portion of that sector, necessarily the newcomers will go to those who pay too much and who are subsidising those who pay nothing. I agree with you, this is the reason why in the transition period everybody is talking about a reserved area, where the newcomers can go. This is precisely the discussion we are talking about, this is the controlled and progressive approach. We are in favour of that control led and progressive approach because we know you cannot change an organisation of 200,000 people just like that. We want it to be controlled and gradual. The only thing we say is that 150 grams is only 3 per cent of the opening, and that is a little below.

Viscount Brookeborough

376. We are really on the same theme, prices. Can I just make a point, the post and the Universal Service is a more basic privilege to individuals everywhere in the country than anything else. I know many houses that do not have water, many house that do not have electricity, many do not have cars, many who do not have television, however they get their mail delivered. Is the effect not, as we have seen through other markets, regardless of how slow we go or how much we try and work out these formulas that ultimately the consumer is going to have to pay more in this country than it does at present for the uniform tariff, accepting that he may be some distance away from the collecting and delivering centres?

(*Senator Bodson*) May I react very openly? If I wore the hat of an electricity company in this country I would be ashamed to know that not everyone has access to electricity and I would make sure as a private person, the head of a publicly traded company that everyone gets the minimum amount of electricity delivered for nothing. This is very important, and this is way it is done in other countries. Frankly speaking, I believe in the market economy but I do not think that the market economy can be held responsible for the failures of people. It is absolutely totally unacceptable to me that some people do not have water, some people do not have electricity in their house. As a group of rich people—because we are all rich, our societies are rich—we should organise ourselves in such a way that everyone would receive a minimum of electricity, of gas and water. When you are saying that individually the prices will go up, I say no. I say it is up to the Government to define what the Government wants in those Universal Service Obligations, and the operators will be forced to respect what the Government say. If I were in Government I would say, "I want this to be delivered at a very low price, maybe once a day instead of twice a day". At least I would maintain a minimum amount of service at a price which I would determine myself. The Government has got to define the scope, the framework in which the private operators do work. This is the way to do it.

377. Already you see large variations in places such as Sweden. In Sweden they have VAT to cope with it. However, the VAT cannot be the total problem.

(*Senator Bodson*) VAT is a very important issue. It is a technical one as far as the different prices in Sweden are concerned. I cannot speak for the Swedish Government. The Swedish Government has the possibility to say that it wants the prices to be the same all over Sweden, if the Swedish Government decides to do so, maybe they do not. As far as Sweden is concerned I would like to draw your attention to one factor, this is a very important factor. A lot of people use Sweden as a negative example of what liberalisation can mean. Do not forget, the density of the population in Sweden is 26 inhabitants per square kilometre, it is ten times more in this country. Therefore, when you look at your operation as a whole, as an operator, as an industry, as a company, you will look at the average density. It means that you have ten times more customers per square kilometre in England than you have in Sweden.

Chairman

378. If we may pick up on Sweden, the density of the population has not changed greatly pre-liberalisation to what has happened, yet the price has changed very substantially, indeed, following liberalisation, upwards.

(*Senator Bodson*) You are absolutely correct. Everyone is talking about Sweden. There is a Report from the University of Toulouse, I have not read that study, what I read in the Report of the Swedish Postal Sector is that the price increases that took place between 1993 and 1995 were due to the introduction of the VAT, this is what we talked about. The following year in 1996 there was a six per cent increase. In 1997 Sweden managed to use a loophole in the price mechanism that led to an increase in price for a single letter by almost 30 per cent. This is what they write themselves in their own report. The loophole no longer exists and the price has not risen since 1997. Now you have to try and pass judgment on the level of prices in Sweden compared to the level of prices in other European counties. I will only give you one example, first class mail 100 grams—the only information I have available—is in this county 41 pence, in Sweden it is 69 pence, which means that it is around 70 per cent more. The density of the population is what it is. Therefore, I personally have a very hard time to say whether or not it is justified.

Viscount Brookeborough

379. Can I just make the point, the density of the population is one thing but also the geographical shape of the country is entirely another. You could have X million people distributed throughout an area, for instance, Holland or Belgium but in this country we are much closer, although not similar in total density geographically to a Swedish type situation because we have people living so far away. I realise you talk about how much it costs to get a letter from A to B. It is not only the average density, because you can put them all up instead of out.

(*Senator Bodson*) I do entirely agree with you, that the density is the first element to take into account when you pass judgment on the price in one country. I am not saying that this is the only element, distribution is obviously another factor, and I agree entirely with you, but those who are comparing the prices without even looking at the density are probably making a mistake. If we want go one step forward, because you were asking me questions about whether or not the competition in the sector was fair. In Germany it is 20 per cent above the Swedish tariff and they have a density which is comparable to England and probably a population which is well above England's. Therefore, you can really ask yourself, is there, under the pretext of Universal Service Obligation, evidence of a lot of money being made and being used to create an empire. Frankly speaking, if I was head of the German office I would do exactly the same thing. As the boss of the corporation you have to take advantage of the law. Now that I have become senator I do want the law to be as precise and specific as possible to make sure that those businessmen do not take advantage of us.

380. Can I just turn to information technology and e-mails and various other forms of competition. This is beginning to put a certain amount of stress on postal services or least it is changing the market to a certain extent, how much do you think it is going to continue to do so? Do you not think that for them to cope with that problem at the moment they might be well left to do that on its own rather than having liberalisation too fast in addition?

(*Senator Bodson*) The way you are asking the question is already pushing me in one direction. I am going to go for it, I have to apologise for that.

381. Go for it.

(*Senator Bodson*) Let me put this way, I am the Chairman within the Belgium Federation of Employers', the Chairman of a special committee on e-commerce, which means I am not a specialist but I have some information. I have a feeling that the e-commerce, that e-business, the Internet is going to have a major impact on the way we live in the future, we have not yet really perceived that. That impact, because it a change, is perceived as a threat by most of the unions in the postal sector. Sometimes I say to myself, it is no threat, it is going to increase, to the contrary, the importance of your sector. It is more a threat for great distribution, the distribution of goods, department stores, and so forth. I think a lot of things are going to go through the post office and there will not be intermediary inventories as we have today. Therefore, I am saying maybe I should say to them, do not worry. As I want the sector to change and as I want them to be more attentive to be preoccupations of the customer I say to them, yes it might be a threat, therefore you better adapt because I want to push in the direction of adapting themselves. If you ask me what I really believe, I do not think we will see a very big impact on the postal sector within the next five years. A lot of letters are sent by e-mail which would reduce the volume. There was a normal increase in volume over the last year, we have seen that. In the United States and in Canada for the first time we see some of those letters. Business to consumer, banks to customers we saw some of those letters disappear because the banks are communicating directly with their customer through the Internet but it has not had a major impact on the value being treated by the postal sector. Therefore, I do not see that to be a major threat in the short-term future. In the long-term it is going to be major. Because it is going to be major I am saying that as politicians we have a responsibility to force those monopolies that we have organised, with very good reasons in the past. We have a responsibility to force them to change and to prepare for change. What is a drama in our economy is when the changes are brutal. If those changes are not imposed on them, if they are not forced to evolve slowly with the market then one day they will be faced with something totally different and the change will be very, very hard to manage. The social cost will be very hard. It is much better to say to the unions, look we have seven years to adapt, let us work out a programme over seven years. Over seven years you can modify an organisation 100 per cent, if you want eight I am prepared to give you eight. If from one day to another suddenly the competition explodes and the new technology changes your business totally, then you are faced with a drama and you cannot manage it.

Chairman

382. You talked earlier about organising yourself to counter some of the forces which were very well organised to the post change. I presume you have put the trade unions in that category.

(*Senator Bodson*) As unions I do not think they are members of any organisation but I know a lot of union leaders who are part of those who are really arguing against liberalisation. Therefore, you know, I have full respect for that because they sometimes try to protect their affiliates by taking the position they are taking. I believe in my own experience that the protection would be much more efficient and much better if, in fact, think were accepting that the sector will be changed, whether it is five years, ten years or 15 years, I do not know. One day it will change and if we have not prepared ourselves it will be a brutal change. That brutal change will be impossible to manage. We start today because we know that we have a fixed date, this is the reason why we want a fixed date, just to get the dynamics going in the other direction.

383. The unions in the United Kingdom say they are not opposed to liberalisation. They are very concerned that hasty liberalisation will precipitate a heavy loss of jobs but if is taken at a gentle pace and it is phased in over a good period of time then maybe they can cope with it. Is there a contradiction

15 *November 2000]*   SENATOR PHILIPPE BODSON AND MR AXEL RINDBORG   *[Continued*

Chairman *contd.*]

between maintaining jobs at the present levels and liberalisation?

(*Senator Bodson*) This a very difficult question because it depends on the answer you are giving on the impact of the technological change and the way we are doing business in the world. I have to make a distinction between employment in the sector and employment in the post. Employment in the sector, I tend to think that is going to go up. It depends how you define the sector, if you look at sector of just the mail, the letters which we are sending to one another will go down probably but if we look at the sector, if we include logistics, the little books, the records, the CDs, and so forth I think employment might go up. Maybe the old monopolies, the old incumbents will go down because they will have to adapt to the new technologies. I am not so concerned about total employment.

384. We are now coming to the end of our session. I am just wondering if there is anything you would like to put us which we have not raised with you on which you would like to express a view and go on the record for it. Do not feel forced.

(*Mr Rindborg*) We would also, if possible, like to make a written submission. We do not have a text with us today, would it be possible for us to send it to you later?

Chairman: We are very happy to receive that.

Viscount Brookeborough

385. When you talk about the changes that will come which might mean fewer letters, are you really thinking of interactive digital tv as opposed PCs?

(*Senator Bodson*) Your question is getting so precise and specific.

386. Or something different. It is along those lines, where people can sit down and talk to each other.

(*Senator Bodson*) Specialists in the industry all have a different opinion, I know that something will happen, whether it will be the net, whether IP, the evolution of the IP now, or whether it will be the tv, I do not know, I do not know exactly. There is a major convergence there and it is very hard to say when the final product will come.

Chairman

387. Could I ask you, if you prepare a paper for us, could you get it to us very quickly because we are coming towards the end of our deliberation.

(*Mr Rindborg*) End of this week or early next week.

388. End of this week would be better.

(*Mr Rindborg*) By e-mail.

389. Most of our business is being done by e-mail. Thank you very much for making the journey to see us. I hope it has been worthwhile for you, it has been very interesting for us. Certainly, you are looking in the globe to 20 years on, 2020. It is fascinating some of the ideas that you have been thinking about and very interesting for us. We are grateful to you for coming today. Thank you very much.

(*Senator Bodson*) I was very honoured to be invited.

WRITTEN EVIDENCE

Memorandum by the Association of International Courier and Express Services (AICES)

EXECUTIVE SUMMARY

1. AICES recognises the need for the European Commission to find common ground in favour of further liberalisation, but is disappointed that the final proposals have been diluted in comparison to earlier drafts. The Commission was widely expected to propose the full liberalisation of direct mail as of 2003, but the final proposal presented by Commissioner Bolkenstein reserves the vast majority of direct mail items (items up to 50g) for Europe's monopoly holders.

2. AICES is encouraged by the reduction of the reserved area for domestic mail from 350g to 50g and by the confirmation of continued competition in the market of outgoing cross-border mail. However, the express industry is extremely disappointed that full liberalisation of direct mail has been abandoned—again contrary to earlier drafts of the Directive.

3. The level of liberalisation proposed is the bare minimum necessary and AICES is very concerned that the Directive in its current draft could be significantly watered down as it goes through the legislative process.

4. While the intent of the draft Directive is undoubtedly progressive, the effect may prove to be regressive, as the lack of a deadline may delay necessary modernisation by postal operators, and will force the current market potential to seek alternative outlets.

5. AICES is surprised and disappointed by the response of the Royal Mail, particularly as it is to gain new commercial freedoms by its new status as a PLC. The Royal Mail fails to recognise that liberalisation does not imply lost revenue for the public postal operator, it provides the impetus for market growth, to the benefit of public and private operators alike.

6. The lack of a final date for full liberalisation is a concern, as it implies not only delays in much needed reforms of the public postal operators, but also a delay in the completion of the Single Market and continued insecurity for private operator start-ups.

7. Without a final date for liberalisation, postal operators will delay modernisation, consumers and business customers will suffer the consequences of delayed improvements in efficiency and service, and new market entrants will not have the security they require to make investments.

8. AICES hope that the British Government and elected representatives in Europe will vehemently contest any attempts to further dilute the proposals and ensure that British consumers have the benefits of choice and low prices that liberalisation will undoubtedly bring.

ABOUT AICES

9. AICES is the trade organisation in the United Kingdom for companies handling international express documents and package shipments. AICES membership—which includes household names such as DHL, FedEx, TNT and UPS—employs tens of thousands of people and is responsible for over 95 per cent of the international courier and express shipments moved through the UK every day. Our services provide the "just-in-time" information and goods that organisations from banks to hospitals rely upon.

10. AICES has a long-standing relationship with the Department of Trade and Industry and has played an active role in the development of its proposals for the future of the Post Office. We broadly welcomed the proposals in the Government's White Paper "Post Office Reform: A World Class Service for the 21st Century" and ensured elected representatives from all political parties were kept informed of our members' concerns during the passage of the Postal Service Bill, which has now received Royal Assent.

11. The rest of this paper outlines AICES's reaction to the draft proposal and outlines some areas that can be addressed in order to achieve increased performance of postal operators, market growth, better postal services for business and citizens alike as well as ensuring fairer competition.

BENEFITS OF INCREASED COMPETITION

12. Customers increasingly want a wider range of new services with a good price/quality ratio, and also freedom of choice between service providers worldwide. The following points advocate that need for further opening of the postal market in Europe:

— The Single Market for postal services should be completed, as it is for all other sectors.

— The price/quality ratio of the postal product must be improved. Increased competition can and will guarantee this.

— The development of new products will be stimulated.

— Increased competition will stimulate the reform of public postal operators into efficient, cost-aware, and above all customer-oriented, companies.

— The abolition of monopolies will end distortions of competition between alternative segments of the communications market.

A Coherent Rationale for Liberalisation

13. Making e-commerce development possible—The successful development of e-commerce requires efficient, reliable, liberalised delivery networks. Users of electronic commerce should have freedom of choice and diversity of delivery according to their needs. This requires the complete liberalisation of postal and express delivery. In order to ensure consumer trust in electronic commerce, it is essential that consumers who order goods electronically receive those goods in an efficient and reliable way.

14. Liberalisation benefits employment—The "safeguarding employment" argument is often used by inefficient postal operators to preserve existing monopolies. It is clear from other economic sectors that liberalisation leads to market growth. We see no reason why this principle would not apply to the postal sector, and benefit employment in that sector. Employment is currently decreasing in the public postal sector by 0.8 per cent a year, but this is not a result of market opening but rather of technological shifts and a drive for greater efficiency. The aim of liberalisation is to bring improved services, which should ultimately result in increasing employment.

15. Guaranteeing the universal service provision—The Commission's current proposal does not change the obligations of universal service. AICES repeats that universal service and a fully liberalised market are not mutually exclusive, and that they can co-exist perfectly. However, universal service should meet the most important criterion: the provision of a good and affordable basic postal service. The concern is that if postal services lag behind the communications market as a whole, they risk losing the very basis on which the social role is built. The current Commission proposals liberalises a mere 20 per cent of the currently reserved area, which is sufficient to guarantee the universal service obligation.

Achieving Real and Beneficial Change

16. Without a timetable there is no incentive to improve services—AICES believes that the Directive should include 1 January 2007, as a final date for the full liberalisation of EU postal services. Without a final date, the public postal operators will have no real incentive to improve their services and take advantage of the dynamics of the internal market. In addition, this open-ended situation fails to provide the necessary market security to allow for new market entrants from private industry to innovate, invest in the postal sector and create employment opportunities.

17. Reduced weight and price limit for items of domestic correspondence—AICES favours full liberalisation of the market for items of domestic correspondence by completely abolishing the current weight and price limits. The price and weight limit (2.5x the price/50g) as proposed by the Commission is only a modest step in the right direction. AICES considers this the absolute minimum necessary at this time.

18. Positive move on outbound cross-border mail—AICES welcomes the Commission's proposal to de jure liberalise outbound cross-border mail. This will stimulate communication and mail flows between the EU's citizens and enterprises. Since the cross border mail streams are already de facto liberalised in all Member States, this demonstrates that a dynamic market does not wait for regulation.

19. High time to set free inbound cross-border mail—AICES appeals for a re-examination of the issue of inbound cross border mail. We strongly oppose the view that it is necessary to maintain a reservation to this market, since this is not necessary in order to safeguard the universal service, as was already determined in the Directive 97/67/EC from 1997. We are convinced that control mechanisms can be put in place in order to prevent situations whereby mailers seek to avoid the higher domestic tariffs in certain countries.

20. Liberalisation of direct mail allows huge growth potential to be realised—Europe's direct mail market has a huge potential for growth. In a fully liberalised market, public post offices will respond more rapidly and effectively to the demand for more creative and cost-effective direct mail campaigns. Full liberalisation will lead the way to improved services in terms of reliability and range. It will encourage public post offices to be more efficient, flexible and customer-oriented. If the public postal operators and private industry are not free to develop this means of advertising, it will be substituted by other means of communication. Six Member States have already opened the direct mail market to competition, without in any way threatening the universal service. The full liberalisation of direct mail would allow public postal operators and private industry alike to further develop this dynamic means of communication.

21. No cross-subsidisation of competitive services—Cross subsidisation, where income from the reserved area is used to subsidise the development of competitive services, causes huge distortions of competition in the postal market. The Commission's Postal Notice (OJ 98/C 39/02) on the Application of the Competition Rules to the Postal Sector makes it clear that it is prohibited for a dominant postal operator to subsidise competitive activities from monopoly revenue. The Commission proposal must be consistent with the Postal Notice: clarification of the current proposal is needed in order to prohibit the cross-subsidisation from the

reserved area to the non-universal service area, as well as illegal cross-subsidisation to the universal service area.

22. Special Services—AICES considers that the Commission proposal to exclude "special services" from the postal monopoly (irrespective of price and weight limits) codifies existing case law and jurisprudence of the Commission and the European Court of Justice. Therefore, we would like to stress the importance of maintaining this proposed provision as a guarantee of legal certainty.

23. Express Services—AICES fully supports the Commission's recognition that express services fall outside the universal service, thus confirming established case law of the European Court of Justice.

24. Government-Mandated complaints procedures—The Commission has proposed that Government-mandated complaints procedures also be applied to services outside the universal service. AICES consider it inappropriate for the Commission to propose that Government-mandated complaints procedures be applied to such services, irrespective of the service provider. Such services are already subject to longstanding commercial arrangements. It cannot be the business of Government to regulate freely competitive services, irrespective of the provider.

14 September 2000

Memorandum by the Consumers in Europe Group (CEG)

CEG is an independent UK umbrella body for 34 UK organisations with an interest in the effects of EU policies on UK consumers.

1. INTRODUCTION

1.1 The postal services in the EU Member States play a very important economic and social role. The public has a right to expect a postal service that is universally available, reliable and affordable. The postal services in Member States remain largely in the hands of unwieldy national monopolies. The European Commission has been trying for almost 10 years to find a way of liberalising an uncompetitive, monopolistic industry, whilst ensuring that it continues to generate the economic returns necessary to pay for a universal service, available in terms of access and cost to all. In May 2000 the Commission published a draft Directive proposing a further liberalisation of the market from January 2003.[1]

2. THE ISSUES FOR UK CONSUMERS

2.1 The fundamental social requirement of a postal service is the maintenance of a universal (nationwide) service operating throughout one Member State or between any two Member States, of any service or range of services—for example, letters, printed matter, parcels and so on,—up to a certain weight or price limit. This service must be reliable, efficient and affordable, and offered to all to a published quality standard.

2.2 In addition, UK consumers wish to maintain a single postage rate throughout the UK for each service making up the universal service (single unitary tariff) and to retain the choice of first or second class mail.

2.3 Another issue of concern to UK consumers is the social importance of the continued existence of post offices, especially in rural areas. The National Federation of Women's Institutes (a CEG member organisation) and others have emphasised the importance of post offices in rural communities, particularly for the elderly, the poor and the excluded.[2]

3. THE SITUATION IN THE UK

3.1 At the moment the Post Office retains the monopoly on the delivery of all letters costing under £1. This is the Post Office's "reserved area". The Post Office has welcomed "sensible competition and deregulation" and suggested in 1992 that the threshold for the reserved service could be reduced gradually—starting with a drop to 50 pence[3]. However, the threshold remains at £1.

3.2 The reserved area enables the Post Office to supply a universal service with a speed-based tier system split between first and second class deliveries. The second class service, which enables mail to be handled in off-peak periods, is a scheduled service that is supposed to meet specified delivery standards. UK consumers therefore have a wider choice of services than consumers in most other European countries.

3.3 The social role of rural and deprived inner city post offices is very important for UK consumers, particularly older and less well-off consumers. The UK government announced at the end of June its intention

---

[1] COM(2000) 319 final of 30.5.2000.
[2] Home and Country, June 2000.
[3] EC opens the post to the market, The Independent of 17/6/92, p.27.

of maintaining the rural network and preventing any unavoidable closures of rural post offices by establishing new subsidies. It also announced plans for a Universal Bank to provide basic banking services and encourage post offices to act as internet access centres.[4]

4. A Comparison of Member States

4.1 Postal services account for a large sector of the economy of the European Union: the annual turnover amounts to 80 billion euros, or 1.4 per cent of the GDP of the EU, and operators employ 1.4 million people.[5] Currently, public service providers have about 97 per cent of this revenue, which would be reduced to around 80 per cent under the Commission's new proposals.[6]

4.2 Postal administrations in the EU provide services in all three product areas—letters, express and parcels. The private operators cover mainly express and parcel services, but offer some cross-border letter services. National letter services below a certain weight or price remain the domain of the national post offices and are known as the "reserved areas". The UK is the sole Member State to base its reserved letter area on price: all others use a maximum weight definition.

4.3 There are wide differences in the definitions of weight and dimensions and in the cost of sending letters, postcards and packages between and within all Member States. Some EU countries retain a statutory monopoly covering areas, such as parcel delivery, which others have opened up to competition. Postal services in Sweden are completely liberalised and the universal service has been maintained. Finland has also liberalised all letter post, including direct mail and cross-border mail. The Netherlands has opened up direct mail and outgoing cross-border mail and Spain has liberalised all direct mail and local mail. Germany and Denmark have also both deregulated more than required by the 1997 Directive.

4.4 A Financial Times report[7] states that, although Sweden completely deregulated postal services in 1993, competition has been slow to develop: the Swedish post office (Posten) still retains a monopoly since it is the only service to offer a nationwide delivery service, in spite of there now being 60 authorised postal operators in Sweden. Mail volumes have not grown in Sweden due to the development of e-mail. Posten retains 95 per cent of the total market for letters but, whilst it has become more efficient, consumers have not benefited in terms of lower prices.

4.5 The Bureau Européen des Unions de Consommateurs (BEUC) reports[8] contradictory lessons on liberalisation from the Swedish and Finnish consumer organisations (Sveriges Konsumentråd and Suomen Kuluttajaliitto). Liberalisation in Sweden seems to have led to a decline in the quality of service (increased uncertainty about the time for mail to arrive), whilst experience in Finland has proved beneficial to consumers, enhancing the quality of service and keeping stamp prices even.

4.6 France has a slightly smaller number of post offices than the UK, although 80 per cent of the network consists of main post offices staffed by public sector employees. Most post offices offer a full range of financial services making "La Poste" the second-largest bank in the country in terms of current accounts.[9] The French government is not keen to change the status quo and grants a number of subsidies, tax breaks and cross-subsidies in order to maintain the network and to provide financial services to poorer people.[10]

4.7 Post offices in nearly all Member States provide financial services, although the extent of these services varies considerably.

4.8 Postal administrations in all EU Member States apply the principle of a single unitary tariff for national letter deliveries. Some geographical cross-subsidisation is obviously necessary to achieve this single tariff since costs have to be averaged out. Any losses of individual services—particularly those offering preferential tariffs eg printed paper distribution—have to be funded either by central funding or cross-subsidies from profitable areas. Such cross-funding is therefore at the expense of the consumer of the profitable service who is paying a higher price to cross-subsidise the customer of another service.

5. The Commission's 1992 Green Paper

5.1 On 13 May 1992 the Commission adopted a Green Paper on the Development of the Single Market for Postal Services. The Green Paper stated that the fundamental objective was to ensure the continuation of the universal service, which must be provided at an affordable price, have good quality of service and be accessible to everyone.

---

[4] Counter Revolution—Modernising the Post Office Network, A Performance and Innovation Unit Report, June 2000.

[5] Europe's last post, The Economist, May 13 2000, p.97.

[6] European Commission Press Release IP/00/541 of 30.05.00 "Postal services: Commission proposes to speed completion of Internal Market".

[7] Financial Times of 07.06.00. "Deregulation in Sweden has failed to deliver".

[8] BEUC's Comments on the Commission's Proposal for a Directive amending Directive 97/67/EC with regard to further opening to competition of Community Postal Services, BEUC/284/2000.

[9] Financial Times of 29.06.00. "Europe delivers some solutions".

[10] Counter Revolution—Modernising the Post Office Network, PIU, June 2000.

5.2 The Green Paper concluded that, in order to ensure the universal service, it would be necessary to have some restriction of the free market. Some reserved services would be operated by the national postal administrations, but these would be strictly proportional to the universal service objective. At the same time the reserved services would carry out certain harmonisation measures to ensure that the universal service operated effectively in all Member States.

6. THE 1997 DIRECTIVE ON POSTAL SERVICES

6.1 After years of discussion, the European Commission finally put forward a proposal for a Directive in November 1995, establishing common rules for the development of EU postal services and the improvement of quality of service. The proposal was accompanied by a draft Notice on the application of the competition rules to the postal sector.

6.2 The Directive was eventually adopted in 1997[11] in a substantially watered-down form, having failed to open up the state monopolies. The Directive obliges Member States to adopt a minimum harmonised standard for the universal service, notably maintaining a quality service throughout the country with guaranteed regular deliveries at affordable prices.[12] The Directive also harmonises the maximum scope of the sector which may, where appropriate, be reserved for Member States in order to guarantee that the universal service is maintained. In order to guarantee the financial viability of the universal service, the Directive agreed that the monopoly could continue for letters weighing less than 350 grams, which meant that an extra 3 per cent of letter volumes and 5 per cent of operator's revenues would be opened up to competition.[13]

6.3 The Directive also requires the creation of national regulatory authorities that are independent of the postal operators. The Postal Services Commission has recently been established in the UK as the Post Office regulator.

7. THE COMMISSION'S NEW PROPOSALS[14]

7.1 Article 7 of the 1997 Directive required the Commission to undertake a review of the postal sector, which the Commission began at the beginning of 1998. The Bureau Européen des Unions de Consommateurs (BEUC) concluded that the Commission's study failed in its objective and that it did not adequately consult with consumer and user organisations to find out consumers' attitudes to postal services and their quality.[15]

7.2 On 30 May 2000 the European Commission tabled a draft Directive on further liberalisation of the postal sector which, if adopted, will open up more services to competition from private operators. The proposal would require Member States to:

— by 1 January 2003, reduce the weight limits on letters and direct mail (addressed advertising mail or "junk" mail) from 350g to 50g and to reduce the price limits from five times the basic standard tariff to 2.5 times;

— open up fully to competition outward cross-border and express mail services. The Commission is not proposing specific liberalising measures for inward cross-border mail.

In addition, on the basis of new proposals to be tabled before the end of 2004, the Commission may decide fully to liberalise the sector before the end of 2007.

7.3 The new proposals make no changes to the universal service obligation. The Internal Market Commissioner, Frits Bolkenstein, has given firm assurances that a universal service will be maintained, and safeguards for this are already laid down in the existing Directive. In its explanatory memorandum the Commission states that "there is furthermore no evidence that a substantial market opening would compromise the requirement in the Postal Directive for "affordable tariffs". Uniform tariffs in some cases can easily evolve into a "uniform structure of tariffs" to take account of different categories of users as is usually already the case for business customers." The explanatory memorandum states that the experiences of Sweden and Spain, both of which have some degree of liberalised mail, shows that to date the uniform tariff for individual customers has not been abandoned by the universal service providers despite full or substantial market opening. The explanatory memorandum continues to state that a "rigidly imposed uniform tariff for all customers is not a compulsory part of the Postal Directive framework and this proposal reflects that fact."

7.4 The Commission's new proposals state that "cross-subsidisation of universal services outside the reserved area out of revenues from services in the reserved area shall be prohibited except to the extent to which it is shown to be strictly necessary to fulfil specific universal service obligations imposed in the competitive area".

---

[11] Directive 97/67/EC of 15 December 1997 on Common rules for the development of Community postal services and the improvement of quality of service.
[12] The universal service covers the collection, transport and distribution of address mail items and books, catalogues, newspapers and periodicals up to 2 kg and addressed postal packages of up to 20 kg, and also a service for registered and insured items.
[13] Europe's last post, The Economist, May 13 2000, pp. 97–99.
[14] COM(2000) 319 final of 30.5.2000.
[15] BEUC position on the next stage of liberalisation of the Postal Services, BEUC/378/98 of 5.1.99.

7.5 According to the Commission, the new 50 grams weight limit will open up a further 16 per cent of the EU market (in terms of universal service providers' total postal revenues) to competition. Currently the maximum area that can be reserved, represents on average in the Community 70 per cent of revenues. Setting a 100 grams limit would have opened up the market by 9 per cent. BEUC is advocating a 20 grams weight limit since "20 grams letters represent the most important part of mail from and to residential consumers and the proposal is unlikely to create real competition in this segment".[16]

7.6 As some Member States have already opened up their postal markets further than proposed by the Commission, the impact of the proposal on the revenues of the universal service providers will vary from one Member State to another. The Commission estimates that, under this proposal, Member States could still maintain a reserved area representing, on average, 50 per cent of the universal providers' revenue from postal services: currently, on average 70 per cent of their revenue is derived from reserved services.

7.7 The social function of postal services and the maintenance of rural post offices are important in all Member States. The Commission recognises the vital social importance of the post office network in its Explanatory Memorandum but makes no recommendation for maintaining the networks in the proposal.

8. CEG's VIEWS

CEG stresses the absolute importance to consumers of ensuring the maintenance of the universal service.

The principle of a single unitary tariff for national letter deliveries in each Member State should be maintained.

The universal second class mail system in the UK must be continued. The abandonment of the second class service would mean a vital loss of consumer choice, which would be particularly felt by those on lower incomes.

CEG believes that the letter monopoly held by most European post offices should be reduced as far as possible, in order to encourage lower prices, better service and more choice for consumers.

CEG favours a step-by-step approach to liberalisation, reducing the monopoly of the universal service providers for letters and direct mail to 150 grams as a first step, with further reductions depending on the outcome of the Commission's review of the situation at the end of 2004. However, CEG considers that 2004 may be too early for a full assessment.

The reserved area should be strictly proportional to the cost of providing the universal service. Cross-subsidisation of universal services outside the reserved area out of revenues from services in the reserved area should be prohibited.

CEG considers that complete transparency of costs of the universal service provider(s) is vital to ensure that any funding to fulfil universal service obligations is justified.

CEG would like the Commission to provide strict guidelines for the operation, transparency and control of the compensation fund which each Member State is allowed to set up to ensure the maintenance of the universal service in the event that the reserved area cannot cover the universal service provider's costs.

CEG has urged the Commission to provide a definition of "affordable" as specified in the 1997 Postal Services Directive which defines the universal service as being available for all users at affordable prices.

CEG would like to see quality standards for the universal service agreed by CEN as soon as possible in order to facilitate cross-border services.

27 September 2000

Letter by Mr W Maschke, Deutsche Post

On behalf of Mr. Zumwinkel I have the pleasure to enclose a copy of a common statement signed by TNT-Post Group, Posten AB, Finland Post and Deutsche Post AG on the European Commission's proposal on further liberalisation of the European postal market. The statement was transmitted to Commissioner Bolkestein in June.

Even though Deutsche Post as the other signatory posts would have favoured a more determined approach (by setting a final date for complete liberalisation) we support the Commission's proposal as a well balanced compromise that should be acceptable to all involved.

4 September 2000

---

[16] Draft BEUC's Comments on the Commission's proposal for a Directive amending Directive 97/67/EC with regard to further opening to competition of Community Postal Services.

Annex

Revision of the European Union Directive 97/67/EC on common rules for the development of the internal market of Community postal services and the improvement of quality of service of 15 December 1997—Commission's proposal of 30 May 2000.

COMMON STATEMENT: 30 JUNE 2000

Deutsche Post AG, TNT Post Group NV, Posten AB and Finland Post Ltd are all in favour of a full and swift, yet gradual and controlled, liberalisation of the European postal market.

Against this background the four public postal operators generally welcome the Commission's proposal of 30 May 2000 opening up a further (although limited) share of the postal sector. Given the difficulty of creating competition and finding an appropriate balance between the different interest involved, this intermediate step being proposed by the European Commission and the timetable being set is understandable.

However it is disappointing to see that no final date for full liberalisation has been set. As already pointed out in the common position paper of 14 February 2000, Deutsche Post AG, TNT Post Group NV, Posten AB and Finland Post Ltd take the view that a final date for full liberalisation must be set. A clear timetable with a final date is essential to give the necessary planning and investment security to the market. Only a clearly defined timetable will put the incumbents into a position to meet the fast and dramatically changing challenges of the postal market and the demanding customer requirements.

The four postal operators see the Commission's proposal as the minimum step to be taken in 2003, which should not be further watered down concerning content and time-table.

Letter by Anton van der Lande, Chairman, EEA Postal Committee

The EEA welcomes the Commission proposal to further open the postal market, as well as the creation of legal certainty through the definition of special and express services.

However, the EEA regrets that the proposal does not adequately address the need for increased competition in Europe's postal market. This letter outlines areas of the proposal that have to be addressed in order to achieve increased performance of postal operators, market growth, better postal services for business and citizens alike as well as ensuring fairer competition.

1. The EEA believes that the post-2003 reduction of the reservable area to 50g/2.5x the price limit of domestic mail to be a step in the right direction, although a minimal one. This limit opens a mere 20 per cent of the currently reserved postal market to additional competition. Public post offices will not lose this market share automatically, they will simply have to compete for it. This competition will take place between public postal operators as well as with domestic private operators.

2. The EEA considers that direct mail should be fully liberalised as of 2003, in order to realise the full growth potential of this sector.

3. The EEA welcomes the liberalisation of outbound cross-border mail, and believes that it is high time to liberalise inbound cross-border mail as well.

4. The full opening to competition of all express mail services is welcomed.

5. The omission of a final date for full liberalisation allows post offices to further postpone crucial modernisation, and also prevents the completion of the Single Market. Furthermore, such an open-ended situation fails to provide the necessary market security to allow for new market entrants from private industry to invest in the postal sector.

6. Finally, the Commission has proposed that Government-mandated complaints procedures be applied also to services outside the universal service. It is wholly inappropriate for the Commission to propose that Government-mandated complaints procedures be applied to such services irrespective of the service provider. Such services are already subject to longstanding commercial arrangements. It cannot be the business of Government to regulate freely competitive services, irrespective of the service provider.

The attached position paper provides you with what we believe to be persuasive arguments that advocate a final date on 1 January 2007 and full liberalisation of domestic mail, direct mail and cross border mail.

14 September 2000

Annex

Position paper on the European Commission's proposal for the further opening of the postal market in Europe

INTRODUCTION

The European Express Association (EEA) welcomes the Commission proposal to further liberalise the postal market. However, the EEA regrets that the proposal does not adequately address the need for further liberalisation of Europe's postal market. The following paper outlines the EEA's reaction to the proposal and outlines some areas that can be addressed in order to achieve increased performance of postal operators, market growth, better postal services for business and citizens alike as well as ensuring fairer competition.

Benefits of increased competition

Customers increasingly want a wider range of new services with a good price/quality ratio, and also freedom of choice between service providers world-wide. The following points advocate that need for further opening of the postal market in Europe:

— The Single Market for postal services should be completed, like it is for all other sectors.
— The price/quality ratio of the postal product must be improved. Increased competition can and will guarantee this.
— The development of new products will be stimulated.
— Increased competition will stimulate the reform of public postal operators into efficient, cost-aware, and above all customer-oriented, companies.
— The abolition of monopolies will end distortions of competition between alternative segments of the communications market.

EEA POSITION

Without a timetable there is no incentive to improve services

The EEA believes that the Directive should include 1 January 2007, as a final date for the full liberalisation of EU postal services. Without a final date, the public postal operators will have no real incentive to improve their services and take advantage of the dynamics of the internal market. In addition, this open-ended situation fails to provide the necessary market security to allow for new market entrants from private industry to innovate, invest in the postal sector and create employment opportunities.

Reduced weight and price limit for items of domestic correspondence

The EEA favours full liberalisation of the market for items of domestic correspondence by completely abolishing the current weight and price limits. The price and weight limit (2.5x the price/50g) as proposed by the Commission is only a modest step in the right direction. The EEA considers this the absolute minimum necessary at this time.

Positive move on outbound cross-border mail

The EEA welcomes the Commission's proposal to de jure liberalise outbound cross-border mail. This will stimulate communication and mail flows between the EU's citizens and enterprises. Since the cross border mail streams are already de facto liberalised in all Member States, this demonstrates that a dynamic market does not wait for regulation.

High time to set free inbound cross-border mail

The EEA appeals for a re-examination of the issue of inbound cross border mail. We strongly oppose the view that it is necessary to maintain a reservation to this market, since this is not necessary in order to safeguard the universal service, as was already determined in the Directive 97/67/EC from 1997. We are convinced that control mechanisms can be put in place in order to prevent situations whereby mailers seek to avoid the higher domestic tariffs in certain countries.

Liberalisation of direct mail allows huge growth potential to be realised

Europe's direct mail market has a huge potential for growth. In a fully liberalised market, public post offices will respond more rapidly and effectively to the demand for more creative and cost-effective direct mail campaigns. Full liberalisation will lead the way to improved services in terms of reliability and range. It will encourage public post offices to be more efficient, flexible and customer-oriented. If the public postal operators and private industry are not free to develop this means of advertising, it will be substituted by other means of communication. Six Member States have already opened the direct mail market to competition, without in any way threatening the universal service. The full liberalisation of direct mail would allow public postal operators and private industry alike to further develop this dynamic means of communication.

No cross-subsidisation of competitive services

Cross subsidisation, where income from the reserved area is used to subsidise the development of competitive services, causes huge distortions of competition in the postal market. The Commission's Postal Notice (OJ 98/C 39/02) on the Application of the Competition Rules to the Postal Sector, makes it clear that it is prohibited for a dominant postal operator to subsidise competitive activities from monopoly revenue. The Commission proposal must be consistent with the Postal Notice: clarification of the current proposal is needed in order to prohibit the cross-subsidisation from the reserved area to the non-universal service area, as well as illegal cross-subsidisation to the universal service area.

Special Services

The EEA considers that the Commission proposal to exclude "special services" from the postal monopoly (irrespective of price and weight limits) codifies existing case law and jurisprudence of the Commission and the European Court of Justice. Therefore, the EEA would like to stress the importance of maintaining this proposed provision as a guarantee of legal certainty.

Express Services

The EEA fully supports the Commission's recognition that express services fall outside the universal service, thus confirming established case law of the European Court of Justice.

RATIONALE FOR INCREASED COMPETITION

Making e-commerce development possible

The successful development of e-commerce requires efficient, reliable, liberalised delivery networks. Users of electronic commerce should have freedom of choice and diversity of delivery according to their needs. This requires the complete liberalisation of postal and express delivery. In order to ensure consumer trust in electronic commerce, it is essential that consumers who order goods electronically receive those goods in an efficient and reliable way.

Liberalisation benefits employment

The "safeguarding employment" argument is often used by inefficient postal operators to preserve existing monopolies. It is clear from other economic sectors that liberalisation leads to market growth. We see no reason why this principle would not apply to the postal sector, and benefit employment in that sector. Employment is currently decreasing in the public postal sector by 0.8 per cent a year, but this is not a result of market opening but rather of technological shifts and a drive for greater efficiency. The aim of liberalisation is to bring improved services, which should ultimately result in increasing employment.

Guaranteeing the universal service provision

The Commission's current proposal does not change the obligations of universal service. The EEA repeats that universal service and a fully liberalised market are not mutually exclusive, and that they can co-exist perfectly. However, universal service should meet the most important criterion: the provision of a good and affordable basic postal service. The concern is that if postal services lag behind the communications market as a whole, they risk losing the very basis on which the social role is built. The current Commission proposal liberalises a mere 20 per cent of the currently reserved area, which is sufficient to guarantee the universal service obligation.

More About the European Express Association

The EEA represents express delivery companies and associations in Europe including DHL, FedEx, TNT Post Group (TPG) and United Parcel Service (UPS). As such it represents express delivery companies and associations, both large and small, in Europe. The express industry in Europe employs some 400,000 European men and women who work in companies ranging from large multinationals to small city couriers. Europe's express delivery sector is dynamic: jobs provided by EEA members alone have risen from 18,000 in 1989 to currently around 100,000. European men and women working in the express sector deliver more than 450 million packages per year.

Memorandum by La Poste, France

Question 1: What benefits are likely to result from the proposed liberalisation measures?

The French post office had encouraged and welcomed the adoption of directive 97/67/EC dated 15 December 1997 in that it achieved a balance between the guaranteed sustainability of the universal service and a gradual and controlled opening up of the market. Its effects have already been very positive and in particular have led to a noticeable improvement in service quality in cross-border relationships.

The French post office which already earns approximately 50 per cent of its turnover in competition and employs 306,000 people, hopes for a set of rules that will guarantee its legal certainty as well as its economic viability. Following the example of other European post offices (position taken by PostEurop in February 2000), the French post office accepts a new stage of liberalisation in 2003 on condition that this is on the basis of simple rules that are easily controllable and not likely to involve a multiplication of contentious proceedings.

The effects of current proposals from the European Commission on the overall postal sector have not been measured by reliable and full impact assessments.

The few examples of total liberalisation of postal markets in Europe (such as in Sweden) require great caution with regard to the benefits of liberalisation. In fact, neither the consumers (the stamp rate has increased by 72 per cent since 1993), nor employment (fallen by 25 per cent since 1993 with the Swedish operator), nor the Swedish post office itself which is in a financial loss situation for 1999, nor the overall sector (postal market growth in Sweden is stagnant), have benefited from the total and brutal opening to competition.

In other words, on the hand, negative effects of liberalisation can be observed through examples. On the other, no benefits of liberalisation have been steadily forecasted yet.

In this context, the French Post Office approves the European Commission's approach in its aim to maintain a reserved sector and to fix its contours on the basis of the twofold limits of weight and price. It does however have the strongest reservations on the following points:

— The weight/price limits proposed are too low.
— The introduction of new concepts of special services and traditional services.
— The announcement of new proposals before 2004 without assessment of measures expected to come into effect in 2003.

The French Post Office therefore expresses its doubts on the effectiveness of the majority of measures proposed.

Question 2: What problems could result from the proposed liberalisation, particularly in terms of maintenance of a universal service with an affordable and uniform tariff structure?

The Union's political objectives are to guarantee sustainability in the supply of a universal quality service, at affordable and even uniform prices, accessible to all and everywhere. Such objectives must remain a priority and must not be put in doubt by a liberalisation at any cost. It is in fact necessary to have a simple and easily controllable framework of regulations in order to preserve the viability of post offices, which are alone capable of guaranteeing the universal service.

The French post office thinks that, in its current version of 30 May 2000, the directive proposed by the Commission is not satisfactory since it introduces measures the application of which would be likely to generate risks for the sustainable supply of the universal service at a uniform tariff.

Adaptability of the universal service and appearance of new concepts: special services/basic services

The Commission's approach on the new concept for special services/basic services is unexpected and has not been the subject of any consultation or survey. This proposal casts doubt, without the slightest prior analysis of the consequences, on one of the fundamental principles of the universal service, that of the service's adaptability particularly in line with technological developments or customer requirements (article 5 paragraph 5 of the 97/67 directive). In fact, any extra item added to the so-called traditional service would make it a special service, placed outside of the universal service and therefore liberalised, whatever the weight/price limits.

Legal certainty

In addition to the problem of the universal service's capacity to develop, liberalisation of the so-called special services in particular poses a real problem of legal certainty, given that the list of so-called special services is not restrictive and there is no provision for intervention by any authority to define what is a special service and what is not. It will also be noted that the Commission is moving away in the definition of express services from the one that it itself proposed in its Communication of 1998 on the application of rules of competition to the postal sector by removing the reference to pricing.

Economic balance of the universal service provider

The Corbeau judgement recognises the notion of specific (or special) service being inseparable from the service of general economic interest. Nonetheless, such services can be offered in competition solely if they do not affect the economic balance of the economic general interest service and its provider.

In this way, the Commission's proposal jeopardises the universal service and the principle of adaptability, as well as the economic balance of its service provider.

The French post office remains attentive to the question of the scope of the universal service. It believes that there is reason to reassert that a quality universal service must have a potential for development and incorporate technological innovations in line with customer requirements as provided for in article 5 of the 97/67 directive.

Weight/price limits

The French post office supports the idea that the most appropriate method for a progressive and controlled opening of postal services to competition is a gradual lowering of weight and price thresholds. This method, applied in an appropriate manner, would considerably reduce the risks of cream-skimming and would enable uniform tariffs to be maintained within the reserved sector alone.

The French post office however believes that reducing the reserved sector to 50g is not acceptable because such a major opening would run the risk of weighing heavily on its accounts, at a time when it must finance the modernisation of its production tool as well as invest in new technologies in order to prepare for the future.

In fact, to justify this threshold, the Commission bases its reasoning on averages and does not look into the question of possible margin losses, caused by opening the market. This superficial analysis does not take into account the behaviour of newcomers, attracted by increased opportunities of turnover on a significantly larger market, any more than entry strategies onto only the profitable market segments. In addition, this would signify the end of the uniform tariff for all services offered in competition. The consequences of the Commission's proposal have not therefore been correctly assessed.

In addition, the French post office believes that accepting the 50g threshold would be an implicit admission that any new phase of liberalisation would lead to total liberalisation, even though no impact assessment makes it possible to contend the compatibility of total liberalisation with maintaining a quality universal service of quality with uniform pricing.

The French post office, like most other European operators, would be ready to accept weight/price limits brought down to 150g and three times the base tariff.

The timetable for review

The Commission's proposal goes against the principle of a gradual and controlled opening making it possible to durably guarantee the provision of a universal service. In fact, if the timetable proposed by the Commission were to be adopted, the Commission would have the possibility, from the moment the review directive comes into effect, ie from 2003 and before 2004, to make new proposals for liberalisation without assessing the effects of the measures proposed and their impact on the universal service.

In fact, firstly, the date of 31 December 2002 as deadline for implementation is too close, secondly, the period between this date and the subsequent stage of implementing a new phase also appears too short. Experience shows that the proposed timescales is incompatible with the necessity, for the Commission, to analyse the consequences of the new phase of liberalisation, before making new proposals. It would seem reasonable to programme a period for assessment of at least three years prior to putting forward new proposals.

In any event, the French post office believes that the Commission should be invited to present a report on the effects of this new directive and accompany its proposals with the results of in-depth impact assessments, conducted in an open and transparent manner with the sector's main leaders.

Question 3: Are any measures not identified in the Commission's proposals which would help to secure the Community's stated aimed for postal services?

Nullity

The principle of the directive's nullity in the event of disagreement between the European Parliament and the Council was provided with a view to facilitating the search for a compromise in the negotiation of a common position between member States. However, the Commission, in its proposal, gives absolutely no explanation of what is involved by the principle of nullity. In fact, the European Commission's proposal carriers a substantial risk of casting doubt on the regulatory framework and its normative qualities. The community postal acquis, which includes the directive organising the internal market of postal services, case-law and article 16 EC relating to services of general economic interest, cannot be repudiated by such a provision. The Commission introduces, with the notion of nullity, a strong element of legal uncertainty prejudicial to the whole postal sector.

In addition, this proposal reveals a major contradiction. In fact, the Commission cannot plead for the universal service at the same time as proposing the removal of the regulatory framework which guarantees it in the event of disagreement on review of the directive.

Again, since the Universal Postal Union Congress, held in Peking in September 1999, all member countries of the organisation committed themselves to guaranteeing a world-wide universal service in terms of cross-border postal relations. Would it be coherent for the Member States of the European Union to ensure such a service with third party countries but not within the community after having promoted it on an international scale?

Relationships with third party countries

The European market today is the market most open to competition in the postal sector world-wide. In comparable countries such as the United States, Japan or Switzerland, the monopoly is guaranteed within the following limits:

— Japan: 2kg.
— Switzerland: 2kg including parcels.
— USA: USD 3 (this monopoly changes in line with the weight of items dispatched and can for example reach USD 6 for a package weighing 1kg).

The continued opening up of the European market under conditions would therefore be to the detriment of European interests, which would, in addition, be weakened in negotiations at the WTO.

17 October 2000

Memorandum by the National Federation of Subpostmasters (NFSP)

Liberalisation tends to be irreversible and therefore needs to be carefully thought out before implementation.

The Post Office states that a reduction of the level of the reserved area to 50g may virtually eliminate all their profits.

The Post Office could be left unable to maintain a viable business or sustain a universal service for customers if the reserved area is reduced to 50g.

Studies suggest that competition results in the end of uniform pricing and a big increase in postage prices.

Compensation funds for the universal service are thought to be unworkable.

NFSP is concerned that too radical a liberalisation will result in a serious reduction of the funding available via the Post Office to support sub post offices.

Sub post offices provide crucial social and economic services, particularly for older people, disabled people, people on low incomes and rural communities.

The deterioration of the universal service, uniform and affordable postal tariffs and the closure of local post offices would subject the most vulnerable people in our society to further social exclusion.

NFSP believes that the reduction of the reserved price limit to 50g is too radical. Any reduction should be more gradual and require a thorough review of its consequences before further liberalisation.

1. Introduction

1.1 The European Commission proposes to open up further parts of the postal services market to competition in January 2003, amending Directive 97/67/EC. This involves reducing the monopoly on existing weight/price limits for letters and full opening to competition of outward cross-border mail and express mail services. The National Federation of Subpostmasters has been asked to comment on these proposals.

2. The National Federation of Subpostmasters

2.1 The National Federation of Subpostmasters represents nearly 18,000 subpostmasters throughout the United Kingdom. Sub post offices make up 97 per cent of the national network of post offices and are run by private business people, subpostmasters, most of whom run their post office business alongside another retail business.

2.2 The physical network of post offices is part of the UK Post Office network that also runs mail and parcel delivery and collection through Royal Mail and Parcelforce Worldwide.

3. Liberalisation

3.1 The European Commission (EC) is keen on the further opening up of the postal sector to competition in order to help the sector's development. The EC recognises the postal sector as offering a key communications infrastructure with high economic and social importance. It is a sector that needs to develop with the major changes taking place in communications, advertising and transportation logistics. The EC holds that liberalisation will promote innovation, greater choice and better pricing.

3.2 The National Federation of Subpostmasters (NFSP) totally supports the modernisation of the postal sector so that it can take full advantage of new technology and deliver an efficient high quality service to members of the public and businesses. However, NFSP is concerned as to whether liberalisation will in fact produce benefits in efficiency, service quality and cost reduction, leading to reductions in price and increases in choice for all customers.

4. Reduction of the Reserved Weight/Price Limit

4.1 In the interests of furthering liberalisation of postal services the EC proposes reducing the price/weight limit reserved by Member States to their universal service providers from the current level of 350 grams and 5 times the basic standard tariff to 50 grams and 2.5 times the basic standard tariff.

4.2 The EC holds that the reduction of the reserved area to 50g represents a gradual and controlled approach to reducing limits. Items weighing between 50 and 350 grams represent 16 per cent of the revenues universal service providers derive from postal services. Moreover, the EC states, only a small part of the 16 per cent will be accessible to new entrants in postal services because of the cost and time needed to establish a parallel distribution network. A limit of 100 grams, for example, would not be satisfactory as this would represent a "mere" 9 per cent of market opening that would not provide sufficient benefits from competition.[1]

4.3 The National Federation of Subpostmasters (NFSP) along with many other stakeholders is very concerned about the proposed reduction of the reserved limit to 50 grams. As the Association of European Public Postal Operators (PostEurop) points out, liberalisation tends to be an irreversible process and therefore should be dealt with gradually, ensuring that the impact of each stage is well understood.[2] Neither PostEurop, the UK Post Office nor the Communication Workers' Union believe that a reduction to 50g is a sufficiently gradual and controlled liberalisation. All three bodies support a next stage of liberalisation at a reduction of the level of the reserved area to 150g, rather than the 50g proposed by the EC.

4.4 The UK Post Office states that it would be unable to guarantee current levels of universal service provision if the level of the reserved area were to fall below 150g. The Post Office cites a sophisticated economic model that estimates the financial impact on the postal service following liberalisation, assuming the need to continue providing a universal service at a uniform tariff. The model estimates a loss of profit to the Post Office of £50–£150 million if the monopoly were reduced to 150g. However, a reduction to 50g would result in a loss of profit of £130–£430 million. A 150g limit would result in a loss of about 25 per cent of business profits, but a 50g limit would virtually eliminate all profits.[3]

4.5 NFSP has great reservations over reducing the reserved limit to 50g, given the widespread doubts over the effects of this proposal, and the potentially extremely serious consequences for the Post Office.

5. Universal Service, Uniform and Affordable Tariff

5.1 The Universal Service Obligation includes the requirement of at least one delivery to each postal address in the UK and at least one collection of postal packets from collection points every working day. The obligation also requires the provision of affordable postal services at an affordable uniform public tariff, ie that the price of sending a letter within the UK is the same irrespective of where it is posted to and from. This is a service that the UK Government has committed to continuing.[4]

5.2 The EC states that experience of deregulation of postal markets shows there is no contradiction between the gradual introduction of competitors and maintaining and improving the universal service "providing the universal service provider has the necessary commercial and pricing flexibility. . .".[5] The EC also claims that there is no evidence that a substantial market opening would compromise the requirement for affordable tariffs. Moreover, universal service providers can cross-subsidise universal services which are non-reserve with revenue from reserved services insofar that it is needed to provide the universal service. Additionally, the universal service providers' financial performance has improved significantly over recent years; and the costs of providing service in areas which are not commercially appealing amount to 5 per cent, on average, of the postal revenues of the universal service providers.

5.3 NFSP completely supports the socially crucial universal service and uniform tariff. However, NFSP is deeply concerned about the impact of these important obligations alongside the proposed liberalisation of postal services. The Post Office stresses that the obligation to provide universal service at a uniform tariff would "severely damage the ability of the Post Office to make the profit level required to maintain a viable business".[6] The universal service is an obligation and would not be provided by operators for purely commercial reasons. This obligation permits a geographical cross-subsidy. Urban areas, which tend to have a high volume of mail in a relatively small geographical area and therefore postal service costs are proportionately less, effectively subsidise the more expensive geographically dispersed rural areas.

5.4 A major concern is that a form of competition that allowed competitors to concentrate their activities on the markets with low operating costs and charge lower prices than the uniform tariff, would undermine the Post Office's ability to use revenues from low cost areas to support high cost rural customers. Profits used currently to subsidise rural consumers would instead be taken by competitors. The Post Office affirms that this form of "cherry-picking" competition is a particular threat as the Post Office depends on a few very large and increasingly powerful customers for a major part of its revenue. The EC estimate of 16 per cent of universal service providers' market share as subject to competition is therefore too simplistic an analysis, given the advantage to competitors due to the high profit opportunities provided by the uniform tariff.

5.5 A study carried out by the University of Toulouse also suggests that following the entry of competition, uniform price breaks down and disappears. Prices to rural customers may increase by over three times the original uniform price.[7] Sweden is often referred to as a good example of a fully liberalised market. However, the price of first class letters in Sweden has more than doubled between 1988 and 1998. In the UK the price has only increased by 37 per cent over the same period, which (even given the imposition of 25 per cent VAT in 1995 on postage in Sweden) is considerably less.[8] Additionally, business mailers have to contend with 40 different prices for deliveries to different cities in Sweden.

6. COMPENSATION

6.1 The Postal Directive already allows for the possibility for Member States to establish a compensation fund for cases where they believe that universal service obligations represent an unfair burden on their universal service providers. However, neither the UK Post Office nor PostEurop are convinced that a compensation fund is a workable solution. Compensation funds as a means of funding the universal service have not been investigated fully. Operating a compensation fund is likely to be complex, involving substantial data gathering, monitoring of volumes, costs and revenues for all providers.

7. SPECIAL SERVICES AND EXPRESS MAIL

7.1 The EC also proposes to open all special services to competition, regardless of price and weight. These are defined as any service that is quite distinct from the standard universal letter mail service. This includes express services and other special services offering "added-value" features. NFSP shares concerns with the Post Office that this results in a lack of clarity over the boundaries of the reserved area. Ultimately this could result in the development of spurious features to an ordinary letter service taking mail out of the reserved area. Clearly, the concern here is that this causes an additional loss of revenue to the Post Office, further endangering the provision of the universal service.

8. THE SUB POST OFFICE NETWORK

8.1 The primary concern for NFSP is that too radical a liberalisation will result in a reduction of the funding available to support the post offices themselves. Sub post offices are part of Post Office network. One of the main sources of expenditure of the Post Office network is payments to subpostmasters for running sub post offices. Most sub post offices also have an associated retail business with both part of the business being mutually dependent on the returns from the other part of the business. Measures that seriously damage the ability of the Post Office to make sufficient profits to maintain a viable business will inevitably have negative effect on the physical network of post offices.

8.2 Post offices are currently embarking on a process of radical change due to a series of challenges to their traditional lines of business. There are a wide range of new opportunities for post offices to seize, particularly in banking, e-commerce and the provision of government services. At this important time for our post offices, further financial pressures are likely to be critical.

8.3 The Post Office network reaches into every urban community and nearly every sizeable rural settlement, with 94 per cent of people in the UK living within one mile of a post office. Twenty eight million customers make 45 million visits to post offices every week. Post offices offer a range of 170 different services and products including banking services, cash management for businesses, bill payment, pension and other benefit payments, insurance services, car tax and TV licences, mail and distribution, passport renewal applications.

8.4 Much recent evidence has highlighted the crucial social and economic roles local post offices play in their communities.[9] Not only do post offices provide a wide range of postal, government and commercial services, but often their very existence helps keep open retail outlets in rural and deprived urban areas. Commonly the shop attached to a post office is the last shop in the village. Post offices, frequently the only local place to take out cash, make a special contribution to local economies. People able to access cash often spend it in other local businesses. Post offices also provide access to cash for local businesses themselves.

8.5 Subpostmasters and post offices also play an invaluable role in many communities by providing support for vulnerable residents, including older and disabled people. For example, subpostmasters frequently interpret official letters, field lost property, take messages and offer emotional support.

8.6 Post offices also act as a focal point for communities. For instance, post offices give people a place to congregate. Post offices are also used by the police, local authorities and tourist attractions to display information.

8.7 A recent Countryside Agency report on rural post offices suggests that if a local post office closed, the time taken for a customer to travel to the nearest post office would more than double. Only half as many people would still be able to walk to the post office and 30 per cent more post office users would travel to the post office by car. Monthly travel costs would increase by an average of £1.35 per user. A post office closure would result in a loss of an average of £19,000 per year to shops formerly attached to the post office. It is likely that such shops, and other local businesses, may also have to close. The Countryside Agency estimates that the closure of a post office in a typical settlement of 500–1,000 people is likely to impose an economic resource cut of over £52,000 per annum to the local community.[10]

8.8 Clearly, the closure of a local post office not only seriously impedes people's access to the wide range of post office services, but has more extensive knock-on effects. People most liable to be worst affected are those who are already vulnerable to social and financial exclusion, such as older and disabled people and people on low incomes. These groups will often find it difficult to access a post office that is further away, due to increases in costs of transport and difficulties in physically reaching the service. Moreover, it tends to be older people and the less well-off who use post offices most. The practical effects are likely to be far-reaching, culminating in increasing social isolation and all the problems that brings to individuals, communities and society in general.

8.9 Post offices are crucial to sustaining the vitality and viability of communities. Closure of post offices and other key local services results in greater isolation of villages and further ghettoisation of deprived urban areas.

9. CONCLUSION

9.1 Whilst fully endorsing the modernisation of the postal service, NFSP is deeply concerned about the EC's current proposals of further liberalisation. In particular, NFSP is apprehensive that a reduction of the reserved weight limit to 50 grams seriously undermines the financial viability of the Post Office.

9.2 The fact that the UK Post Office itself suggests that the EC's proposals would potentially eliminate the Post Office's profitability has extremely worrying implications. Instead, profits would be taken by competitors who would neither provide a universal service nor uniform tariffs. The Post Office would be left handling the expensive unprofitable part of the UK's postal services and, ultimately, would be in danger of being financially unable to provide a universal service.

9.3 Critically, the ensuing loss of revenue is very likely to have a highly negative effect on the post office network. Many sub post offices already operate on very low margins. NFSP is concerned that any further financial pressures would result in the very closures of post offices that Government, the UK Post Office, subpostmasters and the general public have been fighting against.

9.4 The people most seriously affected by the deterioration of the universal service, uniform and affordable postal tariffs and the closure of local post offices would be older people, disabled people, people on low incomes and rural communities. These groups, the most vulnerable in our society, would thus be subject to even further social exclusion.

9.5 NFSP believes that to reduce the reserved price limit to 50g is too radical a step that is likely to have very undesirable consequences. Any reduction should therefore be more gradual and require a thorough review of its consequences before further liberalisation.

REFERENCES

1. Commission of the European Communities, May 2000, Proposal for a European Parliament and Council Directive Amending Directive 97/67/EC with Regard to the Further Opening to Competition of Community Postal Services: Explanatory Memorandum.

2. PostEurop, February 2000, Review of Directive 97/67/EC.

3. The Post Office, May 2000, Competition in Posts and the Universal Service: Getting the Balance Right.

4. Department of Trade and Industry, July 1999, Post Office Reform: A World Class Service for the 21st Century.

5. Commission of the European Communities, May 2000, Proposal for a European Parliament and Council Directive Amending Directive 97/67/EC with Regard to the Further Opening to Competition of Community Postal Services: Explanatory Memorandum.

6. The Post Office, May 2000, Competition in Posts and the Universal Service: Getting the Balance Right.

7. The Post Office, April 2000, Uniform Pricing and Postal Market Liberalisation.

8. Communication Workers Union, April 2000, Swedish Postal Experience.

9. Performance and Innovation Unit, June 2000, Counter Revolution: Modernising the Post Office Network.

10. The Countryside Agency, July 2000, The Economic Significance of Post Offices in Rural Areas.

12 September 2000

Memorandum by Posten AB, Sweden

INTRODUCTION

Seven years ago, in 1993, the Swedish monopoly on letters was abolished in one single step. This was done before any sector specific legislation or regulatory body had been put in place and since then, admittance to the postal market has been free.

One year after the liberalisation, on 1 March 1994, the Swedish Postal Services Act was implemented and a postal unit was formed within the regulatory body for telecom, today. The National Post and Telecom Agency. The Postal Service Act sets out the general rules concerning the provision of the universal service and it is stated that the responsibility for the nation-wide and universal postal service legally rests with the State. To fulfil this responsibility the Swedish Government has assigned Posten AB to be the Swedish universal service provider. This has been done by special conditions in the licence to pursue postal business and by a separate agreement between the Government and Posten AB.

According to the special licence conditions imposed on Posten AB the company has to provide one clearance and one distribution of postal items up to 20 kg, every working day, at all access and distribution points. This means that every[17] household and company, irrespective of where in Sweden it is situated, is entitled to postal service once a day five days a week. The Postal Service Act also stipulates that single letter items shall be conveyed at uniform and reasonable prices.

FURTHER LIBERALISATION

Regardless of any regulatory change or liberalisation, the letters market has, for the past 10–15 years, already been facing considerate and fast growing competition, a competition primarily coming from alternative methods of communication such as fax, e-mail, broadcasting and now recently the Internet. This development will undoubtedly continue to grow in the future and generate a significant and potential impact on the postal industry. However, the swift development of the telecommunications market, exponential development of the Internet and e-commerce market is not to be seen as a threat but as an opportunity for the postal industry to expand.

The technological development does also give rise to changes in customers need and demand for services and there is a considerable trend in the development of special or "tailor-made" services which go far beyond the standard letters services offered today. Postal operators are therefore, not only obliged to adapt to new technology but also to changing customer demands (both private and business customers) for different and more swift means of communications and logistics services.

A further business potential is the emerging e-commerce market that creates a fast growing need for ever-present physical delivery networks and logistics services. This development will significantly change the transportation and logistics industries and create substantial possibilities of market expansion for European postal operators. These operators are today in the possession of high standard national and international networks, well suited to provide all kinds of logistics services required by e-commerce companies. Therefore to enable the postal operators to take advantage of their assets and skills it is urgent to create possibilities for them to define and establish their market positioning in the new economy.

All these are facts that the postal operators are well aware of. Consequently, in recent years, many of them have engaged in extensive restructuring and modernisation of their organisation and services. They have used the new information and communication technologies to improve the efficiency of their existing postal services as well as to launch new types of neighbouring service. Some of the postal administrations, enjoying a domestic monopoly, have also moved significantly to make acquisitions. This situation gives small-and medium-sized operators little if any chance of positioning themselves as nothing but some form of regional or strategic ally for big companies. Thus, there is a great risk that "free competition" will be nothing but printed words on a paper and that the dynamic effects of the developing market fail to appear. Therefore, to avoid this situation in the internal market it is necessary to adapt further and swift regulatory changes, harmonising the conditions of providing postal services. Furthermore, it is utter importance that all postal operators are given equal conditions for making business as their competitors. These conditions can be based on similar access to the financial market, equal application of taxes and other regulations giving competitors the commercial freedoms needed in the accelerating communications and logistics market.

---

[17] Some minor exceptions are allowed in remote rural areas where the post is delivered 2–4 days a week.

CONCLUSIONS

In the light of the above and in answer to the ongoing discussions concerning the impact of liberalisation in already de-regulated markets Posten AB would like to stress two important perspectives:

— To safeguard the universal service the European postal industry must be given the possibility to compete on equal terms, as other service providers, in the expanding European communications and logistics markets. It is therefore important to enable the European postal operators to meet future technology and markets by giving them the necessary conditions to modernise and to be competitive. Therefore, the liberalisation of the European postal sector must be put into effect as swiftly as possible. A prolonged process will jeopardise the long-time future of the postal sector, including employment, affordable prices and last but not the least the universal service it self.

— By harmonising and liberalising the postal market it will be possible to maintain and even improve the universal service. Our view is that it is important to concentrate more on the contents of the postal service than on the structure of how to offer a service. Therefore, a flexible organisation enabling postal operators to adopt to market changes, quickly shifting customer demands and different local solutions for service, is the best way to safeguard the maintenance of universal services to all citizens.

To conclude we want to stress that it is important to continue in the direction of liberalisation initiated by Directive 97/67/EC and to keep up with the pace suggested by the Commission in their latest proposal. If the Community wants to profit from the dynamics of the technological development and there is to be any result at all of the liberalisation of the internal postal market, it is utmost important that:

— The price and weight limits are not set higher then those proposed by the Commission; and

— that the transposition period must be fixed at a date not later than 1 January 2007; and

— that the date under no circumstances can be negotiated, once it has been decided.

Finally, we would like to conclude by quoting the Swedish National Post and Telecom Agency's statement in their latest report[18] on the Swedish liberalisation:

"There is nothing in the Swedish experience that may indicate that competition in the entire postal market should be regarded as a problem. Instead it should be considered a solution to the challenges facing the Postal World in a new environment dominated by Information Technology and globalisation."

13 September 2000

Memorandum by the Royal National Institute for the Blind

1. INTRODUCTION

The Royal National Institute for the Blind (RNIB) is the largest organisation in the UK providing direct services for blind and partially sighted people. In addition to its work in this country, RNIB is also a leading partner in the European Blind Union (EBU) and in turn the World Blind Union (WBU).

2. SUMMARY OF THE MAIN POINTS OF RNIB'S EVIDENCE

This evidence is submitted in my capacity as Chairman of the Royal National Institute for the Blind but also draws heavily on my experience as President of the European Blind Union and as Chairman of the World Blind Union's Working Group on Postal Services. The central concern of blind and partially sighted people and their organisations is that any moves towards further liberalisation of postal services should not threaten the continuation of vital freepost Articles for the Blind services, which help to counteract the exclusion many visually impaired people meet by being unable to access information which the rest of society takes for granted. Therefore this evidence corresponds most closely to the Sub-Committee's second question, regarding possible problems which could result from the proposed liberalisation. As the experience of visually impaired people in New Zealand has demonstrated in recent years, concerns about freepost/articles for the blind schemes being threatened by badly handled liberalisation are far from theoretical. In addition, visually impaired people share the general public's concerns that universal service be continued in the postal sector.

3. The current postage free Articles for the Blind Scheme in the United Kingdom operates under the Inland Post Scheme, dating from 1969. The Articles for the Blind Scheme principally enables the sending of communication items, such as information in Braille, audio tape format or computer disk for visually impaired people who cannot access traditional print or other formats. In addition, organisations of or for the blind, including RNIB, make special arrangements with the Post Office to enable certain goods items to be sent under the Scheme. The Scheme operates weight and dimension limits.

4. Government commitment to safeguarding Articles for the Blind has been expressed by both the Conservative and Labour administrations of the last decade, for example when the Conservative Government

---

[18] National Post and Telecom Agency, Postal Affairs Department, THE LIBERALISED SWEDISH POSTAL MARKET—and the situation seven years after the abolition of the monopoly, 10 July 2000 Available at www.pts.se

introduced its 1994 Green Paper on the future of the Post Office, and more recently when the 2000 Postal Services Bill included reference to free postal services for blind and partially sighted people.

5. In contrast to this background of domestic political support for Articles for the Blind, at EU level such commitment has been less forthcoming. Following lobbying by the European Blind Union, the European Parliament did demonstrate support for such schemes by amending the 1995 Directive proposal, to ensure that liberalisation would not threaten freepost schemes in the different Member States. However the European Commission was not enthusiastic about such amendments. The compromise found was for the Commission to introduce a new recital to allow for Member States to continue such schemes.

6. Again in contrast to the UK's commitment to Articles for the Blind, at the level of the Universal Postal Union there is less support for such schemes, as evidenced by opposition raised at the UPU Congress at Beijing in 1999 to the continuation of the international concession system for literature for blind people. It is in response to this worrying trend towards a less socially-responsible attitude that I was asked to chair the newly established World Blind Union working group on postal services. The WBU also takes part in the UPU's advisory group for non-governmental organisations, to press for blind and partially sighted people's needs for access to the postal system.

7. A practical example of how well founded are visually impaired people's worries over badly handled postal liberalisation comes from the Commonwealth. When the New Zealand Post Office transferred their country's Articles for the Blind scheme into a type of sponsorship, the department responsible took the view that the scheme did not provide good value for money and ended it. Although this decision was then reviewed, the New Zealand Government has felt is necessary to step in and provide short term funding, leaving the future of the Scheme extremely uncertain. This kind of experience in such a similar country to the UK, pursuing the road of liberalisation on which the EU as a whole seems set, shows the need to secure Articles for the Blind schemes in any such moves. Not only would this avoid unnecessary dislocation to the lives of visually impaired people who rely on the present system, it would also prevent the need for the kind of Government emergency measures caused by the problems encountered during the process in New Zealand.

8. In addition to specific concerns about the potential risk to Articles for the Blind, liberalisation if pursued needs to address more general public interest concerns which visually impaired people share. For example, universal service including nationwide collection and door to door delivery, the existence of plenty of points to post mail and maintaining the delivery of time sensitive items needed for people's livelihoods are all relevant to visually impaired people, whose mobility needs and relatively lower income levels mean that universal and affordable postal services are crucial.

CONCLUSION

9. RNIB does not take a view on whether the postal sector should be liberalised/privatised or not. Our concern is that regardless of the ownership pattern in the sector, services such as Articles for the Blind and universal service features vital to the inclusion of visually impaired people in the everyday life of the country need to be safeguarded. The prospect of New Zealand style problems is very real if changes in the sector do not include steps to secure such services. The possibility that progress in the postal sector into the 21st Century might mean blind people on low incomes paying the high costs of Braille postage for example, is one which we trust the UK Government will work to avoid in its negotiations in the EU on this subject. Promoting the continuance, if not the extension, of such features of the UK postal system into the rest of the EU and the world would give the UK an ideal opportunity to lead the arguments for proper inclusion of disabled people in their societies. The opportunity afforded by the European Commission's proposal in this area to argue for such inclusion is one we hope the Government will welcome as we do.

14 September 2000

Letter by Brian Simpson, MEP

My views on the Commission proposals concur very much with those outlined to you by the Communication Workers Union in their evidence.

However, I would like to make a few relevant points on specific proposals put forward by the Commission whilst stressing the threat to UK postal workers jobs that I believe this Directive poses.

Firstly, we must remember that the existing Directive calls for controlled and gradual liberalisation. A cut in the reserved area from 350g to 50g in one move is, in my opinion, neither controlled or gradual.

Secondly, the UK Postal Services Commission must ensure that any of its decisions are consistent with EU decisions.

Thirdly, the proposal to reduce the reserved area to 50g puts at risk the financing of the universal service throughout the United Kingdom. It is my view that in order to ensure a viable universal service throughout all parts of the United Kingdom, a reserved area of 150g is required, including direct mail.

Fourthly, the Directive proposed to introduce a new definition of Special Services but then fails to define what a Special Service would be. This is clearly a new concept and in my mind needs further study to ensure that the Special Service additions proposed do not put at risk the viability of the reserved area and subsequently the universal service.

Fifthly, we have to recognise that this proposal moves us closer to a fully liberalised postal service. Whilst I accept that the "status quo" is not an option, the timescales envisaged for this and subsequent steps is important. It is my view that the implementation of step one (150g) could be done by 2004 with a further consideration of the reserved area size undertaken at that time for future proposals.

Finally, the Directive proposes a compensation fund to support the universal service. Frankly if you allow national post operators to have a reserved area large enough to deliver a universal service, then the need for such a fund disappears. This to me is a "smoke screen" put up by the Commission to hide the fact that they know a reserved area of 50g cannot guarantee to deliver a universal service for all.

2 October 2000

Memorandum by Ross Clark, Journalist, The Spectator

1. I visited Mount Pleasant Sorting Office in London on the afternoon of Monday, 6 November at my own request in connection with a piece I had been asked to write on the Royal Mail for the Spectator magazine, subsequently published in issue dated 11 November. The magazine had a particular interest in the subject having received a large number of letters from subscribers complaining about the late arrival of the magazine through the post.

2. My researches established:

2.1 That subscription copies of the magazine are delivered, already sorted, to Chelmsford sorting office on Thursday mornings. They are then taken, by the Royal Mail, to a sorting office in Hatfield.

2.2 Copies bound for London addresses are then taken by the Royal Mail to Mount Pleasant, from where they are distributed.

2.3 Since the magazine is posted first class, it ought to arrive on the following working day, Friday. But the experience of many readers is that it does not arrive, even in London, until the Saturday, or, in some cases, the following Tuesday. My own subscription copy, posted to my home address in Cambridgeshire, also frequently fails to arrive on Friday mornings.

2.4 Because of the unpredictability of the post, many magazines, for example the Economist, have been forced to go to the extra expense of delivering London-bound subscription copies directly to Mount Pleasant. This is a practice which the Spectator is to take up early in the New Year.

3. On arrival at Mount Pleasant I was shown the sorting operations by Mr Vince Calouri, manager of the office. While there was some evidence of new technology employed at Mount Pleasant, it is disjointed and appears to be designed to ensure the continued employment of 4,000 staff. A quarter of all mail, I was told, was sorted entirely by hand.

3.1 The sorting operations are carried out over two floors. The lower floor was almost wholly given over to manual operations, some of which would clearly have lent themselves to mechanisation. For example, first class post is separated from second class post by a dozen or so workers at a bench.

3.2 The process was a lot less ordered than one might have expected. I was expecting a "production line", with letters entering at one end and emerging, sorted, at the other. But the machinery was not linked together in an efficient form; instead letters were taken from place to place in trolleys. In one place a machine was spewing letters onto the floor. Some parcels were being handled roughly, being thrown into baskets several feet away.

4. The sorting office has a very caring attitude towards poorly addressed items of post. The most impressive part of the operation was the reading, by human eye, of items which the sorting machine had been unable to read: a roomful of workers sat at computer consoles, studying images of envelopes and, using their knowledge of post codes, keying in the destinations. It seemed to me that this was a labour-intensive operation by nature, and that the employment of technology in this field would not have involved the loss of many jobs. Was this the reason, I wondered, why this was the one part of the operation where technology had been allowed to flourish?

5. I was unsatisfied by the answer given to my question "why isn't the entire sorting operation mechanised?" Mr Calouri told me that while that is how you would approach the problem if you were building on a greenfield site, there wasn't enough room on the Mount Pleasant site to automate the entire operation; since Mount Pleasant occupies almost an entire precinct between Farringdon Road and Gray's Inn Road I found this unconvincing.

SUMMARY

6. It seemed to me that Mount Pleasant sorting office had not even begun to employ technology to its full potential; that while there was some machinery in use, it was disjointed and incomplete; a quarter of all mail was sorted by hand. The reason, I suspect, has more to do with labour relations and the desire to keep

employed 4,000 staff, than with the given explanation, that the place is not big enough for a fully automated sorting operation.

6.1 I felt that the sorting operations took great care over poorly addressed items of post, but that they did not give a good deal to Spectator subscriptions and other well-addressed items of mail. London, I understand from conversations with the Post Office National Users Council, has one of the worst records of punctual delivery. This seems iniquitous given that post addressed from one part of London to another must be heavily subsidising mail sent from one rural district to another. As a resident of a rural district myself, I would be concerned if the flat-rate charging structure for mail was to be entirely dismantled, though it does seem unfair that businesses based in London and other cities are not allowed access to private postal services which could be cheaper and more reliable.

Memorandum by United Parcel Service (UPS)

1. SUMMARY OF MAIN POINTS

UPS welcomes the Commission's Proposal to further open to competition EU Postal services, as well as to create legal certainty.

UPS considers the Proposal to reduce the reserved area for items of domestic correspondence to 50 grams/ 2.5 times the basic standard tariff to be the bare minimum necessary.

UPS regrets that the Commission has not proposed the full liberalisation of direct mail services despite the recommendation of the Commission's Services to this effect.

UPS welcomes the complete liberalisation of outbound cross-border mail and express mail services.

2. BENEFITS OF LIBERALISATION

The Single Market for postal services should be completed as for other sectors.

The price/quality ratio of postal products should be improved. Increased competition can bring this about.

Liberalisation will stimulate the development of new products and encourage innovation in the postal sector.

Increased competition will stimulate the reform of public postal operators into more efficient, cost-aware, and above all customer-oriented, companies.

The abolition of monopolies will end distortions of competition between alternative segments of the communications market.

3. FULL LIBERALISATION OF POSTAL SERVICES IS REQUIRED

UPS believes that the Directive should include 1 January 2007, as a final date for the full liberalisation of EU postal services. Without a final date, public postal operators will have no real incentive to improve their services and take advantage of the dynamics of the internal market. In addition, the current open-ended situation fails to provide the necessary market security to allow for new market entrants from private industry to innovate, invest in the postal sector and create employment opportunities.

4. REDUCED WEIGHT AND PRICE LIMIT FOR ITEMS OF DOMESTIC CORRESPONDENCE

UPS favours the full liberalisation of the market for items of domestic correspondence by abolishing the current weight and price limits. The price and weight limit (2.5x the price/50g) proposed by the Commission can only be described as a modest step in the right direction.

5. LIBERALISATION OF OUTBOUND CROSS-BORDER MAIL

UPS welcomes the Commission's proposal to de jure liberalise outbound cross-border mail. This will stimulate communication and mail flows between the EU's citizens and enterprises. Since the cross-border mail streams are already de facto liberalised in Member States, this provides legal certainty for operators.

6. LIBERALISATION OF DIRECT MAIL

Europe's direct mail market has a tremendous potential for growth. The Commission's own studies show that the direct mail segment of the mail market is likely to grow substantially in a situation of full liberalisation. The failure to liberalise this market segment is likely to lead to stagnation followed by decline and substitution by other means of communication. Only competition in the direct mail segment will encourage innovation, the development of new services and a higher quality of service meeting the exacting needs of customers and staving off competition from other means of communication such as newspapers advertising, tv advertising, billboards or the internet.

Furthermore six Member States have already opened their direct mail market to competition, without in any way threatening the universal service. The full liberalisation of direct mail would allow public postal operators and private industry alike to further develop this dynamic means of communication.

7. No Cross-Subsidisation of Competitive Services

Cross subsidisation, where income from the reserved area is used to subsidise competitive services, causes huge distortions of competition in the postal market. The Commission's Postal Notice (OJ 98/C 39/02) on the Application of the Competition Rules to the Postal Sector, makes it clear that it is prohibited for a dominant postal operator to subsidise competitive activities from monopoly revenue. The Commission proposal must be consistent with the Postal Notice. Clarification of the current proposal is needed since the Commission's proposed text relates only to cross-subsidisation of universal services and omits any reference to the cross-subsidisation of services outside the universal service being prohibited.

8. Special Services and Express Services

UPS considers that the Commission proposal to exclude "special services" from the postal monopoly and from universal service codifies existing case law and jurisprudence of the Commission and the European Court of Justice. Therefore, UPS would like to stress the importance of maintaining this proposed provision as a guarantee of legal certainty.

UPS fully supports the Commission's recognition that express services fall outside the universal service and may not be reserved, thus confirming established case law of the European Court of Justice.

9. Complaints Procedures

The Commission has proposed that Government-mandated complaints procedures be applied also to services outside the universal service. It is wholly inappropriate for the Commission to propose that Government-mandated complaints procedures be applied to such services irrespective of the service provider. Such services are already subject to longstanding commercial arrangements. It cannot be the business of Government to regulate freely competitive services, irrespective of the service provider. This was clearly accepted by the Government in the White Paper on Post Office Reform which stated on pages 6–7:

> "It is therefore the Government's intention that regulation should focus primarily on the Post Office and any others operating in the monopoly area, leaving the rest of the market free to operate as now in the largely unregulated environment."

10. Making E-Commerce Development Possible

The successful development of e-commerce requires efficient, reliable, liberalised delivery networks. Users of electronic commerce should have freedom of choice and diversity of delivery according to their needs. This requires the complete liberalisation of postal and express delivery services. In order to ensure consumer trust in electronic commerce, it is essential that consumers who order goods electronically receive those goods in an efficient and reliable way.

11. Liberalisation Benefits Employment

The "safeguarding employment" argument is often used by inefficient postal operators to preserve existing monopolies. It is clear from other economic sectors that liberalisation leads to market growth. We see no reason why this principle would not apply to the postal sector, and benefit employment in that sector. Employment is currently decreasing in the public postal sector by 0.8 per cent a year, but this is not a result of market opening but rather of technological shifts and a drive for greater efficiency. The aim of liberalisation is to bring improved services, which should ultimately result in increasing employment.

12. Guaranteeing the Universal Service Provision

The Commission's current proposal does not change the obligations of universal service as set out in the Directive. Universal service and a fully liberalised market are not mutually exclusive, and they can co-exist perfectly. The current Commission proposal opens to competition only 20 per cent of the revenues which universal service providers derive from postal services. The incumbent operators will not suddenly lose this revenue and may well retain 80–90 per cent of the market opened to competition.

14 September 2000